# PEARLS
# IN THE LANDSCAPE

# PEARLS IN THE LANDSCAPE

## The Conservation and Management of Ponds

*Chris Probert*

FARMING PRESS

*First published 1989*

Copyright © Chris Probert, 1989

British Library Cataloguing in Publication Data
Probert, Christopher D.
  Pearls in the landscape: the conservation and
  management of ponds.
  1. Great Britain. Ponds. Management
  I. Title
  333.78'4

ISBN 0-85236-198-X


Published by Farming Press Books
4 Friars Courtyard, 30–32 Princes Street
Ipswich IP1 1RJ, United Kingdom

*Distributed in North America
by Diamond Farm Enterprises
Box 537, Alexandria Bay, NY 13607, USA*

Phototypeset by Galleon Photosetting, Ipswich
Printed and bound in Great Britain by
Butler & Tanner Ltd, Frome and London

# Contents

Colour plates 1–24 are between pages 118 and 119

# Acknowledgements

I would like to thank everyone who has helped me with the preparation of this book. As I travelled around the country looking at ponds and talking to farmers, advisers and researchers, I was constantly impressed with and fascinated by the level of knowledge and enthusiasm displayed by everyone whom I met.

My requests for assistance were very quickly and generously answered in all parts of the country, and a number of individuals deserve special mention.

The following experts all very kindly gave up their time and shared their knowledge and enthusiasm with me:

Mrs Jane Warmington, Mrs Juliet Hawkins and Mr Richard McMullen, Farming and Wildlife Advisory Group

Dr Harry Gracey, Department of Agriculture, Northern Ireland

Dr Mary Swann and Dr Robert Oldham, Nature Conservancy Council and Leicester Polytechnic National Amphibian Survey

Mr Michael Street, ARC Wildfowl Centre

Dr Hugh Dawson, Freshwater Biological Association

Dr Jeremy Biggs, Pond Action

Mr Pip Barrett, Aquatic Weeds Unit

Mr Andre Berry, Coed Cymru

Mrs Deborah Priddy, Essex County Council Archaeological Department

Mrs Margaret Palmer and Dr Chris Newbold, Nature Conservancy Council

Mr Alex Behrendt, Two Lakes Fishery

Mr Trevor Lay, Waveney Wildfowl

Dr John Worthy, National Rivers Authority Anglian Region

Thanks are also due to:

Norfolk FWAG and the Terrestrial Ecology Research Fund who very kindly permitted use to be made of their material in Appendix 3.

Hertfordshire County Council and the North Hertfordshire Museums

Natural History Department for permission to reproduce their pond survey and assessment card at Appendix 3.

The Ministry of Agriculture, Fisheries and Food for consent to reproduce material from Booklet 2078, *Guidelines for the Use of Herbicides on Weeds in or near Watercourses and Lakes.*

Mr Nick Ratcliffe of Kings Legend Ltd, Leiston, for the supply of drawing equipment.

I would also like to record my very grateful thanks to Messrs Robert Orford, David Blundell and Johan van der Berg of Miles Waterscapes Ltd, who very generously supplied me with technical information and drawings for use in Chapter 4.

The illustrations were provided by:

*Plates:* the author except:

    1.3, Aerofilms Ltd

    1.6 and 6.5, Dr Harry Gracey

    3.7, Department of Agriculture, Northern Ireland

*Figures:* the author except:

    1.1, 2.3–2.7, 2.9–2.13, Mrs Jane Warmington

    4.1–4.8, Miles Waterscapes Ltd

I am indebted to Mr David Allen and Sandoz Products Ltd (Agro-chemicals), United Framlingham Farmers Ltd, Mrs Ellen Woodruffe and particularly Mrs Sue Norris, who worked extremely hard and cheerfully, processing the various drafts of each chapter and meeting all my impossible deadlines—thank you very much.

Finally, I owe a special debt of gratitude to my wife, Margaret, who inspired and supported me throughout the preparation of this book and to whom this book is dedicated.

CHRIS PROBERT
*Martlesham Heath, Ipswich*
*May 1989*

# PEARLS
# IN THE LANDSCAPE

*Chapter 1*

# Ponds

Water has always been important to the people of the United Kingdom. From earliest times the island races have been protected against invaders from abroad by the surrounding seas, while the many thousands of natural and man-made waterways criss-crossing the countryside have been of inestimable value as features of the landscape and have helped to revolutionise the development of communications, trade and industry. The marvellous lakes of North-West England have inspired some of the country's greatest writers, while the Lake District, together with the Scottish lochs, attracts tourists from all over the world to look at the natural beauty of Britain. In recent years, lakes, rivers and canals have all had an impact on the development of the great new leisure industry and there is little doubt that water (and even its source—rain!) has had—and will continue to have—a major effect on the lives of the people of Britain and Northern Ireland. Yet, in the midst of this rich history and the invaluable contribution made to society by water, the humble pond is often forgotten. Nevertheless, it has a most fascinating background and possesses the potential to bring pleasure to both young and old, town and country dweller alike, at the same time sustaining some of the country's most exciting and attractive plants and animals.

The pond has been a feature of the countryside since time immemorial, playing a significant part throughout the centuries in the development and sustenance of agriculture and the establishment of industry. It has also formed an important focus of social life for the village community, a role which is seldom fully appreciated in today's changing landscape.

The word 'pond' conjures up a multitude of different visions—for many people based on childhood memories, for others perhaps inspired by film, television and magazine or even more simply as a recollection of shimmering water glimpsed from the window of a car or train during a journey through the United Kingdom. The idyllic picture of a tranquil village pond, supporting the local duck population and fringed by flowering irises or reedbeds, set against a backcloth of village green, traditional cottages and the parish church, is probably to most people a

1

vivid idea of what a pond should look like. Sadly, this romantic notion is more often than not an image portrayed only on the front of a chocolate box or featured in glossy natural history programmes made for television. Too many of the ponds which remain today are far from idyllic, isolated in the corner of a field or on the edge of an area of woodland, with little management and no hope of recovery.

This is a sad situation, but one for which the blame cannot be laid at any one door. Ponds are almost certainly one of the most under-utilised, semi-natural resources in the United Kingdom today, both in terms of their potential for wildlife conservation (whether they be on a farm, in a garden, or in some other location) and with regard to their suitability for management as part of a farm or rural business. With a greater understanding of ponds and the management techniques necessary both to encourage wildlife and to utilise the water, more ponds could be enhanced and new ones developed to the benefit of the countryside as a whole.

## WHAT IS A POND?

The question 'What is a pond?' has been much debated. Of necessity, a pond must be an expanse of still as opposed to flowing water, although to confuse the issue, a stream may flow into a pond and an outlet take moving water away. If it is accepted that a pond is a stillwater, albeit with inflow and outflow, this explanation remains somewhat confusing, because stillwaters range in size from tiny garden ponds and small water-retaining hollows through to lakes, with many stages in between. Thus a further refinement is required to the definition that 'a pond is an area of stillwater'.

A consensus holds that a pond is an area of stillwater which is shallow enough to enable light to percolate to the floor of the pond, encouraging aquatic plants to grow throughout the water. This differentiates between ponds and deeper areas of stillwater which can be classified as lakes. Because most light energy is absorbed in the top 3 metres of water, a good rule of thumb guide is to consider that 'a pond is an area of stillwater no deeper than 3 metres'.

Unfortunately, this is still not a totally exhaustive answer to the question 'what is a pond?', because very large expanses of shallow stillwater are commonly described as lakes. So, to go one stage further, if the feature has a large surface area and its shoreline suffers from serious wave erosion caused by the wind, it should be considered a 'lake', as opposed to a 'pond'.

The definition of a pond as being 'a stillwater less than 3 metres deep and not subject to serious wave erosion of the banks' will thus exclude the majority of stillwaters created on farms exclusively to store water for irrigation and which are often in excess of 1 hectare in size. In so doing, the definition provides a convenient cut-off point for practical pond creation, because the technology required to develop high capacity water storage is of necessity extremely complex, in many cases governed by legislation in the form of the Reservoirs Act 1985. This requires the design of all lakes capable of storing in excess of 25,000 cubic metres of water above the level of the adjoining land to be supervised and certified by an engineer approved by the Department of the Environment.

For the purposes of this book, ponds are therefore held to be 'stillwaters no deeper than 3 metres and ranging in size from a few square metres to 0.405 hectares'. Although the principles of design, conservation and management outlined in the book are also equally relevant to larger expanses of water such as lakes, reservoirs and flooded gravel pits, the constructional techniques described may require modification in the case of reservoirs and areas of water over 0.405 hectares in size.

## THE ORIGINS OF PONDS

Some ponds developed naturally thousands of years ago, particularly in the north and west where geology and climate enabled water to collect naturally and become a permanent feature of the landscape. Other natural ponds develop where a meandering river changes its course and cuts off part of its old channel, which still retains water and forms a pond; these ponds are described by geographers as 'oxbow lakes', further confounding the definition of a pond! Many of these natural features are in fact too big to be accurately described as ponds, nevertheless natural ponds do exist but are certainly far less common than man-made features, man having been responsible over the centuries for the creation of the vast majority of ponds in this country.

The name pond is derived from the Anglo-Saxon term meaning pound or pen as used to hold livestock—thus the pond was considered to be an enclosure created to hold water, probably by impounding a water course.

Historically, one of the basic essentials for human settlement was water. Because of this, man either built his home near to a natural water collection point or he constructed ponds to store the water on which he depended for his survival. These water stores were not just for domestic supply. The rural economy was naturally based on agriculture and livestock were a vital part of it; the animals themselves also needed to drink, whether they were grazing near to the village or were being driven to market for sale. Where roads between settlements and markets did not cross rivers or streams, ponds were often constructed so that the animals could drink en route and,

*Plate 1.1    A Norfolk marl pit, now a significant landscape feature on account of the surrounding trees.*

in due course, small settlements frequently grew up around these meeting places. As farming developed and it became possible for more farmers to keep livestock through the winter months, ponds adjacent to farmsteads became commonplace. These not only provided drinking water for the animals, but also acted as reservoirs of water to fight the fires which were frequent destroyers of straw ricks, timber framed buildings and thatched roofs.

Away from the farmstead, holes were dug to drain water off the surrounding land, thus enabling better quality crops to be produced. These drainage holes became ponds, many of which remain today. Some holes were created to store water for use on the crops during dry summers—the forerunners of modern irrigation reservoirs. Land improvements other than drainage also resulted in the development of ponds. In particular, marling, or the digging of clay which was spread onto light, sandy land improving fertility, left large holes in the ground. Because these were dug into clay soils, they quickly flooded, and became ponds, while in the same fashion old peat or gravel workings often filled with water as did holes left in the ground after the excavation of building materials. Old marl pits can often be found in pairs or larger groups. The original marl pit would fill with water and, when a new one was required, the second would be dug adjacent to the first with only a narrow bank separating the two. These interesting relics of old farming systems can still be found in many areas.

Between 1700 and 1850 many hundreds of Private Enclosure Acts were passed by Parliament, each Act enabling landowners to re-apportion their local common and meadowlands. The boundaries of the new enclosures or 'fields' were marked by hedgerows or walls, so that the movements of grazing livestock could be controlled. Whereas prior to Enclosures, the sheep and cattle had roamed the countryside drinking at village ponds, streams and ditches, now that they were fenced in to fields, drinking places had to be provided for them. Many such 'enclosure' ponds remain today, often at the junction of fields where one pond was created to serve several enclosures. (See colour plate 1.)

One particular form of field pond worthy of special description is the dew pond. Dew ponds occur mainly on chalk downland and are mostly circular in shape and fairly shallow. Because of the lack of good natural supplies of water and the difficulties of storing water over chalk, special

*Plate 1.2   A neglected dew pond.*

types of pond had to be developed to collect direct rainfall and run-off from surrounding catchment areas. These clay-lined ponds providing water for livestock are steeped in tradition. Sometimes called cloud or mist ponds, they were for a long time thought to be filled by atmospheric condensation. It is now known that the ingenious method of construction provided for a large catchment area to collect water, at the same time keeping evaporation to a minimum, thus enabling satisfactory water levels to be retained within the pond. A number of dew ponds remain today, but many have fallen into neglect because they have become redundant with the development of piped field water supplies. They are well worth restoring if only on account of their historical value.

Ponds also served an important purpose as providers of fresh food. Wild duck were caught using curiously shaped decoy ponds, a few of which can still be seen in their original form, with funnel shaped pipes, or arms, into which the duck were lured and trapped before being killed and sent to the local market. Fishponds were once important features of

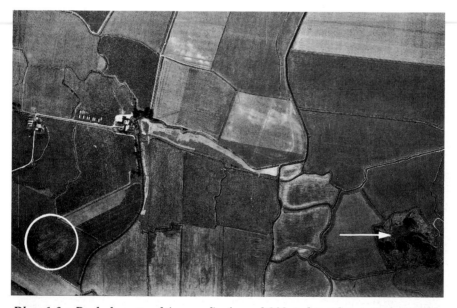

*Plate 1.3   Duck decoy pond (arrowed). Around 200 such ponds were constructed in Britain. This example, on the Dengie marshes in Essex, was one of 31 created in that county. Annual catches of between 700 and 3000 duck were reported from this pond when it was in use. The site of a second pond, now infilled, can be seen circled (Aerofilms Ltd).*

rural communities and a large number of these can still be found, although often only the outlines remain, usually identifiable due to their proximity to fortified farmhouses, monastic ruins or manors. Often constructed in a series, with two or three ponds grouped together and covering a large area with very sophisticated water control systems, these stew ponds served a valuable function providing a means of producing food. The concept of fish farming in ponds was introduced to Britain by the Normans and these ponds were originally considered as status symbols associated with landownership. Bream were reared in the earliest ponds, and carp became more commonplace in the fifteenth and sixteenth centuries.

Many old fishponds are classed as medieval moated sites and these, together with manorial or moated farmstead complexes, are quite common features of the landscape. The estimated number of recorded moated sites in England and Wales is in excess of 5,000, although a great many of these no longer hold water and survive simply as earthworks. The better examples are often protected as Scheduled Ancient Monuments in conjunction with their associated buildings, an impressive reminder of the grandeur of the countryside in times past.

*Plate 1.4   Overgrown medieval fish ponds. One of the channels used to control water flow is still clearly visible.*

Plate 1.5   Moat Hall, Parham, Suffolk. A sixteenth-century hall and moat on a much older site. Both features are protected by listing.

Plate 1.6   The ice house at the Greenmount College of Agriculture and Horticulture in County Antrim. (Dr H. Gracey)

8

Long before the days when refrigerators were household items, owners of large country houses sometimes built ice houses, where ice collected from ponds in winter could be stored for a considerable time for use in warm weather. If no suitable supply of water was available, ponds would be constructed to act as a source of ice.

Throughout the country, ponds were regularly constructed to support industry and provide a means of generating energy. The production of linen, particularly in the North of Britain and Northern Ireland, required ponds for the retting of flax. Oblong ponds known as lint holes were made, in which bundles of flax were submerged for ten to fourteen days so that the woody matter and cellular tissues surrounding the fibres could decompose, prior to the flax being dried and processed to produce linen. Ponds were also created to store water used to drive waterwheels or power the tilt hammers of iron forges; these ponds were often produced simply by damming a stream so that a constant supply of water could be made available throughout the year.

A number of ponds also serviced power of a different kind. Shallow, hard based areas of water were needed as standings during hot weather for horses and carts, to refresh the horses and soak the wooden cartwheels, contracting the iron tyres back on to the rims. Many of these ponds can

*Plate 1.7  A pond created to store water used for driving water wheels at the Llywernog Silver Mine, Wales.*

*Plate 1.8   Copy of an old photograph of horses using a Norfolk farm pond during the early part of this century. A farm building now stands over the site of the pond.*

still be seen in farmyards around the country as nostalgic reminders of the days, not so long past, when horses worked the land.

With such a rich history, ponds provide most important records of the ways in which our ancestors lived and worked. Man's activities have provided an unique legacy in the form of ponds of all shapes, sizes and functions, but it is a legacy which unhappily in recent years has fallen into serious decay.

## NUMBERS OF PONDS

It is virtually impossible to obtain accurate figures as to the number of ponds which remain in existence today. The physical difficulty of actually counting the number of stillwaters (including garden ponds) in the United Kingdom—even using aerial surveys—coupled with the need to try and differentiate between ponds and lakes, makes the operation a virtual non-starter even for the most serious of pond enthusiasts.

Ordnance Survey data collected between 1930 and 1960 provides a rough figure for the number of ponds in England and Wales as being in the order of 338,000. Dr Oliver Rackham has assessed the number of ponds larger than 6 metres across, using Ordnance Survey maps dating from the 1920s, and reckons that there were 340,000 ponds, lakes and wet pits in England and Wales at that time. He further calculates that in 1880 there were some 800,000 ponds in England and Wales, or fourteen ponds to the square mile. Dr Rackham's work also demonstrates the regional differences in pond distribution, with fewer ponds in the upland regions of England and Wales and more in the South, East and Midland areas; the greatest concentrations occurred in south and mid-Norfolk, north-east Suffolk and parts of Cheshire.

Many specialised sample surveys to assess the present number of ponds have been undertaken in recent years. One of the most comprehensive was carried out by the Ministry of Agriculture, Fisheries and Food in 1985. Results from this survey showed that there were about 170,000 ponds on farms in England and Wales. It was estimated by MAFF that 54,500 English farms (42 per cent of the total number of farms) had ponds up to 2,000 square metres in size and that each of these farms had an average of three ponds. 32 per cent of the farmers who had ponds on their land indicated in response to the survey that they had created or removed ponds during the five years prior to 1985, but the emphasis was found to have been on creation rather than destruction of ponds, with 19,000 gains against 10,000 losses. The figures for Wales provided by the same survey showed that only 27 per cent of farms (about 7,400) were estimated to have ponds, with an average of two each. On these 7,400 farms, 2,700 ponds had been created within the five years prior to the survey, against losses of some 800 ponds.

More localised surveys have been undertaken in recent years relating specifically to ponds on agricultural land and these show interesting results. The well publicised countryside survey carried out by the Stanton (Suffolk) branch of the National Farmers' Union (also in 1985), canvassed union members in 28 parishes covering almost 50 square miles. The agricultural land involved amounted to 12,340 hectares and covered most of the farms within the survey area.

The Stanton survey found that 433 ponds and 12 moats (plus 6 lakes or reservoirs) were present on the 126 participating farms. As a result of the survey, it was suggested that there were in excess of 11,000 ponds on Suffolk farms. Records kept by the United Framlingham Farmers Countryside Management Group (part of a Suffolk farming co-operative) show that on the 56 participating farms covering 11,330 hectares there are over 350 ponds. Both East Anglian surveys indicate that ponds on the region's highly productive cereal farms are not perhaps in such short supply as the casual observer might be led to believe and that not all of the landscape features and wildlife habitats on these farms have given way to the plough in recent years.

These records must be viewed in context because, as Dr Rackham showed, this area is favoured with a very high density of ponds. Survey work carried out in one of the other pond-rich counties, Cheshire, showed that some 110,000 ponds existed in the county, almost 30 per cent of the remaining national total.

Seemingly encouraging statistics derived from surveys such as these must, however, be viewed with some caution. While it is good that large numbers of ponds can still be found on farmland in some areas, no allowance can be made within a statistical survey for either the quality of those ponds, in terms of their ecological value, or the use to which they might be put. However, the numbers are significant, particularly in the case of the MAFF survey with regard to new pond creation, because the potential for the future is considerable if newly excavated ponds are well maintained.

Elsewhere, research has been conducted by many County Councils and other organisations to assess the rate of pond loss and the numbers of ponds remaining in particular areas. A sample survey conducted by Bedfordshire County Council Planning Department during 1978–9 showed that between 75 and 80 per cent of the ponds marked on the Ordnance Survey sheets of 1902 had disappeared by the late 1970s, either totally destroyed or rendered useless through neglect.

By comparing the 1882 six inch Ordnance Survey sheets with the 1978 1:10000 series maps, Hertfordshire County Council assessed that there were 7,007 ponds in the county in 1882, that number having fallen to 3,595 by 1978. The loss is believed to relate primarily to the decline in the traditional role of ponds in the rural economy. On a pessimistic note, the County Council suggested that the remaining ponds were under considerable threat from destruction, pollution, development, dumping, land drainage and neglect.

A study carried out in Hampshire has revealed an overall 24 per cent loss of ponds in six surveyed areas. Ordnance Survey sheets produced in 1904 and 1931 were compared with map evidence from 1960 and 1972 and showed that the greatest losses during the intervening period were of farm and field ponds as opposed to village and heathland ponds, although there had been a 14 per cent overall loss of ponds within villages, mainly due to housing developments.

The Nottinghamshire Biological Records Centre estimate that 90 per cent of the ponds occurring on agricultural land in that county have disappeared during the past 50 years, mainly due to changes in land use, in particular a rising trend towards arable farming as opposed to grassland and livestock farming. By contrast, however, a survey carried out in the

Loughborough district of North Leicestershire showed that in 1934, 958 field ponds existed in the district. By 1979, this number had decreased to 370, an overall loss of 60 per cent in 45 years. In this case, it was considered that the losses were largely due to natural succession, encouraged by livestock trampling around the edges of the ponds in grassland areas, following the advent of piped field water supplies.

A study carried out for the Nature Conservancy Council to look at marl pits in the Lower Dee Valley of Clywd concluded that 32 per cent of these ponds had disappeared by 1969, while research carried out at the Monks Wood Experimental Station in Huntingdonshire (now the Institute of Terrestrial Ecology) demonstrates how pond numbers have fluctuated over the years. In a study area of 2,000 hectares there were 112 ponds in 1764, this number having risen to 152 by 1890. Only 103 remained by 1950 and by 1969 the number had fallen to 67, representing an overall loss of ponds of 56 per cent since 1890, and a 35 per cent drop in pond numbers between 1950 and 1967.

These and other statistics collected in recent years provide evidence of a serious decline in pond numbers throughout the country, with many areas having lost between one-third and a half of their ponds over the past 100 years. Some of these losses have been inevitable, with the necessary changes in farming technology which have occurred since World War II. With the advent of larger machines working on farms, field sizes have had to be increased and the well documented loss of hedgerows around the country also resulted in a decline in the number of ponds. Old enclosure ponds created at the junctions of several fields disappeared together with the hedges, while field drainage superseded the need for pits to collect water and many ponds were lost as part of complex land drainage schemes. It is interesting to note that the United Framlingham Farmers' survey showed that many of the remaining ponds were found adjacent to surviving hedges or next to woodlands, tracks and roads—features retained on the farms—with few ponds still present in the centre of fields, where they would pose obstacles to farming.

Piped water supplies for grazing livestock have reduced the need for standing water in fields and as traditional drinking ponds have become redundant, so the management which is so vital for their survival has been neglected. These old ponds are often considered as hazards to livestock and have been infilled, or they are gradually lost as they become overgrown with plants and slowly revert to marshy ground through the process of natural succession (see p. 29). Ponds have also been seen as hazards for children and some near to farmsteads have been filled in, while many deep pits which were formerly ponds have become tips, providing a convenient disposal point for farm or domestic rubbish, but an undesirable one if located close to public roads.

*Plate 1.9   Pond loss due to agricultural intensification.*

*Plate 1.10   This pond is being destroyed by fly tipping.*

14

Not all pond losses can be attributed to agriculture—urban development has been responsible for the disappearance of many ponds. The construction of roads, housing estates and industrial complexes on green land will inevitably have resulted in widespread loss of ponds, but notwithstanding all of these reasons for pond losses, the sad fact is that yet another major part of the nation's heritage has been destroyed, mainly on account of man's activities, leaving society much poorer and with potentially disastrous effects on wildlife.

The well publicised loss of hedgerows around the country has resulted in a far greater appreciation of the problems facing the rural environment and is leading to major improvements in hedgerow management for the benefit of all. It can only be hoped that increased awareness of the dramatic decline in pond numbers and the problems facing those which remain will have a similar effect, with more old ponds being properly restored or maintained and greater encouragement given to the creation of new features.

## Ponds and Wildlife

Without doubt, the most important single contribution to the countryside made by ponds today is towards nature conservation. Any pond, whether it be small, butyl-lined and situated in the corner of a garden or a half hectare farm pond, is capable of providing valuable habitat for wildlife, although the bigger the pond, the better. This is simply because there is greater opportunity for variety in a large pond which will attract more wildlife and at the same time provide larger scale habitats. Likewise, old ponds are the most valuable for wildlife assuming that they are properly managed. The older the pond, the more time plants and animals have had to colonise and to become well established.

Many forms of wildlife require fresh water or its associated habitats for survival. Ponds support a wide range of fauna and flora; it has been suggested that over 1,000 species can occur in ponds, while the surrounding areas will support many more plants and animals which will derive value from the proximity of water. There are approximately 1,750 species of flowering plant and fern native to Great Britain, excluding Northern Ireland. (Native or indigenous plants are those which have always occurred in Britain and which have not been introduced from abroad.) About one-third of these plants are associated with wetland habitats such as open water, bog, fen and marsh. Aquatic or wetland plants which would not survive on a farm or in a garden unless water were present make a vital contribution to nature conservation, while representatives of all the major animal groups—protozoa, invertebrates, fishes, amphibians, reptiles, birds and mammals can be found in or around fresh water.

The decline in pond numbers which has been described in this chapter has adversely affected all of these forms of wildlife, with loss of species from many areas and reductions in the distribution of others around the country. This trend was highlighted by the survey of field ponds in North Leicestershire, outlined in the previous section. In addition to recording the loss of ponds in the area, it was also noted that while there were 87 species of aquatic plant in the locality prior to 1900, only 77 were present in 1979, with the distribution of a further 11 species reduced. These losses were attributable to a lack of pond management.

In terms of ponds and plants, it appears that the larger the pond, the better the diversity of species. Small ponds such as those in gardens, with a surface area of less than 20 m$^2$, tend to provide very uniform conditions, whereas those over 100 m$^2$ offer greater opportunities for a wider range of plants to become established.

The overall value of ponds to wildlife is best seen by looking at some of the various types of animal which are associated with water.

## Dragonflies and Damselflies

Dragonflies and damselflies are some of the most exciting forms of wildlife found around ponds. They are also among the oldest orders of life, their ancestors having flown over 300 million years ago. There are thirty-seven resident breeding species of dragonfly in Britain, excluding the smaller damselflies, with the best breeding sites for these insects being small areas of acidic stillwater in the lowlands, normally found on heathland. It is essential that ponds supporting dragonflies and damselflies do not dry out during the summer months, so very shallow pools are often unsuitable, but any moderately sized pond with good surrounding habitat should encourage these beautiful creatures. Because of their predatory habits—they require plenty of smaller insects to eat—and conspicuous presence, they are more likely to be seen where the quality of the pond and its environs is high, providing plenty of suitable food.

The value of ponds to dragonflies is considerable; the Nature Conservancy Council's review of nature conservation in Great Britain published in 1984 specifically refers to dragonflies, listing the extinction, vulnerability and decline of resident breeding species in the country since 1950. The ruddy sympetrum, a dragonfly once common in the southern half of the British Isles, is shown by the Nature Conservancy Council as a declining species because of the loss of ponds and the removal of emergent vegetation around the edge of ponds in the interests of improving fishing and amenity. There is little doubt that the loss of ponds throughout Britain has resulted in many species of dragonfly and damselfly becoming far less widely distributed. Notes on pond design to encourage these insects can be found in Chapter 3.

## Birds

Ponds are often too small to encourage breeding birds, but they do have an influence on the wellbeing of many species which need to visit water, for instance swallows and martins which obtain materials for nest building from wet areas. Song thrushes will feed around the margins of ponds and recorded observations from one small, butyl-lined garden pond showed that regular visitors to drink during the summer months included stock dove, wood pigeon, goldfinch, hawfinch, blackbird, willow warbler and blackcap. A small clump of sedges, no more than a metre in diameter adjacent to the same pond, also encouraged a pair of sedge warblers to nest successfully, a demonstration that even very small ponds can have major significance for both common and uncommon species of bird (see plate 5.2, p. 105). A much larger butyl-lined pond created at the headquarters of the Royal Society for the Protection of Birds attracted thirty species of bird to drink or bathe in the water within four months of the pond being completed.

It is quite common to find birds such as mallard and moorhen nesting around larger ponds, especially in the case of the mallard if conditions on the bankside are suitable. Hints on the design of ponds and their surroundings to encourage wildfowl are given in Chapter 3. Moorhens appear to prefer ponds with plenty of reeds and rushes around the edges and also seem to have more breeding success when there is good cover in the form of scrub surrounding the pond, to protect them from predators.

Where reedbeds and scrub areas form part of the margins of larger ponds in the 0.4 hectare size range, other species of bird such as warblers and reed buntings may be more easily encouraged but, as with mallard, this will largely depend on the quality of the surrounding habitat and not just on the pond itself. Teal can often be found using farm ponds during the winter and tufted duck are frequent visitors to open ponds, while ponds with associated marshy areas are quite likely to attract common snipe.

## Amphibians and Reptiles

Like dragonflies, amphibians are good indicators of the quality of a pond. Many well managed stillwaters should be a haven for frogs, toads and possibly even newts. In England and Wales, it is also possible that one of the more common reptiles, the grass-snake, may be found living around the margins of the pond in areas of good ground cover and feeding both in and out of the water, its diet including all types of amphibian.

There are six amphibians native to Britain:

Common frog
Common toad
Natterjack toad (now rare and only found in sandy coastal areas)

Smooth or common newt
Palmate newt
Warty or great crested newt

The natterjack toad and great crested newt are both fully protected species under the provisions of the Wildlife and Countryside Act 1981 (see Chapter 8, Ponds, Wildlife and the Law) and any pond or its surrounding area where either species may be present must not be disturbed. Prior to any management being carried out on such areas, specialist advice must be obtained, from either the Nature Conservancy Council or local County Wildlife Trust.

Amphibians spend only a relatively short period of time actually in the water during the spring breeding season. As with birds and dragonflies, the conditions around the perimeter of the pond are of considerable importance if these animals are to be encouraged to remain at the pond or to colonise a new feature.

Unfortunately, many ponds providing safe homes for amphibians have disappeared in recent years and more sites are threatened. A recent survey commissioned by the Nature Conservancy Council and conducted by Leicester Polytechnic estimated that there are now 6,000 breeding sites for great crested newts, mainly in the south and east of Britain, 2 per cent of the newts' breeding sites having been lost between 1980 and 1985.

The Nature Conservancy Council's survey 'The Status of the Common Amphibians and Reptiles in Britain', published in 1983, records the demise of the native amphibians in relation to pond loss, with the greatest emphasis placed on the decline of the great crested newt, which has suffered more than other, more common species. However, while traditional breeding sites have disappeared, the increasing interest in pond creation amongst the owners of Britain's 405,000 hectares of gardens may help to redress the balance in favour of species such as the common frog. This has benefited considerably from the development of suitable ponds in gardens; it appears that there are now more frogs in some suburban areas than in the surrounding countryside.

More specific information on the design of ponds for amphibian conservation is provided in Chapter 3.

## Water beetles

Any pond watcher will frequently see beetles in and around the water. These fascinating insects are often some of the first colonisers of new ponds, able to disperse easily from other stillwaters because of their ability to fly.

One of the most exciting of the many common beetles found in ponds is the great diving beetle. Growing up to 35 mm long, it is unmistakable as it moves swiftly through the water in search of food. The females lay their eggs in holes made in underwater plants and both larvae and adults feed on small invertebrates, as well as attacking amphibians and small fish.

Figure 1.1   Great diving beetle

Another easily recognised water beetle is the whirligig. This is much smaller than the great diving beetle, only 5 mm long, but its behaviour, whirling round and round on the surface of the pond and feeding on smaller insects which have fallen on to the water, makes it instantly identifiable. An interesting inhabitant of ponds which are rich in organic matter is the screech beetle. More commonly found in southern areas, this beetle is about 12 mm long. It makes the squeak for which it is named by rubbing the tip of its abdomen against its forewings when it is alarmed. The screech beetle, too, is carnivorous, feeding on small invertebrates which it finds in the mud on the floor of the pond. The larvae of all three of these beetles pupate out of the water, either in the mud around the pond or on emergent plants.

The largest of the water beetles, the great silver beetle (named because of the air bubble which covers its thorax and abdomen when it is underwater and which gives it its silvery appearance), is sadly now becoming much less common because of the loss of its favoured habitats, weedy ponds and plant-rich drainage dykes. One of Europe's largest beetles, it can grow to 45 mm in length, scavenging on plant material as well as other insects and water snails, the latter forming the almost exclusive diet of the larvae.

These and many other forms of wildlife are dependent on wetland habitats for their survival. The management of our dwindling stock of ponds is absolutely vital if these once common creatures are not to become uncommon and in many areas be preserved only as memories.

## PONDS IN THE LANDSCAPE

A picturesque, well managed pond in any location provides an attractive addition to the landscape. A sheet of water, bordered by tall, emergent vegetation, with the leaves and colourful flowers of floating plants breaking the water surface, cannot fail to excite the imagination whether it is viewed at close quarters or from afar.

Where the countryside is characterised by hedges, trees and boundary walls or even where few such features relieve the visual monotony of large expanses of cropped land or pasture, a pond helps to provide diversity. The changing colours throughout the seasons and the variety of wildlife which may be seen in conjunction with the water serve to heighten the interest, effects which are enhanced if the pond can be viewed from higher ground. The visual impact is increased where trees grow near the pond: in some agricultural areas, ponds (for instance old marl pits) are clearly identified by clumps of trees growing around the margins—often the only trees for some distance. The natural beauty of the countryside is based on variety, and a landscape without ponds and other areas of water would be much poorer, a feeling admirably summed up by the German authors Kabisch and Hemmerling in the title of their book *Ponds & Pools—Oases in the Landscape*.

*Chapter 2*

# Life in the Water

Some basic knowledge of how life flourishes within stillwaters will add considerably to an owner's enjoyment of a pond. Without an understanding of how the pond works, many of the reasons why it should be managed in any particular way cannot be fully appreciated and mistakes can easily be made, jeopardising either the survival of wildlife or the utilisation of the water.

The terminology relating to the environment tends to include jargon which can sometimes be confusing. Three words in common use are defined below:

*Ecology* is the study of the ways in which plants and animals relate to their environment.

An *ecosystem* is the situation which arises out of the interaction of animals and plants (organisms) both with their environment and with one another.

*Habitat* is the term used to refer to the place where any animal or plant exists; a habitat is the home of that creature or plant.

A pond can be regarded as an ecosystem, providing a variety of habitats for wildlife. The study of the pond and its wildlife is then described as ecology.

Ecosystems come in many forms but the pond is one of the nearest examples which can be found of a closed ecosystem, because the waters of the pond are self-contained and the animals or plants within the water are enclosed in one place. As a whole, the feature is capable of surviving for a long period in some form without outside interference, which makes ponds an extremely important habitat type.

Wildlife within the pond is affected by several factors. Some of these are physical, for example light, temperature, the oxygen content of the water and the acidity or alkalinity of the pond. Other factors result from the interaction between the various organisms within the water and these are described as biotic, for instance the relationship between predators and their prey.

## PHYSICAL FACTORS AFFECTING LIFE IN THE POND

### Light

Light is the major source of energy in most stillwaters. It is vital that light reaches the surface of the water, and yet the amount of available light will vary according to circumstances which are often beyond man's control. Cloud cover, climate, season and the physical aspect of the pond all exert an influence on the amount of light reaching the water surface, but man can also have an effect by ensuring that excessive shade caused by overhanging trees or plants whose leaves cover the surface of the pond does not prevent light striking the water.

Sunlight is the starting point for life within the pond. To create the right conditions for the interaction of the different organisms within any habitat (including a pond) two things are essential: first a continuous energy flow within the ecosystem, and second the recycling of organic matter. Light is the catalyst which starts both processes.

### Temperature

The temperature of the water within the pond is of fundamental importance for the development of life. Cold water is very dense and this adversely affects the distribution of animals within the pond, which move about less at lower temperatures. The deeper the water the cooler it is, so less life is present at great depths. In shallow waters where the temperature is higher, normally around the pond margins, a greater proportion of the animals living in the pond will be found.

A pond which has a range of depths varying from shallows through to deeper regions will have a richer ecosystem, assuming other factors are satisfactory, than a pond with little depth variation.

### Oxygen

Oxygen is absolutely essential to the great majority of living organisms and the volume present in the water is dependent upon a number of criteria:

- Ponds which are in very sheltered locations experience little surface disturbance caused by the wind. Because of this, only very small amounts of oxygen will be absorbed at the water surface.
- The higher the pond lies above sea level, the lower the air pressure, and oxygen solubility is reduced.
- High temperatures cause low volumes of oxygen to be held in water.
- The amount of plant life.

Activities within the pond also influence the amount of oxygen which is available to support life. The decomposition of organic matter such as leaf litter (which builds up in almost every pond) or plant tissue utilises valuable oxygen, while the breakdown of pollutants also requires very large amounts of oxygen, thus reducing the amount available for animal life. The pollutants involved are most obviously chemicals, but also substances such as slurry, silage effluent or milk which can find their way into farm ponds.

The devastation caused to fish populations in rivers, lakes and ponds by chemical spillage is evidence of the destruction which can be caused when all of the oxygen available in the water is suddenly utilised to break down pollutants which possess what are known as high biological oxygen demands.

## Chemical Composition of the Water

All water contains chemicals, but not all chemicals are present in every pond to the same degree. The quantities and types of chemical present in water are dependent on the local geology and the properties of any catchment water running into the pond. For instance, chemicals used on land adjoining a pond may find their way directly into the water or leach through the soil into drainage systems and hence to the pond. Once in the water, they will alter the chemical balance within the pond thus having an impact on the ecosystem.

Using chemical properties as a guide, stillwaters can be classed as:

*Oligotrophic*—poor in nutrients.
*Mesotrophic*—moderately supplied with nutrients.
*Eutrophic*—rich in nutrients.

Oligotrophic waters tend to be virtually sterile, supporting little life. These waters are acidic and are normally located in the north of the United Kingdom and in upland regions where the underlying rocks are very hard and do not release many nutrients into the water. Because of the lack of nutrient, plant growth is poor and this is not conducive to the development of rich pond fauna and flora.

In the south and east, stillwaters tend to be richer in nutrients and are therefore more productive. Ponds in these regions range from mesotrophic through to eutrophic. Ponds in the latter category contain the highest proportions of nutrients and hence the greatest variety of pond life. In extreme cases they are also subject to copious algal growth, which detracts from the value of the pond because it limits light penetration into the water, thus preventing the growth of other plants and encouraging bacteria.

Eutrophic waters are salt rich and alkaline because the flora which flourishes in nutrient rich ponds produces plenty of carbon dioxide, which combines with calcium salts (important constituents of fresh water) to produce calcium carbonate. This encourages the decomposition of organic matter within the pond, which is then recycled back into the water as nutrient, helping to support more life.

Most of the oxygen which is present in water is produced by plants—if there is no vegetation in the pond there is little oxygen. Without oxygen there can be little animal activity; hence the sterility of oligotrophic ponds in relation to more productive eutrophic ones.

## BIOTIC FACTORS AFFECTING LIFE IN THE POND

Life in the pond starts when oxygen is produced within the water as a by-product of a process called photosynthesis, which is carried out by green plants known as primary producers. These green plants photosynthesise using sunlight, to fix green pigment (chlorophyll) and convert carbon dioxide and water into oxygen and glucose. The role of sunlight in the life of a pond is thus crucial, because without light the primary producers would not survive and photosynthesise, so there would be no oxygen.

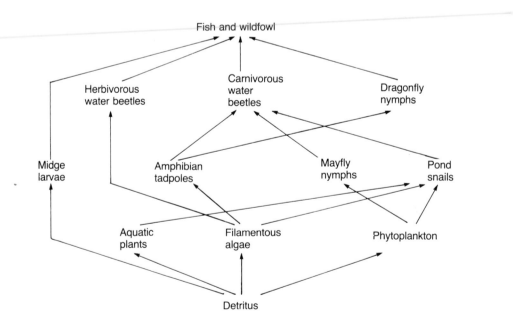

Figure 2.1   Simple food web in a pond

Nutrient which is generated by this process provides food for organisms within the water. In the first instance, these organisms are microscopic freshwater plankton, known as the primary consumers. These in turn become food for secondary consumers. The primary consumers within the pond are herbivorous, only feeding on plant material, while the secondary consumers are carnivorous, feeding on other animals.

This is the start of the freshwater food web which leads via many intermediate stages to duck, fish and ultimately to man. The energy flow continues as living organisms within the pond die, because their bodies decompose through the action of bacteria and their remains are then recycled as inorganic substances back into the system.

Life within the pond is not standardised, however, because while the fundamental processes remain similar there are several different regions in the pond where physical and biotic factors interact in varying ways, thus helping to create the amazing diversity of life in the water and making the study of pondlife so fascinating and exciting.

## THE PLANT ZONES

Plants adapt in different ways to water. Some species cannot survive actually growing in water, while others are able to thrive with either their roots or the entire plant submerged beneath the surface. Classification of plants according to the various zones of a pond is difficult because of these extremes and the intermediate stages which occur in between.

A brief look at any pond will reveal the way in which the flora is zoned. Around the edges of the pond, grasses and herbaceous plants on drier ground (terrestrial habitats) will give way to tall reeds or rushes at the water's edge. The surface of the pond will be characterised by the floating leaves of lilies or pondweeds beneath which submerged, free floating plants will flourish.

The transition from the dry ground surrounding the pond, through to the wet margins and eventually to the water itself is described as a hydrosere. Within this area, terrestrial plants commonly occurring on dry land mingle with wetland species forming marshland. It is marshland which is the first plant zone associated with life in the water.

### Marshland

Plants growing in the marsh surrounding a pond are those which are equally at home either in a very wet field or in the soils occurring around the edge of an area of water. The yellow flag iris is a typical inhabitant of marshes, while the marsh marigold (as its name suggests), otherwise known as the

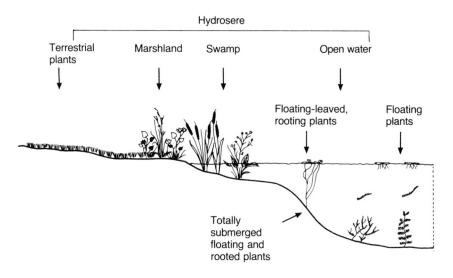

Figure 2.2　Cross-section of a pond showing the plant zones

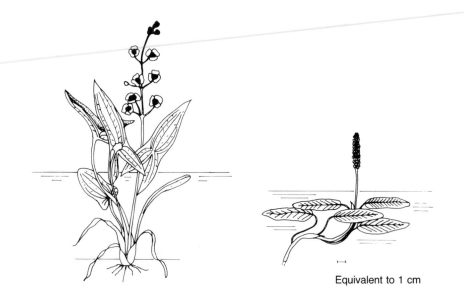

Figure 2.3　Arrowhead

Equivalent to 1 cm

Figure 2.4　Amphibious bistort

kingcup, is a very attractive early flowering species which will establish round most ponds, to be followed into flower later in the season by ragged robin and purple loosestrife, plants which can also be found growing wild in wet meadows. (See colour plates 2–5.)

As the marshland becomes progressively wetter, to the point where the ground is permanently waterlogged, these plants will still occur but the main emphasis turns to emergent species which root in the soils under water but with erect leaves and stems growing up above the water to flower. At this point, the marsh gives way to the swamp zone.

## Swamp

In the swamp, emergent plants are more common than marshland species. Reeds and rushes are typical swamp inhabitants and in larger ponds this zone may be characterised by extensive reedbeds, providing homes for many invertebrates and birds.

Around the water's edge, clumps of bur-reed, water mint, flowering rush, brooklime and water forget-me-not will appear, while further out into the pond colonies of smaller plants will become established. These smaller plants have their roots firmly anchored in mud, but their leaves and flower heads emerge above the surface of the water in summer. They prefer to grow in water less than 225 mm deep and typical species include bogbean, arrowhead, water plantain and amphibious bistort. Because of their growth habits, these plants can also be described as water plants and are typical of the edges of the next zone as well, where the true water plants grow. (See colour plates 6–9.)

## Open Water

As the water depth increases to around 300 mm, a third zone succeeds the swamp. As the pond becomes deeper, so a fascinating range of plants find suitable homes; these are the true aquatics. Species occurring within the third zone can be divided into three distinct groups, based on the way in which they grow. All of these plants still require nutrient, carbon dioxide and oxygen, which they absorb from the water through very thin skins, while some also obtain nutrient from the mud on the floor of the pond via their roots.

The first group of aquatic plants includes those which are rooted on the bottom of the pond but which send up shoots producing leaves and flowers to float on the surface. Of these species, the most obvious and colourful examples are the water lilies. The native white and yellow varieties are the commonest, flourishing in up to 2 m of water on account of their long, flexible stems. Lilies spread very quickly in shallow water by means of

Figure 2.5   Frogbit

Equivalent to 1 cm

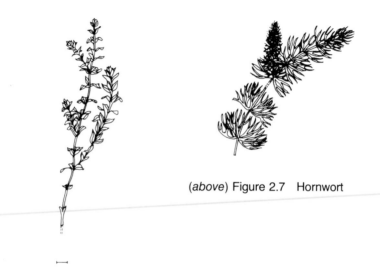

(*above*) Figure 2.7   Hornwort

Equivalent to 1 cm          (*left*) Figure 2.6   Canadian pond weed

seeds, which are easily dispersed throughout the pond. During winter, the individual plants die back below the surface and survive as rhizomes on the bottom, their extensive root systems storing energy. Established colonies of lilies can cause problems during the summer when the surface of the water becomes smothered by their leaves, which cut off light to other plants and organisms which are trying to grow in the water beneath.

The second group of plants occurring in this zone are those which float on the surface of the pond and trail roots below them to obtain nutrient from the water. These plants are not anchored in the mud at the bottom of the pond and they get their oxygen from the air above the water surface. The most common species are the duckweeds, tiny plants with leaves only 2 mm across, which flourish in any area of nutrient rich water. Seeming to appear from nowhere, but often imported by visiting animals or birds, duckweeds very rapidly reproduce and cover the surface of the water, causing severe management problems similar to those created by lilies.

One of the most attractive floating species, frogbit, produces small white flowers during the summer, while the water fern is another example of a rapidly spreading plant (albeit a beautiful one) which also requires control during the summer to prevent surface smothering. Some of the numerous varieties of pondweed can be included in this second category of plants, although some are also major components of the third group of aquatics, those which spend their lives totally underwater.

One of the most common pondweeds, the non-native Canadian pond-weed, falls into this latter category. It is a very adaptable species, which accounts for its success in establishing itself throughout ponds in the United Kingdom. Canadian pondweed is one of the best oxygenating species, hence it has been regularly introduced to ponds, especially smaller ones in gardens. A tiny fragment of Canadian pondweed will quickly grow into a new plant and so, once introduced and established in a pond, it is virtually impossible to eradicate. This can be detrimental to other pond life, because the Canadian pondweed takes over and dominates smaller ponds, often preventing other species from establishing.

Hornwort is a good example of a free-floating plant. Not only is it an excellent oxygenator within the water, but its long, trailing stems with many whorls of leaves, which sometimes reach 1 m in length, provide excellent cover for invertebrates. It does not root in the mud at the bottom of the pond, unlike a species with which it is often confused, water milfoil. This is also a good oxygenator, with most of its growth occurring underwater. The stems sometimes reach 3 m in length and send up flower spikes which break the surface of the pond.

The different species of plants found in and around ponds are too numerous to mention individually, but many typical plants suitable for careful introduction to new ponds are listed in Appendix 2.

**Natural Succession**

Ponds are not static ecosystems. Within the enclosed waters of the pond and around its banks, life is constantly, if slowly, changing. Natural processes steadily alter the nature of the pond, so that over the course of many years the plant zones change and, in the case of some ponds, over a very long period the pond may cease to exist altogether. This process is called natural succession and, as described in the previous chapter, it has been one of the reasons why large numbers of ponds have disappeared during the last century.

While helping to recycle nutrients within the water, the decomposition of dead plant tissue also inevitably leads to accumulations of organic silt at the bottom of the pond. Decaying organic material in water is a product not just of those plants growing in and around the pond but is also the result of leaves blowing into the water—a major problem where the pond is sited in or on the edge of woodland or adjacent to mature trees. Water flowing into the pond will also bring silt and as material from all these sources gradually accumulates so the water depth decreases. This is most noticeable in the early stages around the edges of the pond, especially in the swamp zone, but it should not be confused with seasonal variations in water level—the process of natural succession is incredibly slow and will only manifest itself visually over many years, unless the pond is stream fed.

The reduction in water depth caused by silt accumulations means that there is less space for the true aquatic plants and the swamp zone is able to spread out further into the pond. As the swamp moves forward, so the marshy area becomes drier and more terrestrial plants colonise, together with trees and shrubs which can survive in wet or damp conditions. Willows and alders readily establish under these circumstances to form 'carr' and, given time, the whole pond will gradually become shallower. The swamp will encroach further across the surface and if nature runs its course without man's intervention, the pond will cease to exist as an open water feature, its place taken by an area of marshland.

## ANIMAL LIFE

It is not just the plant zones which are affected by natural succession. The quality and amount of animal life in a pond is governed not just by

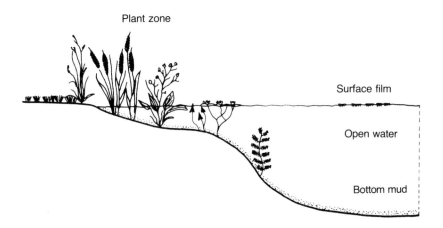

Figure 2.8   Cross-section of a pond showing the zones of animal life

physical characteristics such as water quality but also by zoning. Animal life is not possible without plants, so the richer the diversity of plant life within the water, the more chances there are of finding plenty of animals in the pond. There are four main zones within the pond where animals thrive and each of these must be maintained by management: surface film, plant zone, open water, bottom mud.

## Surface Film

This is a highly complex and very busy place. Many of the creatures living in the water must visit the surface to feed or to take in oxygen, while a number of animals actually live either above the surface film or just beneath it.

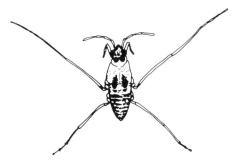

Figure 2.9   Pond skater

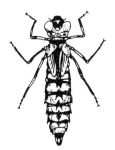

Figure 2.10   Dragonfly nymph

Pond skaters spend their whole lives above the pond, exploiting a phenomenon called surface tension as they move across the face of the water, feeding on insects unfortunate enough to land on the pond or which fall off overhanging vegetation. Water measurers and water crickets are also common inhabitants of this zone. These form the prey, together with pond skaters, of predators such as water boatmen and fish which come up to feed at the surface.

On the underside of the surface film, snails, flatworms and mosquito larvae can be found. They do not emerge out of the water but derive benefit from the same surface tension which supports the pond skaters above them.

## Plant Zone

In terms of animal life in stillwaters, the plant zone is a far more specific habitat than the area previously described under plant zoning (see pp. 25–29).

To the fauna of a pond, the plant zone is confined to the shallow region around the margins of the water where the emergent plants thrive. Because of the lack of depth, the water warms up quickly and light penetration is good. The wealth of photosynthesising plants around the edges of the pond ensures that plenty of oxygen and nutrients are available, so this zone is the most heavily populated part of the pond, teeming with animal life. The mass of vegetation encourages herbivores, which in turn are preyed upon by carnivores, so a wide variety of sizes of animal can be found, including microscopic plankton, dragonfly nymphs, snails, water beetles, amphibians and ultimately fish as the water begins to deepen.

## Open Water

Fish are the animals most normally associated with deep, open water—the parts of the pond away from the fringe vegetation. However, plenty of other life can also be found in the deeper zones, seeking refuge and food amongst the submerged plants and taking advantage of the plentiful algae and plankton rich water.

## Bottom Mud

The mud and detritus found at the bottom of established ponds is not at first sight the most attractive of habitats and yet many animals make their homes there, playing a vital role in the life of the pond by recycling nutrient back into the water.

Chironomid (midge) larvae, favoured food of fish and duck, exist in the mud, feeding on decaying plant tissue, while tubifex worms are also abundant. The larvae of the whirligig beetle stays near to the mud on the

(*above*) Figure 2.12    Tubifex worms

(*left*) Figure 2.11    Midge larva (chironomid)

bed of the pond until it is almost fully grown and dragonfly larvae also burrow in the sediments. Bottom feeding fish thrive on the invertebrates which exist in the mud. Thus this very active area is an essential part of the pond, its inhabitants forming a significant part of the food web.

## ALGAE

No look at life in the pond would be complete without a mention of algae. For many pond owners the problems caused by algae are the most serious that they encounter while looking after their ponds. Prevention is certainly easier than cure, but in all ponds some degree of algal growth is unavoidable and needs to be accepted as part of the normal life cycle.

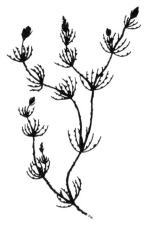

Figure 2.13   Stonewort

Algae are very primitive, non-flowering plants whose spores are present everywhere in air or water. These spores will develop into plants wherever a suitable medium is present and in the case of a pond this medium is, quite naturally, water.

The most common type of algae, and also the most primitive, are the olive greens. These are single celled, minute organisms, capable of multiplying very quickly by cell division to form the algal blooms so dreaded by pond owners. Other types of blue and green algae grow into long filaments, much in evidence during the latter part of the summer and sometimes known as blanket weed or cott.

A more advanced type of filamentous algae, a green algae called cladophera, grows rapidly in polluted water and forms dense mats or rafts of blanket weed which often have to be raked off ponds. The presence of this in a pond is a good indication that something is wrong, normally that the water has been enriched or polluted in some way. Stoneworts are also algae, although they are highly developed forms, and are early colonisers of many new or restored ponds.

Algae thrive on nutrient and sunlight; they are primary food producers and significant generators of oxygen through photosynthesis. Under normal circumstances their presence is inevitable and acceptable, but if excess nutrients in the form of nitrates and phosphates are present in the water, and are not utilised by other plants and animals, the algae will thrive unchecked thus becoming a problem.

Control of algae is described in Chapter 6, Pond Management.

# Chapter 3

# Pond Design

The success of any pond creation or restoration scheme depends on two factors: design of the pond and surrounding areas and subsequent management. This chapter looks at the various ways in which design can influence the quality of a pond, either purely as a wildlife habitat or in terms of an alternative end use.

Any pond which is created primarily for conservation must be planned so that the optimum conditions for the development of the ecological zones described in Chapter 2, Life in the Water, are available. It is not enough to dig a deep hole in the ground and then wait for marvellous results. Something will happen in the pond once it is full of water, but it will not be the balanced effect which is so attractive and desirable.

There are no rules governing the design of ponds, but in general it is essential that plenty of different features are provided, both in and out of the water, because the habitat requirements of the fauna and flora associated with freshwater vary so much from species to species. As a rule of thumb guide, the more diversity in and around the pond the better, otherwise many of the plants and animals which depend on water will not become established, let alone survive.

Despite the limitations of time, money and space which affect most pond schemes, it is well worth trying to include some, if not all of the features described in the following sections when a pond creation or restoration scheme is being planned. The inclusion of as many as are practically possible will help to ensure that the optimum use is made of the site. In addition to these features, special references to the requirements of amphibians, dragonflies and wildfowl are made between pp. 46–55.

Where the pond is to provide a supply of water for livestock or act as a reservoir of water for fire fighting on the farm, special considerations apply which are outlined on pp. 55–57 although, because it is quite possible for the pond to serve several purposes, all of the other design factors should be considered in the planning process.

In every instance, safety aspects must be taken into account. Guidelines for these are provided in Chapter 4, Pond Construction.

## FEATURES TO INCLUDE WHEN PLANNING A POND

The most important features to include in a new pond are an irregular shoreline, islands or nesting platforms, gently sloping banksides, steep areas of bank, variations in water depth and space around the outside of the pond for the development of other habitats.

### Irregular Shoreline

In the past, pond creation was often regarded simply as digging a hole in the ground and allowing it to fill with water. The hole was generally regular in shape with steeply shelving banks which discouraged wildlife.

One of the easiest ways to attract wildlife to a pond is to create the longest possible length of bankside. This enables plenty of plants to become established, providing habitats for lots of small invertebrates which are then eaten by larger animals. As the food web grows, so life in the water begins to flourish.

Given two sites of similar size, a circular pond on one site will have a shorter length of bankside than a pond on the second site which has a very

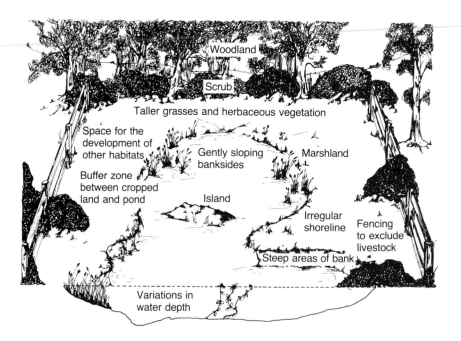

Figure 3.1   Features to include when designing a pond

irregular shoreline, characterised by indented bays and spits protruding into the water. In the second pond, the more visually exciting outline does more than merely allowing space for plants to grow. The bays and spits help to provide areas of calm water on large ponds, because a correctly sited spit will protect the surface of the water in an adjacent bay from the prevailing wind. The shelter created by these irregular shorelines is of considerable importance to dragonflies and damselflies, which prefer relatively undisturbed stands of emergent plants growing around the pond margins.

Breeding wildfowl also derive benefit from indented shorelines. Being territorial, they are more likely to nest successfully if secluded sites are available, therefore the more irregular the outline, the better the potential for duck. (See colour plate 10.)

Naturally, there is more scope for dramatic bankside design on large sites, but even in small, artificially lined ponds some shape variation can be provided, thus increasing the opportunities for wildlife and improving the appearance of the pond. Where the pond has a surface area in excess of 0.25 ha (2,500 m²), the potential may exist for the creation of a small reedbed in a large bay, which might attract birds such as reed and sedge warblers, especially where the adjoining bankside shrubs include hawthorns and willows.

## Islands

The construction of an island serves a number of purposes: it extends the length of shoreline; creates more potential wildfowl breeding sites; helps to alleviate surface disturbance of the water; and encourages seclusion.

The building of an island solely as a breeding site for wildfowl is only really feasible on very large ponds because, unless it is at least 30 m away from the banks and separated from the shore by deep water, predators such as weasels and stoats will be able to cross from dry land. No island is totally safe from mink and if these animals are known to be in the vicinity, control measures are essential.

The optimum shape for an island is either a cross or a crescent. The cross provides the longest possible length of shoreline, while water in at least one of the bays will be sheltered from the prevailing winds. In big ponds, the crescent island is an ideal shape to attract breeding wildfowl. If the mouth of the bay created by the island faces away from the prevailing wind, and the bay itself is very shallow, wildfowl will have good feeding areas as well as safe nesting sites. In the absence of a natural island, for instance in a very deep or artificially lined pond, where the construction of a solid island would pose technical difficulties, a floating nesting platform anchored to the base of the pond is an excellent substitute.

*Plate 3.1   Here a crescent-shaped island has been created in a new pond.*

Creation of natural islands is described in Chapter 4, Pond Construction, and nesting platforms in Chapter 5, Supplementary Habitat Creation.

## Gently Sloping Shorelines

The most significant ecological zone within the pond is shallow water, varying between 150 mm and 600 mm. Characterised by warm temperatures and plentiful plant growth, this part of the pond is the richest in pondlife and it is vital that animals, for instance ducks and amphibians, are given access to it. Ducklings cannot manage steep slopes or a step which is more than 50 mm high, either on entering or leaving the water, and if they are to be successfully reared they must be able to enter the pond to feed, while amphibians must have access to shallow, plant rich waters for spawning.

The best way to create access into the pond is to leave several areas of shoreline, including around any islands, where the banks slope very gently into the water. Where space is a limiting factor, access should be provided on the northern edge of the pond where it will adjoin sunny banksides with a southerly aspect. At least one gentle incline should be created in very small ponds, not only to encourage amphibians but also so that small mammals such as hedgehogs which fall into the water can climb out again. Failing this, a brick or log resting on a shallow ledge near the bank will enable these animals to climb out of the water to safety.

Preformed fibreglass pond liners which have steep sides can be fitted with plastic ramps to provide animals with a means of escape.

## Steep Areas of Bank

In large ponds where there is plenty of scope for creative shaping of the shoreline, it is often possible to provide a 'cliff-face' bank, ideally on the eastern or western side of the pond. This may attract kingfishers and sand martins to nest. The 'cliff-face' needs to rise at least 1.5 m above the top water level, so unless the pond is being excavated into a sloping site or the water level is well below original ground level (necessitating substantial earthmoving) an artificial cliff will have to be constructed.

Techniques for creating 'cliff-face' banks are described in Chapter 5, Supplementary Habitat Creation.

## Variations in Water Depth

### Shallow ledges
The gentle slopes described on p. 38 should lead on to shallow, water covered ledges which are rich in plant and animal life. These should be between 150–600 mm deep. The area of shallows will vary according to the size of the pond. Very small ponds may only have space for a ledge 150 mm deep and 500 mm wide if sufficient deep water is to be provided. In more extensive ponds it should be possible to produce several square metres of shallow water per bay or adjacent to gently graded banks.

Shallows must also be created around solid islands and can be provided in the middle of very large ponds simply by raising the bed of the pond to within a few centimetres of the surface. These areas will be of particular value to wildfowl and wading birds. The minimum depth of water covering shallows should be 50 mm, falling to a maximum depth of 600 mm. An average of around 200 mm is ideal, enabling plants to root but also deep enough to allow pond life to flourish. It is important that the shallow areas are water covered throughout the year, so careful planning is vital to ensure that levels are correct when large ponds are excavated.

### Deep water
The shallow ledges must slope away to deeper parts of the pond. In ponds larger than 100 m$^2$, the shallows should slope down to a depth of 1.5 m and then drop sharply to the bed of the pond. The maximum depth will vary according to the surface area: small ponds are likely to be less than 1 m deep if sloping banks and shallows are to be provided, whereas in ponds over 100 m$^2$ it should be possible to achieve at least 1.5 m. The target depth for ponds larger than this should be between 2.5 and 3 m.

*Plate 3.2   An old pond and ditch prior to restoration.*

*Plate 3.3   The completed pond. Note the shape of the shoreline and the depth variations.*

Depths in excess of 2 m in large ponds are essential for the development of the open water ecological zone, where deep rooting plants can become established and free floating ones have space to flourish. If the pond is not deep enough, the surface to volume ratio is too high and when the shallow water warms up the overall pond temperature rises. If there is no cool, deep water where animals can take refuge, disaster may occur because of oxygen depletion.

In addition to providing better conditions for wildlife, the greater the volume of water in relation to surface area the better, because:

(a) Where the water is deep, the increased volume is better able to dilute any pesticide or fertiliser residues which may accidentally enter the pond, thus helping to reduce their impact on water quality.

(b) Water fluctuations will be fewer, mainly because there is less evaporation of the cooler water. Consistent water levels help to encourage ecological stability.

(c) Long term management of the pond is made easier. Deep water does not become overgrown with plants as quickly as shallow areas, so management is required less frequently, with reduced disturbance to wildlife.

## Space Around the Outside of the Pond for the Development of Other Habitats

Although a pond is the nearest equivalent in wildlife terms to a self contained community, the maximum benefits of the pond to wildlife can only be fully realised if a number of different types of bankside habitat are created. These should be designed not only to encourage the fauna and flora which are directly associated with water, but also to help many of the other species which will be drawn to the pond.

Many ponds which are excellent aquatic environments are often spoiled because insufficient attention is given to the surrounding terrestrial areas. Lack of space is a common reason why the true potential of many ponds is seldom achieved, the area around the pond often being too small to allow grassland, scrub and woodland to become established. Where a bare site is being developed it would be better not to fill the whole area with a pond, but rather to create a small expanse of water with other terrestrial habitats round the edges. This is especially important on farmland, where a buffer zone—for instance a belt of rough grassland or scrub—will help to shelter the pond.

*Buffer zones*
The setting aside of land to form a buffer zone is an ideal way to increase the potential of a pond to support wildlife. In agricultural parlance, 'set-aside'

*Plate 3.4   Development of a field corner habitat. The pond would have been better if it had had a more interesting shape and been located further back into the field corner, thus reducing the volume of water running off the slope into the pond. The space has otherwise been used well, with plenty of room for the development of other habitats.*

means to take land out of production; in the case of the land around a farm pond, this is exactly what is required.

The amount of land necessary to create an adequate buffer zone is impossible to quantify. Much will depend on the location of the pond. Where the pond adjoins an existing valuable habitat or lies in the midst of extensively managed land, a smaller buffer zone will be required than that where the pond is surrounded by intensively managed arable or grassland. A strip of ground 3 m wide around the perimeter of the pond is probably too small, because the wildlife existing in linear features of this size is more liable to predation than that living in more extensive blocks of habitat. Therefore the greater the area which can be set aside and structured as described in the following sections, the better for wildlife.

From the point of view of water quality, the buffer zone will also have major significance. Apart from the obvious advantages of reducing disturbance, and the fact that fertilisers and pesticides will not be applied to the buffer zone (with no risk of accidental direct spillage into the water), certain plants can be used to improve the quality of water running off surrounding land into the pond. Common reed, water plantain, soft rush and water mint are all known to be capable of destroying harmful

*Plate 3.5   A narrow grassland buffer zone between a pond and adjoining arable land.*

*Plate 3.6   An old farm pond with no buffer zone between the water and intensively managed land. It has little value for wildlife.*

bacteria and beds of common reed can be established around the pond to act as denitrifying edges, breaking down nitrate. Nitrate is taken up into the plant body (thus accelerating growth which will need separate control) and is also converted to nitrogen gas by bacteria living in the mud around the rhizomes. Reeds have also been found to be of value in reducing the levels of phosphorus in effluent—an important factor in controlling the growth of algae. See Chapter 6, Pond Management.

By creating buffer zones of these plants in areas where run-off is nutrient rich, the water quality in ponds could be improved. A zone of treatment at least 6 m wide is needed around the fringes of the pond and it will need to be far wider where the pond is on a sloping site or where rainfall is high. At present, there is insufficient information available for precise recommendations to be made about denitrifying edges and further research is needed. One major problem is that much of the loading of water with nutrient occurs in the autumn or early spring, when plant growth is at its lowest and treatment at its least effective.

Having established the need to provide a buffer zone, the main principle to apply when planning a pond is to allow for a succession of vegetation types, progressing from open water to woodland: open water, marshland, grassland, scrub, woodland. The marshland area equates to the water's edge and the swamp zone (including any denitrifying edge), but it does not need to occur all round the pond.

In addition to these areas, other features, described as 'habitat boosters' can be provided to enhance the pond's wildlife value. These are described in Chapter 5, Supplementary Habitat Creation.

*Grassland*
Inland from the water's edge, the ground around the pond ought to be kept clear of trees for at least 2–3 m. On very wet sites, this area may be permanently water-logged, but around large ponds, if there is some dry grassland, at least part of the dry area (preferably on the north bank) should be kept close cropped, as a resting and feeding place for wildfowl.

An occasional tree or bush can be planted (or an existing tree retained) around the perimeter of the pond, but no more than 30 per cent of the water surface should be shaded, otherwise there will be fewer plants and consequently less pondlife able to survive. In addition, there will be a build-up of leaf litter and oxygen depletion will occur. As a guide, bankside trees can be tolerated where the pond diameter is three times greater than the height of the trees.

The limited shade cast by bankside trees is of value. Fish will lie up in shadows on very hot days, and birds will use branches as perches overlooking the water. Insects which fall off leaves will be an extra source of food for predators below and the shade will help to discourage algae and excessive growth of floating and emergent broadleaved plants.

In general, trees should not be planted on the southern or eastern edges of the pond, where they will reduce the amount of sunlight reaching not only the water but also the open bankside habitats.

Two exceptions to this rule are:

1. Where the water supply to the pond is known to be high in nutrient, which will cause eutrophication. In this situation, the planting of trees to the south will reduce the light availability, helping to prevent excessive algal growth (see Chapter 6, Pond Management).
2. Where several ponds occur on the same farm, one could be retained as a shady feature, to provide habitat diversity.

### Scrub

The scrub zone should range from tall grasses and herbs to individual bushes and dense thickets offering excellent cover to small birds and sheltering the pond. Scrub is very important, providing concealed breeding sites for wildfowl, nesting and feeding grounds for other birds and plentiful supplies of food and cover for invertebrates and small mammals. Amphibians will also derive benefit, seeking concealed hibernation sites especially if some rotting logs are left nearby.

As with other bankside features, the area of scrub will depend on the space available. Around very small garden ponds it may only be possible to plant an occasional bush, whereas on farmland quite extensive scrub belts can be created, covering many square metres. The most important consideration is to link the scrub with the open bankside and then, wherever possible, to woodland, so that there is a progression from water into permanent cover.

### Woodland

The presence of woodland makes the whole pond and conservation area bigger, producing a more diverse and stable home for wildlife. Woodland may also provide a link with other features, such as hedges or ditches, which will give cover to birds and mammals moving to and from the pond.

Other than occasional bankside trees, any area of woodland should be at least 20 m back from the water's edge. In a garden where this is normally impossible, boundary trees or hedges will help to imitate some of the conditions provided by woods and copses. Woodland planted too close to a pond will cause shading and lead to a build-up of excessive volumes of leaf litter and nutrient in the water. Conifers should never be planted in close proximity to ponds.

## Pond Design and Amphibian Conservation

The holistic approach to pond design described in the preceding sections is of relevance to the conservation of all the native amphibians with the exception of the natterjack toad.

Frogs, toads and newts all have varying preferences when colonising new or restored ponds. However, it is not only the quality of the pond itself which is crucial, the surrounding bankside conditions are equally significant, as amphibians spend most of their lives on land. Because amphibians travel less than 1 km, successful colonisation of a new or restored pond is only likely (in the absence of spawn introductions) if the species are already present in the area.

### Common Frogs

A major reason for the increase in frog numbers in suburban gardens is the fact that these creatures are capable of breeding successfully in very small ponds, with surface areas as low as 2 m². They will also use ponds which have a tendency to dry out in summer, although the juveniles will only survive if water remains in the pond until metamorphosis has taken place and the young frogs have moved on to dry land.

Whatever the size of the pond, it is more attractive if it has an area of gently sloping bank, plenty of warm, shallow water less than 150 mm deep, and a section which is about 1 m deep. Aquatic vegetation is important, with lots of pondweeds in the water and species such as bur-reed, reed mace and buttercup around the perimeter and growing on the banks. At least 50 per cent of the water surface should be kept clear of floating plants, and overhanging trees or scrub ought to be cut back to allow sunlight to reach the water surface. In the case of new ponds, planting should not be carried out in such a way that shading will result.

Outside the pond, an area of ground large enough to support the adult frog population should be set aside to provide permanent cover, including hibernation sites and sources of food for the frogs while they are living out of the water. As a guide, 20 m² per adult frog should provide sufficient space. The set aside area ought to be at least 2 m wide all round the pond, fenced to exclude grazing livestock and allowed to develop with tall grasses and scrub plus a few areas of shorter grass, from where the frogs can emerge at night to feed. In an ideal situation, the bankside buffer zones described in the preceding sections should be created and will offer benefits to many other plants and animals as well as amphibians.

Frogs will not travel much further than 1 km from the breeding pond and so there must be an adequate area of cover and ample natural food close to the water if the pond is to support a population of these amphibians.

Should the cover be located some distance from the pond, a safe, permanent corridor linking the two must be created. The best solution is to plant a hedge or create a tall grass strip, but an overgrown ditch would also be satisfactory. (See colour plate 11.)

## Common Toads

While many of the guidelines for encouraging frogs apply to toads, the latter are more selective and prefer larger, deeper ponds, usually with a surface area of at least 100 m². Breeding populations of toads tend to be larger than those of frogs and so, in addition to larger ponds, more terrestrial cover must be made available. As a guide, to encourage toads, a minimum of 5 per cent of the land area within a 1 km radius of the pond should be maintained as permanent scrub with taller grasses. Toads will travel longer distances than frogs and good, thick corridors must be provided to link the pond with refuges and feeding areas. (See colour plate 12.)

N.B. The common toad does not occur in Northern Ireland.

## Newts

*Great crested or warty newt*
This protected species prefers mature, large, deep, nutrient rich ponds with plenty of vegetation in and around the water. These very productive ponds also generate large quantities of insects, which are essential food for the newt tadpoles (efts) during the summer.

The newts wrap their eggs in underwater leaves to hide them from predators, preferring to use the decaying leaves from the previous year's growth of great willowherb, reedmace and flag iris. Although copious quantities of vegetation are therefore desirable in the pond, small expanses of open water must also be retained where the males can display in the breeding season.

Newts spend most of their lives out of the water so, as with frogs and toads, plenty of cover must be created nearby. They can travel only about 500 m from the pond and search out damp, dark refuges, on account of their susceptibility to desiccation—they are more prone to this than frogs and toads. Newts are able to travel 70 m per week, and within a 250 m radius of the pond, at least 20 per cent of the ground area should form permanent cover, ideally in the form of long grasses, brambles, scrub (with grasses rather than nettles beneath), open woodland and even dense buttercup patches.

Cropped or close mown grasses and areas of arable land do not provide suitable cover, so where a pond is created or restored in proximity to this type of land use, a buffer zone will be needed, with hedgerow, ditch or grassland corridors linking the pond to suitable refuges. (See colour plate 13.)

*Palmate and common newts*
These species require conditions broadly similar to those supporting the other amphibians. The palmate newt is more common in the north and west, including Scotland, than the common and great crested newt. The common newt is the only newt present in Northern Ireland.

Both common and palmate newts will colonise new ponds, assuming that they already occur in the vicinity. Both are known to use small garden ponds, unlike the great crested newt which prefers the large features more usually found in the wider countryside. Palmate and common newts lay their eggs on the leaves of water crowfoot and frogbit. Neither will use Canadian pondweed—a common species in garden ponds—so if they are to be encouraged, it is essential that there is a variety of plants within the water. Adequate terrestrial grasses and scrub areas are important for both species, acting as cover and providing food in the form of insects, slugs and snails.

Within the limits of its distribution (common over most of England and the Borders, sparse in Wales and the extreme south-west and absent in north Scotland), the smooth newt will also frequent very shallow ponds which have a tendency to dry out in summer. Like the frog, the smooth newt is a species well able to take advantage of the opportunities provided by the spate of new garden ponds created in suburban areas.

## Natterjack Toad

This is a very rare and protected species, now classed as endangered and confined to fewer than forty breeding sites in Britain, mainly on coastal dunes and heathland in Cheshire, Cumbria, south-west Scotland and East Anglia. In 1980 the Nature Conservancy Council estimated that the total adult population over the whole country was only 30,000.

The natterjack toad prefers to spawn in temporary ponds located in heath or dune areas and which retain their water until mid to late July. The size of pond does not seem to be important, ponds with surface areas as small as 1 m$^2$ having been used for spawning. The water should be between 300–500 mm deep, unshaded, with a pH of 6 or just above and not affected by chemical run-off or infestations of filamentous algae. Where ponds are on grazed heathland, livestock access must be restricted to prevent trampling.

Because of the temporary nature of the breeding pools, the lack of established plant or animal life is not a limiting factor. The toads lay their eggs in about 150 mm of water and, after hatching, the larvae feed on whatever plant or animal life they can find, sometimes resorting to cannibalism. Outside the breeding season, the adult toads feed on insects, taking refuge in burrows on the dunes or seeking concealment beneath logs or stones, emerging at dusk to feed.

The optimum terrestrial conditions around the breeding pools are provided by grasses and heathers, interspersed with dry sandy areas. As much as 10–20 ha of this type of habitat is necessary to support a colony of this rare amphibian.

Staff at the headquarters of the Royal Society for the Protection of Birds, at Sandy in Bedfordshire, have succeeded in introducing natterjack toads to their Lodge reserve by creating a butyl-lined pond and ideal terrestrial habitats for the toads. The results of the project will provide valuable knowledge about the conservation of this species.

Further information regarding the natterjack toad can be found in the Nature Conservancy Council Report: 'The ecology and conservation of amphibian and reptile species endangered in Britain'. (See colour plate 14.)

## Fish and Amphibians

Of all the amphibians, the common toad is the species most likely to be able to survive in a pond which has been stocked with fish; neither the adults nor the young are palatable, hence the fish avoid them. Frogs can co-exist with fish, usually where there is plenty of shallow water and vegetation which is inaccessible to the predators. At the opposite end of the scale, the great crested newt cannot survive in a stocked pond, for while the adults and juveniles produce body secretions which help to deter predators, the larvae are unprotected and are easy prey for the fish.

Frogs and common toads will often be found together, as will frogs and smooth newts—quite normal inhabitants of garden ponds. Frogs may also occur in conjunction with great crested newts, although it is more common for the latter to co-exist with the smooth newt.

## POND DESIGN TO ENCOURAGE DRAGONFLIES AND DAMSELFLIES

There are many different species of dragonfly and damselfly, the specific habitat requirements of each tending to vary.

The pond itself is the home of the dragonfly and damselfly larvae, with the adults hunting for food over the surrounding countryside and breeding at the pond. Some common species, such as the southern aeshna, will breed in ponds as small as 25 m$^2$, providing that the pond does not dry up. The green lestes, a damselfly, can breed successfully in ponds of this size even if they lose all their water during the summer. Larger ponds will support more species, but in ponds with a surface area of between 500 and 2,500 m², other factors may be more significant in influencing the range of species. The diversity of plants both in the water and around the pond margins will have an important effect on the numbers present.

## Siting

In order to improve the chances of dragonflies and damselflies colonising a new pond (as well as providing the optimum conditions for them), whenever possible the pond ought to be located within 750 m of an existing wetland which already supports these insects.

## Pond Vegetation

This serves a number of purposes for dragonflies and damselflies:

- Many species lay their eggs in plant tissues.
- Submerged plants provide cover for larvae and offer protection against predators. These plants also shelter smaller invertebrates which in turn are eaten by the larvae.
- Taller plants around the pond margins provide vertical surfaces up which the larvae can climb when they emerge from the water.

Eggs are laid in the tissues of both living and dead water plants. Rigid hornwort, spiked water milfoil and greater reedmace are all favoured species. Larvae have varying preferences for cover within the water—the larvae of the ruddy sympetrum (declining in numbers on account of the loss of emergent vegetation around ponds) are particularly associated with greater reedmace, one of the plants most likely to be cleared as part of a management operation, particularly where there is a fisheries interest.

## Shade

Because the growth of aquatic plants is affected by shade, where water is surrounded by overhanging bushes and trees it is less likely to be attractive to dragonflies and damselflies. These insects will be drawn to sheltered, open pools, where the larvae can flourish in water not more than 2 m deep supporting plenty of emergent, submerged and floating plants. The latter are very important in the case of the red-eyed damselfly, which rarely settles on anything other than floating leaves towards the centre of shallow ponds.

## Habitat Boosters

The presence of a few rotting logs, branches or even tree roots growing around the edge of the pond is also of value to some species. The southern aeshna and brown aeshna both lay their eggs in rotting pieces of wood, while branches and roots provide cover within the water, helping to shelter larvae and attracting other invertebrates. If a log or branch is to be put into a new pond for this purpose, care must be taken to ensure that flexible liners are not punctured.

Fence posts or other vertical structures around the water's edge are also useful, providing surfaces up which larvae can climb, in the same way that plant stems are used.

## Sediments on the Bed of the Pond

The base of the pond is a valuable habitat for many invertebrates and the larvae of some of the 'darter' dragonflies can be found burrowing in sediment, although not in deep layers of silt. To encourage this kind of activity, soil should be placed on the bottom of newly created ponds, especially where flexible liners have been used.

## Terrestrial Habitats

As with other wildlife, it is not only the pond itself which is important to dragonflies and damselflies. The presence of water for breeding and larval development must be backed up by good terrestrial cover to support the adults. Scrub, grassland and wetlands are essential and the larger the area set aside near to the water, the better. If the pond is not surrounded by these kinds of features, corridors to suitable sites must be provided, preferably by hedgerows and ditches.

### POND DESIGN FOR WILDFOWL

The main species of duck which is managed for shooting in the United Kingdom is the mallard. This is a 'dabbling' duck which, together with the teal, feeds in shallow waters and both are likely to be found in the vicinity of most medium to large ponds. Diving duck such as pochard and tufted duck are also of significance and a properly designed pond ought to encourage these as well as mallard and teal.

Duck are quite likely to feed on ponds which lie beneath established flight lines to and from resting places. These are called 'flight ponds', and are the ones which are most commonly used for shooting. It is also possible to encourage wildfowl to nest around ponds which should be shot over less frequently than flight ponds, particularly towards the end of the season. The following design principles should be followed to encourage flighting duck and can also be incorporated into new pond schemes (and restoration plans) to induce duck to become resident around ponds and breed.

The minimum size of pond which can be adequately managed to encourage wildfowl is 0.1 ha (1,000 m²), providing that it is not too far away from a bigger expanse of water which is already used by duck. Large ponds are more attractive than small ones and the greater the expanse of water the better, although there is no relationship between pond size and the number of duck which the pond will support. The most important consideration when encouraging duck is habitat quality, together with proximity to an established stillwater or watercourse.

Many ponds attract duck only in winter because they simply provide roosting places and a supply of food. A pond which is designed primarily for wildfowl must satisfy several requirements if duck are to breed success-fully. The best ponds are well sited, have feeding grounds (for both adult duck and ducklings), good nesting cover and loafing areas on the pond banks where the duck can preen. Predator control is also important.

## Siting

While siting is not a design factor, the location of the pond will have an effect on the overall success of the project. The proximity of larger stillwaters or watercourses supporting wildfowl will help to attract duck on to the new pond. Trees should not be planted where they will impede flightlines on to the water surface. The planting of new woodland near to a pond, or the siting of a new pond near existing woodland, must take account of the prevailing winds and natural flight lines, leaving a 30–35° angle of approach for the duck. For this reason the presence of overhead power cables must also be considered as a limiting factor. Seclusion is important; tracks and roads near the pond may cause disturbance, though this can be alleviated by good screening which will help to shelter most sites and make the pond an acceptable home for wildfowl.

## Feeding Areas

Adult duck find most of their food within the pond itself, eating inver-tebrates such as beetles, freshwater shrimps and larvae, which are all found in the shallow, highly productive waters around the edge. Dabbling species such as mallard and teal cannot feed properly when the floor of the pond is more than 500 mm below the surface, hence the importance of providing

*Plate 3.7 Here a farmer is receiving advice on the construction and management of a new pond in Northern Ireland. Note the varied and visually very interesting shoreline, the islands and the exposed shingle banks which are ideal for wildfowl. (Department of Agriculture, Northern Ireland)*

shallows. This is also the reason why on wet sites a simple scrape pond will suffice to attract not only wildfowl but also other wading birds. For diving duck, the pond should not be more than 2.4 m deep, with an average depth of just over 1 m if the duck are to feed properly.

Wildfowl, especially ducklings, must have easy access into and out of shallow areas to obtain food; gentle gradients between the bank and the water are vital for success. Once ducklings have hatched, they too require a high protein diet during the first few weeks of life. Research carried out by the Game Conservancy Trust shows that they depend heavily on an abundant supply of chironomid larvae (which are present in warm, shallow water) during the first two days after hatching. Where the pond is stocked with fish there will be competition for this type of food. Further research work carried out by the Game Conservancy Trust at the ARC Wildfowl Centre, involving the removal of coarse fish (particularly bream) from flooded gravel pits, has led to an increase in the numbers of chironomid larvae available to ducklings, although the Game Conservancy Trust also reported an increase in the numbers of predatory invertebrates as a result of the loss of fish and increased plant growth. These invertebrates may in turn ultimately compete for food and subsequently reduce the numbers of chironomids again.

The Game Conservancy Trust has investigated the use of barley straw in flooded gravel pits to enrich the floor of the pit and provide more cover and food for invertebrates. Applications as high as 1 kg per m$^2$ of surface area have been used to good effect and, in addition, some control of algae seems to result (see Chapter 6, Pond Management).

### Preening Areas

Dabbling duck prefer to leave the pond to preen and they need safe areas of open bankside for this. Land around the pond should be managed so that there are open spaces which are not overgrown. Spits and islands offer ideal opportunities for the creation of loafing areas which also double up as feeding sites where favoured food plants can be provided.

### Nesting Cover

For nesting, duck favour the tall tussocky conditions provided by herbaceous plants and grasses. Research by the Game Conservancy Trust indicates that plant growth in these areas should be allowed to reach about 600 mm height and, in an ideal situation, vegetation should be left uncut for four to five years so that mature cover starts to develop. This should only be cut back when scrub invasion starts to become a problem. (See colour plate 15.)

Islands are good nesting places if they are free from predators. Alternatively floating platforms can be constructed (see Chapter 5, Supplementary Habitat Creation) which will offer some security.

The provision of good nest sites in the immediate vicinity of the pond is not of such fundamental importance as setting aside loafing and feeding areas. Duck will use suitable nest sites up to 1.2 km from the water, leading their brood to the pond soon after hatching. However, the Game Conservancy Trust has shown that duckling survival decreases in proportion to the distance which the ducklings must travel to feed, so wherever possible suitable nesting cover ought to be created quite close to the feeding grounds.

## DESIGN FOR OTHER USES OF WATER

Wildlife conservation and wildfowling are major reasons for pond creation or restoration in the United Kingdom, but many stillwaters are constructed or maintained primarily for other purposes. The most common of these are: agricultural water supply; storage of water for firefighting; angling and fish rearing; and storage of water for the irrigation of agricultural crops. Angling and fish rearing are covered in more detail in Chapter 7, Pond Utilisation. The storage of water for irrigation is a complex subject, requiring the impoundment or collection of large volumes of water, and is not covered in this book. For interested readers, sources of advice and information are listed in Appendix 6 and Appendix 7.

While many of the principles for pond design outlined in the preceding sections remain relevant for the other uses, there are a number of specific factors which should be taken into account when planning a pond which is to be created for a reason other than or in addition to nature conservation or wildfowling.

### Agricultural Water Supply

The use of ponds as a source of water for grazing livestock has declined in recent years, as more mains water supplies have been piped to field troughs. However, there remains a need in some parts of the country for standing water to be accessible to animals and pond construction or restoration for this purpose still occurs. All the design considerations listed in the main section of this chapter are relevant, but livestock must be given access to the water's edge around only one part of the pond bank, unless more than one field is serviced per pond.

*Drinking bays*

For management purposes a railed or fenced 'drinking bay', which will prevent the animals straying over the whole bankside of the pond and stop them actually getting into the water, is the best form of access from a field. Uncontrolled trampling of vegetation and fouling of the water will very quickly reduce both habitat and water quality.

The drinking bay must have a hard surface, preferably made of hardcore or concrete, to prevent mud which is stirred up by the animals making the water turbid thus reducing light penetration. The hardstanding will also stop hooves puncturing any clay lining. The danger of punctures also renders unsuitable the use of a flexible membrane to line a livestock drinking pond.

*Pumping to field troughs*

To prevent the problems cited above, if it is essential to use pond water for livestock, the optimum solution is to pump water from the pond into an adjacent trough. This avoids the need for access to the pond and its surroundings.

## Storage of Water for Fire Fighting

In the past, inadequate or non-existent supplies of mains water in rural areas have often led to expensive damage to farm buildings, and even the loss of livestock, following an outbreak of fire. With more mains water available, there are now fewer farms needing water storage. Nevertheless, any pond adjacent to a potentially vulnerable feature should be treated as an emergency water supply.

All the design criteria appropriate for conservation ponds can be applied to fire ponds. The main requirements for emergency water storage over and above these are:

- The pond must be capable of holding at least 20,000 litres of water.
- It must not be more than 150 m, and preferably only 100 m, away from the farm buildings.
- A hard road must lead to a firm pumping site within 1.5 m of the pond bank. The road and pumping site must be capable of supporting a fire appliance which may weigh in excess of 10 tonnes.
- A deep sump must be constructed adjacent to the pumping site, so that water can be extracted quickly from the pond. The sump must be constructed so as to prevent any clogging of a suction hose with debris or plant material.
- Any gateway on the access road leading to the pond must be at least 3 m wide.

- The pond must be clearly marked as 'emergency water supply'.

Whenever it is proposed that a pond is to be created (or restored) to serve as a supply of water for fire fighting, advice should be taken from the Fire Prevention Officer of the local Fire Service.

*Chapter 4*

# Pond Construction*

The first step for anyone considering the creation of a new pond is the selection of the most appropriate site. This is not always an easy task and expert advice may be necessary, because the best site from the point of view of engineering may not be the optimum location in terms of any proposed utilisation of the water. At the other end of the scale, the intended use of the pond may dictate where it has to be located, for example a pond which is to act as storage of water for fire fighting must be created very close to the buildings or other features which require protection.

There are many factors which must be considered when a site is being chosen. These can be grouped under two headings, firstly relating to the utilisation of the pond and secondly to water supply and engineering.

## SITING AND UTILISATION

- Is the pond to be created purely for nature conservation?
- Is there a commercial or other objective?

The answers to these questions must be clearly ascertained, as any proposed use of the pond will affect the general geographical location. Only after that can the feasibility of the site be assessed with regard to water supply and engineering.

### Nature Conservation

The best place to create a wildlife pond is a level site adjacent to an old, established habitat such as broadleaved woodland, wetland, hedgerow or meadow. These features will have developed over a long period and there will be plenty of fauna and flora nearby to help colonise the new pond. A pond constructed in a barren environment will take much longer to develop

*The author gratefully acknowledges the technical contribution made by Miles Waterscapes Ltd of Great Ashfield, Suffolk, towards the preparation of this chapter.

as a habitat for wildlife because colonisation will be slow. It is preferable if the site is quiet and secluded, to minimise disturbance to wildlife. A level site is better than a sloping one, to reduce the problems caused by nutrient rich run-off, but where the site does slope, some measures can be taken to improve the water quality as it enters the pond—see Chapter 3, Pond Design.

*A very careful appraisal must be made of the site to check that the existing wildlife value is not greater than that which might be generated once the pond is completed. Valuable habitats such as old meadows or marshlands could easily be destroyed to make way for a new pond when, from the point of view of nature conservation, the original feature was far more significant. If in doubt, expert advice must be obtained.*

## Commercial or Other Uses

### Wildfowl

A secluded site is best to minimise disturbance, especially during the nesting season. If the pond is intended to attract flighting duck it should lie in close proximity to or directly beneath a flightline to a nearby area of water which is already frequented by duck. A clear flightpath on to the pond is also essential and any site which is too close to overhead cables should be avoided.

### Angling and fish rearing

Ponds which are to be stocked with fish must be close to a source of high quality water and be easily accessible to the owner and his employees. Where high value fish are being reared, the choice of a secure site to deter poachers is advisable. If the water is to be let to anglers it must be accessible and the marketability may be improved if there is sufficient space nearby for car parking.

Once suitable sites have been identified, the technical aspects of pond creation must be considered.

## WATER SUPPLY AND ENGINEERING

A number of questions need to be answered:

- Are there any physical obstacles to pond construction?
- Is water available?
- Is the water of sufficiently high quality?
- Will the soils on site retain water?
- Are the soils suitable for embankment construction?

- What volume of water storage can be created in relation to the volume of earth removed?
- Is there easy access for construction vehicles?
- Is the site affected by land drains?
- Where is excavated soil to be put?

## Obstacles to Construction

The presence of any man-made obstacle must be ascertained early on. While overhead cables are clearly visible, underground cables or pipelines may not be well marked. Some overhead lines can be moved (sometimes at considerable cost), but where this is not possible the pond must not be constructed where it will pose a hindrance to the maintenance of cables. The presence of underground pipes or cables will make pond creation impossible.

## Water Availability

The availability of an adequate and reliable source of water is the single most important consideration when planning a pond scheme. Water is necessary not only to fill the new pond but also to keep it topped up. There will be an average annual loss of water from a pond in the United Kingdom of between 300–450 mm per year through surface evaporation, even after allowing for direct rainfall into the pond. This deficit must be made up, otherwise there will be unsightly scarring as mud is exposed around the water's edge and the ecological stability will be adversely affected. In an ideal situation, there should be enough water available to provide some movement within the pond and maintain the water level within 150 mm of the spillway or outflow for at least six months of the year.

The deficit may be increased by broadleaved trees growing too close to the pond. These will draw water from the pond and also intercept ground water which could otherwise help to maintain satisfactory levels.

The amount of water required to fill a pond can be estimated if the surface area is assessed by dividing it into one or more rectangular shapes and using a simple formula to obtain an approximation of water volume:

$$\text{VOLUME} = \frac{H}{3} (A + B + \sqrt{A \times B})$$

where H is the depth of water
A is the top rectangular surface area (length × width)
B is the bottom area (length × width)

If the calculation is based on metres, 1 m³ of volume = 1,000 litres.

Water supplies fall into two categories: natural and artificial. During the course of any investigation into potential sources of water for a new pond, some attempt should be made to tap into local knowledge. People who have lived and worked on the land for many years will have considerable information about local water supplies—which ditches run regularly, which ponds dry up, which watercourses are seasonal and, equally as important, which fields have been drained.

Natural water supplies can be provided via rainfall, stream inflow, underground inflow from a spring, or the water table.

*Rainfall*
When natural supply is being considered for a pond, the catchment area should be assessed as this will have a major effect on water levels. If the local topography is such that adequate rainfall on to surrounding land will adequately supply the pond, this is fine; but where the catchment area is found to be inadequate, alternative sources will need to be identified. It must also be remembered that most water supplies linked to rainfall are variable during any twelve month period.

*Stream inflow*
Surface water from streams can be used to supply a pond, providing that consent is obtained from the National Rivers Authority (see Chapter 8, Ponds, Wildlife and the Law). To create an on-stream pond the watercourse would have to be widened and deepened and an impoundment may need to be constructed to hold back the water. This is often done in a valley, where the valley sides form the pond banks.

*Springs*
Springs often occur along a line where water passes through a permeable layer of soil and flows over the top of an impermeable layer. If the pond can be located below the spring level, a number of sources can be tapped. If the yield is low it can sometimes be increased by excavating deeper into the spring, where the water pressure will be higher.

*Water table*
Soils such as sands and gravels are capable of holding water almost to ground level. In some cases, the water actually flows horizontally through the soil to provide a constant water change in the pond.

Where the water table is high, ponds excavated into heavy soils will fill naturally and retain water. As a check, because soil water levels are likely to vary considerably between summer and winter, test holes should be dug and monitored over a twelve month period. The purpose of this is to determine any changes in level and ensure that the pond will hold water at a relatively constant level throughout the year. A series of test holes 2.5–3.0 m deep should be dug in pairs. One pair is normally sufficient for a pond with a surface area of less than 300 m² unless the site is especially varied. Several pairs will be needed for large ponds.

One hole from each pair should be filled with water to ascertain the rate of loss (if any) from the site, while the other should be allowed to fill of its own accord. Where the empty hole fills slowly on account of low soil permeability, the water level may still rise high enough to provide a good chance of establishing a pond, but if the water level remains low throughout the year the pond will have to be excavated deep to provide a sufficient depth of water. This means that the soil will need to be removed from the site and the banks will require substantial profiling to make the pond visible and attractive to wildlife—all at considerable extra cost.

If the chosen site is near a river, the test holes will show whether there is any connection between the pond site and river water levels. They will also confirm whether the presence of private wells and boreholes (used for water extraction) will affect the levels in the finished pond.

Artificial water supplies can be provided by pumping, by diversion of a watercourse, by land drains, or by collection of surface water.

## Pumping

Water can be pumped into a pond from a watercourse, assuming that an abstraction licence has been issued by the National Rivers Authority. Metered supply is often the only way to fill or top up a garden pond or one where an artificial lining is required.

Where the water table is too low to enable a pond to be constructed, a shallow well can be excavated down to 6 m and water can be pumped up to the pond. This technique can also be used where the water supply is in a different location from the pond, although the project will be expensive because of the extra piping and pumping costs. Wells excavated to greater depths (boreholes) can also provide a source of water for a pond created where clay soil overlies a deeper chalk or clay strata where water is present.

## Diversion of a watercourse (off-stream ponds)

Water can be fed via a channel into a pond created near to a watercourse, in the same way that mill wheels and ponds are supplied. The supply can be controlled so that inflow only occurs when it is needed, for instance to fill or top up the pond. If this method is to be used, the water flow during summer and winter must be checked because many small watercourses only flow seasonally and the pond could be starved of water in the summer, with a disastrous impact on wildlife and visual amenity.

*Land drains*
Land drains can often be diverted to supply water to a pond. It is essential to locate all drains in the vicinity of the pond site prior to construction, even if they are not to be used for water supply. Failure to find all the drains could result in the pond emptying itself—a fault which is difficult to identify and remedy.

*Collection of surface water*
This can be gathered from yards, road or roof collection systems. The high rainfall over many parts of the United Kingdom provides a useful source of water for ponds because substantial amounts run off roofs, yards and roads, although a large volume of this is unsuitable because it picks up pollutants from dairies, livestock yards and silos.

## Water Quality

It is very important to ensure that high quality water is used to supply the pond. Water from any source may be contaminated and, before taking a decision on whether to proceed with construction, it should be tested by chemical and bacterial analysis. These tests can normally be carried out by a local laboratory for a small fee.

Concern is often expressed over the nitrate content of water in agricultural areas but, in addition, effluent and other forms of chemical contamination are very common problems affecting water quality. Even if a water supply is deemed to be of sufficiently high quality at the time of pond construction, the risk of future accidental pollution from a farm or factory upstream should not be discounted, especially where the pond is to be used for angling or fish rearing. With much concern expressed over the cleanliness of the country's rivers, all supplies to a new pond originating in a watercourse ought to be thoroughly investigated.

It is worth bearing in mind the amount of nutrient which could accumulate in an on-stream pond. If the water supply contains even a low concentration of nitrates, for instance 3 mg/litre, where there is a small but constant inflow throughout the year, a very large weight of nitrate will be brought into the pond. This could be beneficial where the objective is to create a coarse fishery because of the resultant increase in natural productivity. On the other hand, if the pond is being constructed for wildlife conservation, the rate of plant growth will be greatly accelerated, necessitating more regular management and therefore disturbance.

Springs, wells and boreholes should provide a reliable source of high quality water but land drains and surface run-off may carry large amounts of nutrient into the pond which could have an adverse effect. Where the pond is to be filled by surface run-off, particularly from agricultural land, there may be a rapid ingress of suspended solid materials following heavy rainfall. This will be undesirable in shallow ponds because accumulations of silt will build up too quickly. The same will apply to stream fed ponds and one solution is to incorporate a silt trap into the design.

## Capability of the Soils to Retain Water

The permeability of the soils covering the proposed site will determine whether some form of waterproof lining is required in the pond. If the soils will naturally retain water the overall cost of the scheme will be lower than if a liner has to be used. Garden topsoil will probably vary very little, but 400 mm below the surface the soils will start to change and over the geographical area which is required for a pond there may be wide ranging conditions which need detailed evaluation.

A visual inspection is not sufficient, because the presence of clay close to the surface, causing the ground to be sticky and waterlogged underfoot in wet conditions, would be misleading if within 500 mm of the surface there were porous soils which would not create a watertight pond following excavation. Trial pits, as used to assess water availability, will also indicate the water retentive properties of the soil. Losses from the pits which are artificially filled with water must be measured. If the level in the pits falls rapidly, this indicates that some form of lining will be needed, whereas if it remains relatively static the clay content of the soil is sufficiently high and water will be retained when a pond is constructed. Where trial pits show both rising and falling water levels, this demonstrates that the water table is fluctuating and the installation of a flexible liner in the pond may prove difficult.

If the tests reveal that a particular site will not naturally retain water, expert advice must be taken unless an alternative, easier to work site is available.

## Soil Suitability for Embankment Construction

Where an embankment is needed, to create above ground water storage or impound a stream, the soils on site must be checked by an expert to determine their suitability for use in a structural barrier. A considerable amount of time and money may be saved if soil samples covering the whole site are sent for analysis to determine plasticity, soil moisture content and permeability.

The soils most commonly used for embankments are those with a moderate clay content. Clays are made up from particles which form a plastic, cohesive mass with a very low permeability rate. If the plasticity is right, clay can be compacted to form excellent impermeable embankments. The best soils to use contain not less than 20 per cent and not more than 30 per cent clay, the remaining volume made up of well graded sands and gravels. This kind of soil remains stable even when there are major changes in its moisture content. When the clay content is too high the soil is prone to crack if it dries out, thus rendering it unsuitable for this type of work. It is possible to use other soils for embankment construction in conjunction with a pond liner which will retain the water.

## Volume of Water Storage in Relation to the Volume of Earth Removed (water to earth ratio)

The volume of water storage provided in a pond, in relation to the amount of earth removed, will directly affect the cost of the project. Good design and expert advice is essential, as is the choice of site.

A pond which is excavated in the form of a simple hole in the ground will have a water to earth ratio of 1 : 1 excluding the freeboard, which is the amount of soil left above water level. If only enough soil is removed from the hole to form water retaining banks above ground level (for instance an off-stream pond) this will improve the ratio and thus the cost.

## Access on to Site

The accessibility of the site will affect the cost of the project. Contractors' equipment is heavy and must be transported as near to the pond as possible, while good access to and from the area is vital if excavated soil is to be moved efficiently.

## Land Drainage Systems

Land drains crossing the pond site must be located and either diverted away from the pond or fed into it to supply water. Old farm plans, drainage maps and local knowledge will help to provide an indication of the way in which the drains run. The next step is to dig a 1.5–2.0 m deep trench at right angles to the lie of the drains. This must be excavated along the whole length of the proposed site unless the exact location of the drains can be pinpointed on an accurate plan.

Once the drains have been found, those leading into the site area can either be allowed to outfall into the new pond at a level above the top water line, or they will have to be diverted. Drains which are to be diverted must be cut 5 m outside the outer edge of the pond construction area and led away in a pipe of similar specification. The isolated lengths of old drain leading to the pond edge must be dug out and compacted with a suitable material, preventing water seepage along the old line of the pipe. Drains running away from the pond should be handled in a similar fashion, although one could be retained as an overflow out of a pond where there is no inflow from a watercourse, providing that the inlet to the pipe is raised to the top water level.

Great care is necessary when blocking drainage systems to ensure that they are properly sealed. Once the pond is full of water there will be considerable pressure on the old pipe lines and any seepage will be very difficult to cure.

Where a pond is to be created on agricultural land which has been mole drained (holes formed in clay soil normally at 600 mm depth and 2.7 m intervals), the moles must also be compacted.

## Soil Disposal

A surprisingly large volume of soil will be excavated during the construction of a pond. Other than soil which is to be used in a structural embankment, the rest of it will have to be either spread on adjoining land or carted away. It is extremely important to choose a site where the soil can be accommodated if it is impractical to remove it to another place. Every time soil is handled the cost of the project increases. If soil is heaped up and compacted on the side of the pond, it is very difficult to move at a later date, should it be decided that it is in the wrong place!

Many ponds, even in gardens, have been spoiled because inadequate thought was given to soil disposal. Regularly graded mounds of earth, seemingly similar to railway embankments, often identify a new pond from a considerable distance. If these are inexpertly landscaped with a few trees sprouting from the summit, they are likely to detract from the finished appearance of the pond and the surrounding countryside. In addition, the construction of a large embankment using soil from a pond could be deemed to be an engineering operation requiring planning consent. See Chapter 8, Ponds, Wildlife and the Law.

The taking of levels and the preparation of a plan will help to ensure that soil banks can be blended in with adjoining landforms. Careful thought when the site is selected, as to the feasibility of on-site soil disposal, will reduce costs and make the pond seem more natural.

## MAKING THE POND

Once a suitable location has been chosen, the method of construction will be dictated by the site characteristics. The nature of the soils will determine whether or not a liner is required, while the means of supplying water to the pond will influence the type of pond which is needed—on-stream, off-stream, hole in the ground or above ground.

From a practical point of view, the simplest pond to construct is the hole in the ground, where the pond is excavated into the water table and fills of its own accord. This type of pond includes the 'scrape pond', which is created to provide good conditions for wildfowl and wading birds. Some provision must be made to handle overflow water but, other than this, construction is straightforward.

The next easiest is the small, artificially lined pond typical of a garden or urban area. This type of pond is filled by pumped water and is topped up from the same source and by rainwater.

Ponds lined with puddled clay and filled by rainwater run-off from surrounding catchment areas seem straightforward to construct, but great care is needed to create a waterproof lining which will stand up to many years of use.

The more sophisticated on-stream, off-stream, above ground and cut and fill ponds all require specialised engineering skills to ensure that they are constructed safely. If there is a choice between having an on-stream or an off-stream pond, the latter provides more scope for imaginative design of the shoreline. It can also be created where it is needed, rather than where an impoundment can be constructed. These advantages are in addition to the potential problems described on p. 63 of siltation and nutrient accumulation which affect on-stream ponds.

Finally (and often the most expensive), large, artificially lined ponds, often constructed as ornamental features, irrigation reservoirs and industrial water stores and less frequently purely for wildlife conservation, require very sophisticated techniques to lay and join flexible membranes.

The best guidance to offer on the building of a new pond is to *seek professional advice*. The expense incurred in taking good advice will almost certainly be recouped by savings in the cost of the work and because the expense of rectifying an error made during construction (especially if it is a fault in an embankment or overspill facility) could be a great deal more than the cost of the original work. A mistake made during construction could also constitute a serious safety hazard, particularly if a failure occurs in an impoundment.

*For these reasons, the information provided in the following sections is for guidance only and should be used to complement, not substitute for, professional advice. Every pond site has unique characteristics and standard guidelines must be properly modified to suit individual circumstances.*

## Taking Levels

The positions and levels of the existing ground contours must be surveyed and recorded. This should be done both in the vicinity of the pond and over the adjacent area. The results will enable the top water level to be determined and a plan can be prepared to show how the pond will blend in with the surrounding countryside and what measures will be needed to landscape the site.

Where the pond is to be fed from a watercourse, levels must also be taken to ensure that water does not accumulate on the upstream side of the pond and cause flooding. Likewise, drainage systems and ditches must be checked to make sure that the pond will not overflow back up ditches and render land drains useless, thus saturating nearby agricultural land.

The levels can be used in the design of the pond, to show how much soil will need to be moved and the height of any embankments. Once this is done it will be possible to calculate how deep the water will be and where the inlets and outlets should be positioned.

## Constructional Techniques

The main factors determining how a pond is to be constructed (excluding the use of liners) are:

- Cost—the cheapest method is usually the quickest.
- The type of equipment which is required.
- The stability of the soils and the flow of water on site.
- The method of soil disposal.

*What machine?*
On a dry site, the pond can be created using a bulldozer to push the soil out of the hole. Although this seems to be a simple procedure it is quite uncommon, because many sites tend to be wet and the bulldozer is not a good machine to use for the final landscaping. A drag-line is more commonly used. Resembling a crane mounted on tracks, with a large bucket on the end of its jib arm, this machine has a very long reach, normally of 20 m but in some cases 30 m. On account of its size, it is not particularly manoeuvrable, especially in confined areas or near woodland, and it cannot operate near to overhead power lines.

The normal tool of the pond contractor is the tracked hydraulic excavator, which is available in many shapes and sizes. Although these machines have a shorter reach than drag-lines they can turn through 360° and, with many of them having very low ground pressures, this makes them invaluable on difficult sites. They are versatile machines; as well as digging the pond, they are equally at home working on a trench, removing scrub and tree roots, or finally finishing off the scheme.

Explosives can also be used, to blast out a pond. This technique is

*Plate 4.1   A tracked hydraulic excavator being used to create a new pond.*

only of value on very wet sites, where a simple hole in the ground can be created with jagged edges and ungraded banks. With more use being made of excavators working from mats, explosives are now less frequently used. In any event very few contractors are licensed for them.

*Site clearance*
Manoeuvring large machinery in confined areas is not cost effective and is very frustrating for plant operators. Prior to starting excavation, the site must be cleared to allow sufficient space for the movement of excavators and also to facilitate the passage of vehicles which are required to haul soil. Where trees are growing close to the working area, limbs which are likely to get damaged should be trimmed off to avoid unnecessary and unsightly scarring. All scrub growth over the site should be removed, to allow the plant operators to see what they are doing and identify marker points.

*Pegging out the site*
Because the machinery involved is so big and the volumes of soil to be moved often vast, very detailed pegging out of large pond sites is generally impractical. The pegs become buried in mud or are quickly knocked over.

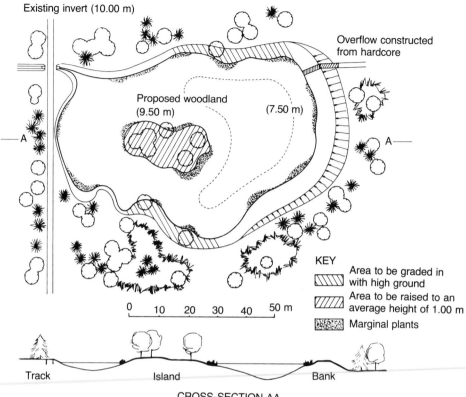

Figure 4.1 Plan for a proposed new pond (*Miles Waterscapes Ltd*)

A few carefully located, tall, coloured poles delineating the site extremities and marking islands, bays or spits should suffice, providing that the plant operators understand their instructions.

The detailed plans showing levels and final landscape form, which are necessary for the initial scheme design, should be simplified when construction starts. Highly elaborate plans are unnecessary; working drawings showing the outline of the pond, cross sections and the location of islands, bays, spits, shallows and deep water will function very well. The plan should also show where topsoil is to be stored and the location of soil banks. Modifications to plans are inevitable once work starts and within a short space of time detailed plans may well be redundant! It is always helpful for the pond owner or his agent to be available for on-site consultation whilst work is in progress so that variations can be agreed quickly.

*Stripping of topsoil*

Excavation should start at the central point of the pond and work outwards. Topsoil should be stripped off first and either hauled off site or placed in a pre-arranged location. Multi-handling may be required on very large sites with resultant increased costs. Once the pond is complete the topsoil is available for re-spreading on to embankments or soil mounds prior to seeding with grasses (see page 104).

*Main excavation*

After topsoil removal, excavation should recommence at the centre of the pond and work to the full depth in one operation. The subsoil should be moved to its pre-arranged storage point.

Where soil stability is low and the site is wet, it may be necessary for the excavator to work from mats, further adding to costs. In some cases the hole may need to be pumped dry as work proceeds so that the operator can accurately gauge progress and grade the underwater surfaces properly. If pumping is required to prevent the site from becoming waterlogged, care must be taken to avoid pollution of nearby watercourses.

On wet sites, soil disposal in the vicinity of the pond will be a problem. Under normal circumstances, the soil from the hole would be spread out prior to levelling or banked up into mounds nearby. Wet soil cannot be heaped up because it slumps and is likely to flow back into the pond. To overcome this, small volumes may have to be excavated and allowed to dry out as work progresses, adding to the length of the job and possibly even requiring more than one visit by the excavator.

*Impoundments and embankments*

If it is necessary to create an impoundment to dam a watercourse, build an embankment above ground level or construct one as part of a cut and fill pond scheme, it is essential that professional advice be taken, because these earthworks require careful design and construction. Embankments are flexible structures. They move as the soil beneath is compressed during construction, when water pushes against them and when the pond is emptied. For this reason, an embankment or impoundment must be built with an impermeable but sufficiently plastic central core which will flex but still have enough strength to stay up.

Around this central core, the inner shoulder of the embankment (the wet side), against which the water pushes, should be constructed of impermeable materials. These will have a minimum number of air voids which will subsequently become water filled thus weakening the structure. The outer shoulder of the embankment must be fabricated of permeable material so that if any water does seep through the structure it can drain away.

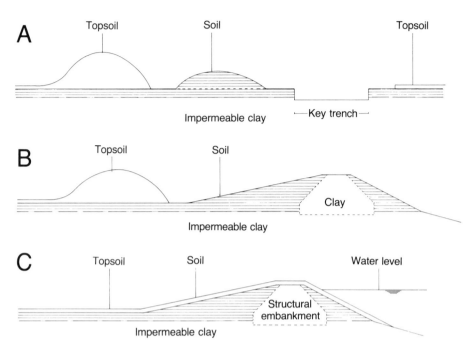

Figure 4.2 Three stages in the construction of an embankment (*Miles Waterscapes Ltd*)

The inner and outer shoulders should finally be covered with topsoil. On the inner face this will help to prevent any water erosion; in the absence of soil, stone facing must be used. The water's edge can then be planted with emergent plants, or log baffles can be established to stop water washing away the soil.

Surfaces exposed above water level on both shoulders can be sown with grasses such as creeping bent and rough stalked meadowgrass, to bind the topsoil and help the embankments blend into their surroundings. Trees and shrubs must not be planted on to embankments because the root systems may penetrate to the central core, weakening the structure and creating channels through which water can pass.

The normal technique used to construct an embankment or impound-ment is to build up the selected soils in layers, taking care to establish a well keyed foundation into the ground beneath. Each layer of soil should not be thicker than 150 mm and should be spread over the entire area of the structure to avoid lines of weakness. The structure should be well consolidated, layer by layer, after spreading. Excavation of soil for use in the embankment should not be permitted adjacent to the structure, as this will weaken the stability of the foundations. As the embankment is

*Plate 4.2 The attractively designed inlet to an on-stream pond in Somerset.*

*Plate 4.3 The impoundment and outlet for the same pond.*

73

built up, the sides must be graded and once it is at its maximum height, the top should be cambered to drain surface water.

The size of the structure will vary according to the site, the constructional materials and the height the embankment needs to be to fulfil its purpose. As a guide, to demonstrate the size and space an embankment may occupy, a structure which is 5 m high will be at least 3.25 m wide across the top. If the embankment is to be 3 m high it will need to be 2.75 m wide across the top. The slope of the inner shoulder should not be steeper than 2.5 horizontal to 1 vertical, and the outer shoulder 2 horizontal to 1 vertical. Many embankments are constructed with even gentler slopes—1 : 4 in some cases.

*Inflow, outflow and overflow arrangements*
Inflow of water into a pond can be created by a variety of methods ranging from the ornamental to the practical, with the source often dictating the method of supply. Where water is to be diverted from a water course into an off-stream pond, the National Rivers Authority may specify that a weir be installed in the stream to ensure that a minimum flow of water can be maintained so that other riparian owners downstream are not disadvantaged. An overflow pipe to a discharge point further downstream will also be required. If an on-stream pond is created by means of an impoundment, a bottom outlet pipe will have to be installed so that residual water flow downstream can be maintained.

No matter how water reaches the pond, adequate provision will have to be made for overflow and, where appropriate, outflow. Many ponds which are created purely for wildlife conservation will not require an outflow (unless embankments have been constructed), because by their nature they are not intended to be emptied. However, ponds designed for fish rearing must be capable of being emptied and refilled at regular intervals, either by pumping or, more preferably on sloping sites, by draining.

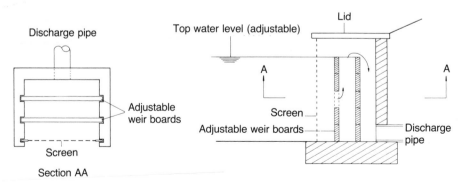

Figure 4.3   Section through monk (*Miles Waterscapes Ltd*)

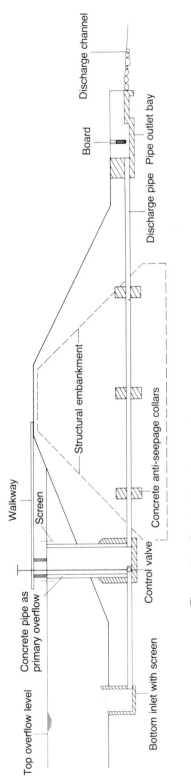

Figure 4.4 Section through dam showing overflow provisions (*Miles Waterscapes Ltd*)

The easiest way to regulate water level or empty a pond is via a monk which enables water to flow out of the pond to an appropriate discharge point such as another pond, stream or ditch. The term 'monk' is given to the type of simple sluice devised by monks in the Middle Ages, who farmed fish using surprisingly sophisticated techniques to control the water supply to their monastic fish ponds.

Bottom outlet pipes installed in an impoundment to provide residual water flows downstream of the pond, can also be used to drain the pond both during construction and on any subsequent occasion. A control valve located in the pond must be used to open and close the pipe. This can be combined with a vertical overflow pipe leading into the bottom outlet.

Overflow facilities range from simple land drainage pipes carrying water into a neighbouring land drainage system or ditch, through to complex

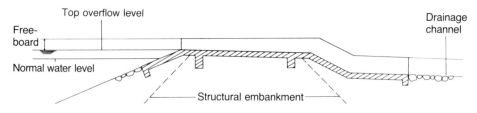

Figure 4.5    Section through reinforced concrete spillway (*Miles Waterscapes Ltd*)

concrete overspill channels bypassing an impoundment and designed to carry floodwater. All overflow and outlet facilities, including the monk, should be screened to prevent the escape of fish.

Spillways and spilltowers are normally associated with lakes rather than ponds, but where water is supplied from a watercourse, additional facilities must be provided to carry floodwaters away from the pond without endangering the dam. It must be stressed that the spillway is designed only to carry water which cannot escape through the primary overflow, such as a vertical pipe leading to the bottom outlet. The crest of the spillway must therefore be higher than the primary overflow but at least 0.6 m lower than the top of the dam.

Spillway channels may be constructed either in stone or concrete. As a more attractive alternative, soil can be used, sown with low maintenance grasses such as fescues and meadow grasses which will bind the soil and provide dense cover. The exact method of construction will depend on the site conditions and the volume of water which might be expected.

*Pipework and outfall protection*

Bottom outlet pipes, together with any other pipework passing into or out of the pond, must be carefully sealed into the surrounding soil and fitted with concrete seepage collars at regular intervals to prevent the trench in which the pipes are laid forming a conduit for water. Any pipework passing under an embankment must also be sufficiently flexible to resist the high loading imposed by soil compaction and the movement of the embankment.

Outfalls at all discharge points must be reinforced to prevent erosion by high water pressure. Discharging water should fall on to either a concrete slipway or a gabion. A gabion is a metal cage filled with large stones and is often used in river management work. In either case, the outfall protection should extend to the floor of the pond or bottom of the watercourse.

All pipework inlets and outlets should be protected with a grating to deter vermin.

*Embankment and pipework maintenance*
Embankments and dams must be inspected regularly to check for seepage and cracks. Some leakage may occur but advice must be taken if excessive amounts of water appear on the outer shoulder. Spillways, monks, outlet, overflow and inlet pipes should be kept clear of debris, particularly where a fish screen has been used. Special attention should be given to all areas of concrete to ensure that foundations are not being undermined.

*Silt traps*
Any pond supplied by flowing water will, in addition to water, receive an influx of silt. Over a long period of time this will accumulate in the pond and cause severe management problems. The rate of siltation could be rapid where the pond is fed directly from a watercourse, especially in times of heavy rain.

Silt traps should be constructed at inlet points on ponds fed from watercourses, because it is much easier to remove silt from a purpose made tank than from the pond. Ditch and drain fed ponds can be fitted with simple silt traps: inflowing water is discharged into a chamber and, as the flow rate is slowed, suspended solids are deposited before the water flows out through a second pipe into the pond. It is vital that silt traps are cleaned regularly to prevent blockages.

Natural silt traps can be created by establishing emergent plants at the point where ditches flow into ponds. These will slow the water rate and encourage silt deposition in the inflow channel, from where it can be removed easily. This technique is an attractive alternative to the more complex installations providing that silt accumulations in the inflow channel are removed regularly, to prevent water backing up and causing flooding. It is also important to make sure that the ditch does not carry so much water during heavy rainfall that it will not be able to escape into the pond fast enough and flooding will again occur.

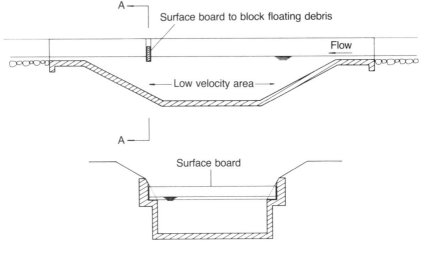

Figure 4.6   Section through a concrete silt trap (*Miles Waterscapes Ltd*)

*Plate 4.4   An on-stream garden pond with no silt trap. The pond is heavily silted around the inlet (foreground). Nutrient rich silt accumulations have combined with shallow, warm water and plenty of sun to cause severe infestations of blanket weed. The only remedy is desilting and the construction of a silt trap.*

78

*Fish ladders*

A fish ladder may be installed at the side of an impoundment on an on-stream pond, to help game fish move upstream through the pond, while still maintaining the water level. The design of the fish ladder is such that the height between pools allows the fish to jump between them, while water is able to flow in a controlled manner from one pool to another, sustaining the supply.

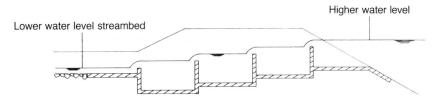

Figure 4.7    Section through reinforced concrete fish ladder (*Miles Waterscapes Ltd*)

*Islands*

The easiest way to create an island when a new pond is being excavated is to leave a block of soil undisturbed in the appropriate location. The island can be shaped and the banks graded to provide the optimum conditions for wildlife and plants can easily be established prior to filling the pond. In large ponds, the stability of this type of island means that in later years, should desilting be required, an earth bridge can be created to enable heavy machinery to cross on to the island and work from it, reaching areas of the pond which are inaccessible from the banks.

If the pond is so small that leaving a solid island during excavation would be a hindrance to machinery, artificial features can be created using techniques which can also be applied in established ponds. An appropriately shaped stockade of stakes can be erected in the pond, with the top of the stockade just above the highest anticipated water level (care is vital to ensure that impermeable soil layers are not ruptured). The interior of the stockade should be filled with non-toxic rubble and topped with soil, which can then be planted with grasses and shrubs or trees. Provided that the rubble core is solid, by the time the stakes rot away the island should be stabilised.

Large diameter culvert or sewer pipes can also be used, turned on to their sides and laid one on top of another until the structure is high enough. The interior should be filled in the same way as stockade islands. Several groups of pipes can be amalgamated to create large islands.

The problem with these artificial islands is that while they can be effectively shaped and landscaped above the water line, it is difficult to provide shallow water offshore and gently sloping banks leading into the water. Wooden or plastic ramps attached to the stakes or culvert pipes will provide access to and from the water, but unless soil can be deposited on the floor of the pond to raise the level nearer to the surface, shallows will have to be sacrificed.

The construction of floating islands is described in Chapter 5, Supplementary Habitat Creation.

*Bank stabilisation*
It is not usual for ponds to suffer from bank erosion, this being a more common feature of lakes. However, in some locations, the soil around the edge of the pond may be eroded by wave action, or fast flowing water entering the pond could affect the bank opposite the entry point. The banks of the pond can be stabilised in a number of ways:

- The simplest method is to encourage the colonisation of emergent plants around the edge of the pond. These will break the force of the water before it reaches any vulnerable soil.
- Log baffles can be floated on the surface of the pond about 1 m from the bank and held in place by stakes. These will prevent wave erosion until plants have become established.
- Wattles or wooden hurdles can be used to shield the most vulnerable or seriously affected parts of the bank, so that soil can be infilled behind them prior to planting.
- Bundles of brushwood staked against the banks will trap silt and help to consolidate weakened shorelines.
- In severe cases, gabions can be used.

## POND LINERS

Lining is essential for ponds created where the soils are permeable or the water table is low. In either situation, the pond will suffer from fluctuating water levels, which will leave undesirable scarring around the water's edge, and it might dry up in hot summers. Pond linings take two forms, they are either natural (clay) or artificial. Artificial linings can be either flexible or rigid.

The use of rigid liners is limited mainly to gardens or urban areas. Preformed fibreglass ponds, readily available in garden centres, can be installed easily and quickly in gardens to provide fresh water; but they are restricted in terms of size and the quality of habitat which can be provided. Concrete is also used, usually in garden or ornamental ponds where a flexible liner might be damaged.

Several factors need to be considered when a liner is being selected: cost of the material; availability of the material; the labour which will be required for installation; the life and durability of the liner; ease of repair; and any proposed utilisation of the pond. Clay is a very cheap lining material when supplies are readily available close to the pond site, but it is bulky and unsuitable on account of cost where it has to be transported any great distance. A flexible liner, while being easier to transport, would be inappropriate where livestock are to be provided with access to the pond for drinking.

## Puddled Clay

Properly puddled clay can be used to create a watertight seal in a pond on permeable soils, as the makers of dew ponds have been demonstrating for centuries. The term 'puddle' means to pound the clay together with water to form a very dense, water resistant mass. Puddling is achieved by trampling the clay or driving heavy machinery to and fro over it, breaking down the structure and removing the air, turning it into a 'plastic' substance.

The pond hole must be excavated and shaped, allowing enough depth for the clay and a covering of soil. If insufficient 'liner allowance' is made, shallow areas of the pond will not be water covered. After excavation, an assessment must be made of the volume of clay which is required, allowing a minimum thickness of 300–1,000 mm over the whole pond (depending on site conditions and the quality of the clay which is to be used). The assessed volume should be increased by 33 per cent to take account of the air which will be removed from the clay during puddling.

Most soil with approximately 30 per cent clay content can be used providing it is stone free. If the clay content is too high, the liner will shrink and crack if the water level falls and the pond will no longer be watertight above the low water mark unless the clay is re-puddled. Prior to puddling the clay, a thin layer of chalk can be laid as a pre-liner. This is said to prevent earthworms burrowing up into the clay from below thus creating lines of weakness. The old dew pond experts sometimes used soot for the same reasons. It has often been suggested that straw should be laid beneath the clay but there appears to be no real reason why this is necessary. Although straw may occasionally have been used in dew ponds to prevent the soil drying out prior to the clay being puddled above it, it was more often used above the clay linings but beneath the soil or flint toppings. The reason for this was to prevent the clay from drying and cracking before the pond filled with water.

If puddling is to be done on foot, very small areas must be tackled in sequence unless a large team of tramplers is available. In a team effort, each person should work on an area of 1 m². As the clay is brought in, a little water should be added and the material puddled until all the air has been forced out.

The lining needs to be puddled in 75 mm layers and built up to the appropriate depth, which should be consistent throughout the whole pond and up the banks to a point just above top water level. If work is interrupted, the completed section of lining must be kept wet or covered with plastic sheeting or straw to prevent drying and cracking. Once the lining is finished, a covering of at least 225 mm of sand or soil should be placed over the top to slow the rate of drying out, protect the clay and provide a rooting medium for aquatic plants which might otherwise penetrate into the clay liner. Traditional dew ponds were finished with a layer of flints to stop animal hooves sinking into the clay.

## Artificial Linings

### Fibreglass

Preformed liners of this material are usually small, up to 4 m in length and 450–600 mm deep. The shapes are characterised by steeply sloping sides and planting ledges. While they cannot provide a wide range of habitat types, they should not be discounted as a means of creating a valuable pond in a garden or school conservation area.

Installation is quite easy. A hole should be dug to correspond with the shape and size of the chosen pond, sharp stones should be removed and the pond placed in position. Backfilling around the sides and base with sand is essential prior to filling the pond, to prevent cracking due to water pressure.

### Concrete

This is a good material to use for lining ponds in garden or urban environments but the difficulties encountered in trying to move or mix large volumes of concrete on remote sites makes it less attractive than flexible liners. Concrete is better than fibreglass in terms of the scope it offers for pond design and shaping. It is also very durable when mixed and laid correctly because it will not dry out or crack if the water level falls and it is not easy to damage a thick layer of concrete!

The construction of a small pond using concrete is reasonably straightforward but reinforcement could be needed, especially on soft ground, to prevent structural cracking. When the hole is excavated, steep falls should be avoided as these will constitute weak points. The dimensions of the hole should allow for a lining of at least 150 mm of concrete and 100–150 mm of soil. The thickness of concrete which is required will depend on the stresses which are likely to be imposed on it—there will be pressure from the water and also from the surrounding ground which is why mesh reinforcement is needed in all but the smallest ponds.

For a pond up to 30 m² two or three layers of wire mesh, such as

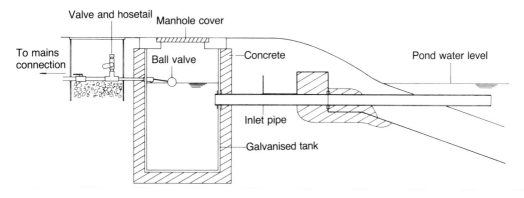

Figure 4.8   Water supply from the mains to a large, lined pond (*Miles Waterscapes Ltd*)

chainlink fencing, should be placed in the hole to cover the entire pond area. Galvanised wire must be used to join each piece of reinforcement together securely. Ferro-cement, a cement mortar consisting of 1 part white Portland cement to 1.5–2.0 parts sharp concreting sand, must be worked well into the mesh to give the required thickness of lining, with at least 20 mm of cover over the reinforcement. A 25 mm rendering coat could be used on top of the lining, together with a waterproofing agent.

The concrete should be laid in one session to avoid weaknesses around joints where the lining dries out in sections. Several days should be allowed for curing, the concrete covered with either plastic sheeting or straw.

After this, the pond should be filled with water and left to stand for three days, to enable free lime and other chemicals present in the cement to leach out. The water must then be pumped out and the concrete washed prior to refilling. It is advisable to allow for further seasoning of the pond before any fauna and flora are introduced. Over a period of at least one month, the pond should be emptied and refilled weekly, with any residues on the concrete scrubbed off. Once the pond is seasoned, soil should be placed on top of the concrete so that plants and animals can become established.

*Flexible linings*
Flexible liners for ponds of all sizes are available in a number of forms. The three main types are polyethylene (polythene), poly vinyl chloride (PVC) and polyisobutilene (butyl rubber). Other more specialised materials can also be used and a brief description of some of these is provided on page 94. There are advantages in using flexible pond liners:

- Liners for ponds less than 30 m × 30 m are relatively portable, can be fabricated in one piece and can be moved to inaccessible sites quite easily.

*Plate 4.5   A pond constructed out of concrete. Note the lack of soil and emergent vegetation.*

*Plate 4.6   Newly created butyl-lined pond. Note the natural appearance and shape of the pond.*

- Sheet liners can be used in irregularly shaped and profiled ponds.
- The skills needed to lay a liner in a small to medium sized pond are not as complicated as those required to lay reinforced concrete.

There are also some disadvantages:

- The lining of large ponds requires professional assistance, especially where sheets have to be joined and inflow and outflow pipes are necessary.
- Where the pond site is in an area with a fluctuating water table, the installation of a flexible liner may be very difficult. If the ground water pressure is too high, the liner will 'balloon' and be forced out of the pond. The liner will revert into position once the water pressure is reduced, but the result can be unsightly and it causes considerable disturbance to pondlife.
- Sheet liners are easily punctured.
- Some flexible liners perish after prolonged exposure to sunlight or frost.

Because of potential problems, the choice of lining material requires very careful thought, and good management is essential once the pond is complete. The three most common flexible lining membranes each have varying characteristics, particularly with regard to durability:

*Polythene* sheets are manufactured in different thicknesses. The black sheeting normally used to cover silage clamps on farms is 500 gauge and is too thin for use in ponds. Polythene liners do not have a long life where they are exposed to sunlight or frost around the water's edge; they must therefore be covered with a good depth of soil for protection and also to enable plants to grow. Under normal conditions, these liners should last many years assuming they are correctly installed in accordance with the manufacturer's instructions.

*PVC* is more expensive and is more resistant to ultra violet degradation than polythene, but if PVC sheets are exposed to direct sunlight, they will lose their plasticity after several years. To avoid this, all exposed surfaces should be well covered with soil above and below water level.

*Butyl rubber* is the most expensive of the three commonly used lining membranes and it also seems to be the most durable, with a proven life expectancy (if correctly used) in excess of 50 years. Polythene and PVC liners have not been in use for so many years and so their longevity is not known.

Sheets are produced in varying thicknesses; 0.75 mm and 1 mm are the most normal for pond linings, although thinner membranes are available. The sheets can be manufactured up to 30 m × 30 m, avoiding the need for jointing (and potential weakness points) in many ponds.

Despite butyl rubber being unaffected by sunlight and frost, all exposed surfaces must still be covered with soil to encourage plants and improve the appearance of the pond.

## Using a Flexible Liner

*Site preparation*
Where the pond is large enough to be mechanically excavated, it should be tackled as if it were an unlined pond. In gardens or on small sites, where the hole has to be dug by hand, it is worth pegging out the shape more carefully.

Wherever possible, the banks of the pond should be very gently graded so that soil placed on top of the liner will stay in position. The steepest gradient where soil will remain *in situ* is 20°, so a gradient of 3 : 1 is the optimum around the pond perimeter. On a large site, this will be no problem, but in a confined space, particularly in a garden, there is often insufficient room to allow for such gentle slopes otherwise the surface area will be too great where the pond is also going to be at least 1 m deep. In this case the alternatives are: to have steeply sloping banks together with at least one gentle incline; or to make a steep sided pond.

In the first instance, the gentle incline will provide ideal conditions for plant establishment, but the steep sides will need planting ledges where soil can be placed to encourage plant growth. A steep sided pond is the least attractive option but if enough shallow ledges are created it will still provide good habitat and appear quite natural.

Inevitably with either option, some of the lining membrane will be exposed above the top water level. This can be disguised by a variety of methods:

- Grasses and trailing plants can be encouraged to grow over the edge of the pond.
- Paving stones can be placed so that they overhang the water around garden ponds.
- Emergent plants can be positioned on ledges to grow up in front of the liner, thus hiding it.

An interesting modification can be made to a steep sided pond surrounded by paving slabs. Ledges covered by the paving stones can be provided at water level as a refuge for amphibians and acting as an escape route. The amphibians are able to climb up a narrow channel between two of the stones thus enabling them to enter and leave the water easily, where they would otherwise be unable to manage steep, slippery sides.

As the pond is dug out, the depth of all areas must be increased to allow for a layer of soil on top of the liner. In a garden pond 75–150 mm of soil

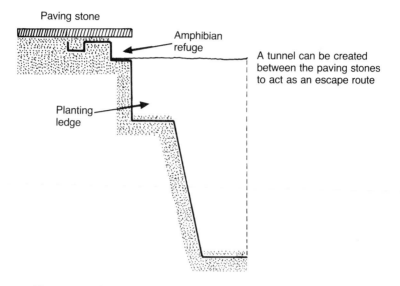

Paving stone

Amphibian refuge

A tunnel can be created
between the paving stones
to act as an escape route

Planting ledge

Figure 4.9   Creating an amphibian refuge in a lined pond

will suffice, but in large ponds where machinery is to be used to spread soil on to the liner a minimum of 300 mm will be required.

If an area of marshland is to be made, the space for this should also be dug out. In garden ponds, the planting ledges must be created at this stage and the liner will be installed once the pond is correctly shaped. Where the surface area of the pond is to be greater than 100 m², it is better to excavate a regularly shaped hole and construct planting areas and bays once the liner is in place. It is far easier to work with a large sheet liner in a regularly shaped hole than it is to ease the membrane on to narrow ledges and round an intricately shaped shoreline. The creation of planting areas and a marshland is described on pp. 92–93.

Finally, thought must be given as to how the sheet is to be anchored around the edges of the hole on completion of the pond. On large sites, where the pond is to be in excess of 300 m² a trench (225 mm × 225 mm) should be dug around the perimeter of the pond at least 1 m back from the water's edge. For smaller ponds, the trench can be closer to the water's edge. Once the pond is full of water, the outer edge of the sheeting will be buried in the trench and held firmly in position. Trenches are often unnecessary round garden ponds (see p. 94–95).

*Assessing the size of liner*
The size of liner required for a pond can be calculated using a simple formula:

Length of liner = overall length of pond (including any artificial marsh and the overlap needed to fit into the anchorage trenches) + twice the maximum depth.

Width of liner = overall width of pond (including any artificial marsh and the overlap needed to fit into the anchorage trenches) + twice the maximum depth.

*Laying a flexible liner*
*In every case, the manufacturer's specific instructions must be closely followed when flexible liners are installed into ponds.*

Immediately prior to laying the membrane, a check must be made to ensure that there are no sharp stones or roots projecting into the hole. Sterilisation of the soil may be needed on some sites before installing the liner, to prevent subsequent weed problems.

Waterproof membranes will be supplied either in a roll or folded and care is needed during transportation and handling to avoid punctures. It is impossible to lay a liner properly in windy or very wet conditions because handling becomes difficult.

As a general guide, some form of pre-lining is advisable. Old plastic sheeting (farm fertiliser sacks are ideal), carpet underlay and fine sand

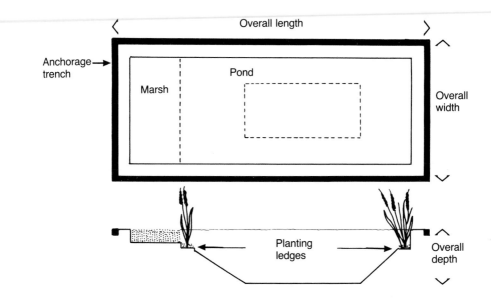

Figure 4.10 The dimensions which are required when calculating the size of a flexible liner

are all good for this purpose, although sand is only appropriate where the bankside gradients will allow it to remain in place. Geotextiles are often used in large scale projects both beneath and above waterproof membranes to provide additional protection, but in view of the cost and sophisticated nature of this type of treatment, professional advice must be taken before using such materials.

Once the pre-liner is in place, the leading edge of the waterproof membrane should be placed on the side of the pond, overlapping the anchor trench. The sheet should then be unrolled or unfolded into the hole. Once it is approximately in place, the lining can be eased into the correct position, any person handling it taking care not to damage the sheeting if it becomes necessary to walk on it.

Polythene and PVC sheets can be folded or allowed to wrinkle as they are moulded to the pond shape. Butyl rubber must be treated with more care. If a lot of slack sheeting remains in the bottom of the pond, a trench may have to be dug either into the pond floor (or the sides) in which the surplus liner can be buried rather than being folded flat.

Where more than one sheet is needed for large projects, the method used to join the material will depend on the type of membrane being used and the manufacturer's instructions. The durability of 'do-it-yourself' joins should never be overestimated. One method is to overlap each sheet by at least 150 mm and apply a double sided mastic tape between overlapping sections; adhesive tape 75 mm wide is then used on the upper surface to cover the join. If possible, a flat piece of wood should be moved beneath the liner as the join is made so that sealing can be done firmly. Specialist contractors or membrane manufacturers who are employed to line ponds will use sophisticated heat sealing techniques which are not available to DIY pond enthusiasts.

If an outlet or inlet pipe has to be run through the lining, the pond can still be made watertight. The membrane must be laid over the end of the pipe, which should project into the pond. Cuts should be made around the pipe end so that the sheet can be eased back round it and securely sealed on to the pipe using adhesive tape. Some manufacturers now supply pipe flanges to help secure inlets and outlets. (See Figure 4.8.)

*Backfilling with soil*

Once the liner is in position, the edges must be temporarily anchored. Bricks or heavy weights placed on the sheet above the top water level mark will prevent it from being dragged under water as it is moulded to the pond shape by water pressure. Once it is anchored, but prior to filling, the liner must be covered with soil. In a small pond, this can easily be done by hand and the soil should be sieved to remove sharp stones. A 75–150 mm deep layer over the whole floor of the pond (or in steep sided ponds on the bed

Plate 4.7   The site for a new pond.

Plate 4.8   The pond with butyl liner in place. Note the marsh (foreground) and the planting ledges.

Plate 4.9    *The pond on completion. A range of plants have been introduced—see Chapter 5.*

Plate 4.10    *Twelve months later. Note the rapid growth of plants, particularly free floating and submerged species.*

and on the surface of the planting ledges) will suffice. The marshy area should also be backfilled.

Where the pond is too large for soil to be introduced by hand, low ground pressure dumper trucks can be used provided that the waterproof lining is protected by a geotextile membrane. The soil should be placed on the edge of the pond and a causeway built out over the geotextile to provide access for the vehicles transporting the soil. Once the soil is tipped on to the membrane, it can be graded into a layer at least 300 mm deep.

### Creating planting areas and bays

Large, regularly shaped holes can easily be turned into attractive ponds once the waterproof lining is in place. Embankments can be created below water using sand bags or large stones (provided that these are placed on top of a protective geotextile). Soil should be built up behind the embankment to create level, shallow areas of water adjacent to the pond banks. These areas can subsequently be planted, the rate of spread of the plants over the remainder of the pond slowed because of the sudden change in water depth. The same technique can be used to create bays and spits, thus varying the appearance of the shoreline. In both cases, the embankments will prevent the soil washing away.

Around those parts of the bank where shallows are not required, a row of stones placed on the liner below water level will help to stop the soil slumping down into the pond, so exposing the liner to ultra violet degradation.

### Creating islands

It is very difficult to form an island during excavation when a flexible waterproof membrane is to be used. However, the floor of the pond can

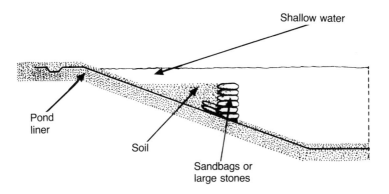

Figure 4.11   Creating planting areas and shallow water in a lined pond

be gently sloped up towards the water surface where the island is required. The liner is then laid as normal with 300–600 mm of rubble and soil placed on top to break the surface, forming the island. As an alternative in a shallow pond, soil should be banked up on top of the liner until it reaches the surface, although some reinforcement in the form of log baffles will be needed around the perimeter of the island just below and above the water surface to prevent erosion. In many instances, the use of a floating raft would be more appropriate, construction of these is described in Chapter 5, Supplementary Habitat Creation.

### Creating a marsh

The creation of a marshland habitat is quite straightforward with a flexible waterproof liner. When the pond is excavated, an extra section should be dug out to a depth of between 225–300 mm. A lip should be left between the marsh area and the main pond, rising above the bottom water level but

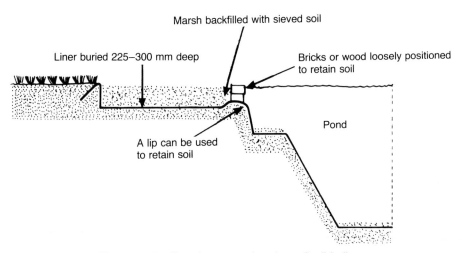

Figure 4.12   Creating a marsh using a flexible liner

finishing below the top water level. This will allow water to flow into the marsh but prevent waterlogged soil slipping back into the pond.

The whole area should be treated as part of the pond for lining purposes and when soil is backfilled on to the pond liner, the marsh should be filled with soil to the level of the surrounding ground. Once the pond is full of water, the marsh will remain saturated by a regular inflow of water. The surplus liner around the edges of the marsh should be treated in the same way as the rest of the pond. Once the marsh is well established and covered with wetland plants, it will be virtually impossible to detect the presence of the liner.

*Plate 4.11    An artificial marsh created in a butyl-lined pond.*

### Filling the pond

The pond should be filled gently via an inlet pipe or hose to prevent soil on the liner being washed down into the bed of the pond.

### Concealing the liner

Once the pond is full of water, trim off any surplus liner overlapping beyond the anchor trench and bury the end in the trench. Exposed sheeting between the trench and the water's edge should be covered by at least 100 mm of soil. There is often no need for a trench around a garden pond; in this case a diagonal cut should be made downwards into the ground (starting above top water level), the surrounding turf can then be eased up and the liner edge tucked into the gap, to be held in place once the turf is firmed up.

## Other Forms of Liner

It is possible to create a waterproof lining for a pond using sodium bentonite, more correctly called Montmorillonite (hydrous aluminium silicate). The use of this material is highly specialised and must be undertaken in strict accordance with the supplier's instructions. Bentonite can be used either in powder or granular form, the material swelling to several times its volume on contact with water to form an impermeable gel which retains water as well as allowing plants to root. Depending on local conditions, this material can be applied either in a continuous layer or mixed with the

Liner inserted into pond bank

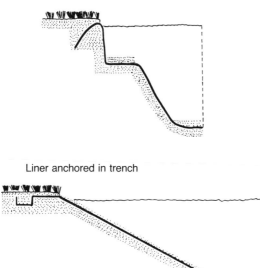

Liner anchored in trench

Figure 4.13   Anchoring a flexible pond liner

soils on site. Because it is chemically inert, it poses no hazard to wildlife if used to line a new pond. Bentonite can also be used to repair leaks in clay lined ponds, but if it is sprinkled on to the surface of the pond and sinks to the bottom as it swells, it may adversely affect animal life within the water.

Reinforced polythene geomembrane sheets are also available for pond lining and have been used successfully in many projects. These liners can be factory welded into sheets up to 1,500 m² and can be joined on site by continuous extrusion welding where a very large pond is being constructed.

## POND REPAIR

The repair of a damaged pond is in most cases a job for experts. Repair to dams, structural embankments, water supply pipes and extensive flexible liners requires professional expertise. Leaks in embankments and clay linings can sometimes be traced using special chemicals and damage repaired once the source of the problem has been identified. Clay linings can be repaired by careful repuddling, while holes in sheet liners can

*Plate 4.12   A warning notice near to a pond is sometimes appropriate.*

occasionally be repaired, assuming they can be found, once the soil has been scraped off the membrane. A patch of a similar lining material should be used for the repair, sealed with mastic tape and coated with bitumen. Failing this, a new liner will have to be installed.

## Pond Construction and Safety

Pond owners should always be aware of the dangers associated with water. While there is no requirement to fence every new pond, some consideration must be given to warning visitors of any danger, and it may be prudent to fence off a pond which is close to a farmyard or house where young children are present. Where public access is anticipated, warning notices can be displayed on fences, posts or trees and lifebelts should be provided close to the pond (see p. 175).

The provision of shallow gradients around the edge of ponds as a design feature to encourage wildlife will also be of value as a safety measure.

## Dealing with Contractors

There are many companies with the machinery capable of creating ponds and lakes, but not many with expertise in the construction of the type of pond which is so valuable for wildlife and the environment. It is very important to find a company with skilled plant operators who can understand the reasons why the pond should be created with a range of interesting features. Before engaging a company to construct a pond, the landowner or his agent should ask to see examples of similar work which that company has undertaken and ensure that skilled plant operators will be assigned to his particular project. If sub-contractors are to be used, for instance to haul soil off site, the landowner must be certain that they too have the relevant experience.

The contractor must be made aware of potential problems (such as those caused by soil conditions) which may be encountered during the work, assuming that the contractor has not been involved with the project since its conception. A full schedule of works should be obtained from the contractor, together with a quotation for the cost of the operations which are to be undertaken. The schedule of works must include details of the final site landscaping. In terms of project costing, the quotation should specify how much the work will cost, any haulage costs incurred moving the machinery on to the site and also whether additional costs will be charged to the landowner if any of the machinery becomes stuck in mud or suffers mechanical breakdown.

Finally, the landowner must agree with the contractor which routes are to be used to gain access to the pond, where soil is to be placed and who is responsible for any damage which may be caused by the contractor, his employees or any sub-contractors, for instance if gateposts or fences are knocked down on access routes or if trees are scraped.

## ONE LAST THING . . .

When the hard work is over and the pond is full of water, do place a seat nearby, so that the true benefit of the pond can be fully appreciated in the ensuing months and years.

*Chapter 5*

# Supplementary Habitat Creation

Any plan for pond creation or restoration should include not only the provision of open water but also the associated bankside habitats described in the chapter on pond design, namely marshland, grassy banks, scrub and trees. In addition, some careful stocking of the water will help to accelerate the development of flourishing plant and animal communities. With insufficient attention paid to these points, the pond may not live up to the owner's expectations, may not look very attractive, probably will not fulfil the original objectives of the management plan and may be more difficult to manage in the long term. In each case, the money spent developing the pond will not have been used effectively.

Once any pond has been created and is full of water, something will happen both in and out of the water as man moves on to another task and nature begins to run its course. Unfortunately, more often than not, a limited number of plants will flourish and eventually dominate the site, to the detriment of other, often more attractive species, thus reducing the habitat diversity. As an example, if willows take hold around the banks of

*Plate 5.1   Shelter is needed around this upland pond to improve the quality of the habitat for wildlife.*

98

the pond and are unmanaged, the area will support fewer species of bird than would be attracted by several different types of shrub. This problem can be overcome by treating the land surrounding the pond as an integral part of the overall scheme and planning its management with care. In some instances, the pond environs may already support plenty of plants and animals as revealed by an initial site assessment, in which case few modifications will be necessary. Where this is not the case, the next part of the pond creation or restoration process can be very exciting, enabling the owner or manager to participate in habitat development and directly influence the way in which the pond matures to support wildlife as well as achieving any other objectives set out in the original plan.

There are four areas around the pond where habitat creation or manipulation should be considered once excavation, desilting or other management operations have been completed:

- Introduction of aquatic plants into the water.
- Establishment of marshland and terrestrial plants around the banks.
- The planting of trees and shrubs on land set back from the pond.
- The provision of artificial 'habitat boosters'.

## INTRODUCTION OF AQUATIC PLANTS

All pond planting programmes should take account of three factors: any anticipated utilisation of the pond; the local conditions; and the water quality.

*Utilisation*   A variety of species can be introduced to a pond created purely for wildlife conservation, whereas if the objective is angling, care will be needed to ensure that the water does not become choked with floating or submerged plants which will hinder the fishermen. If wildfowling is an objective, suitable wildfowl food plants should be selected to encourage duck to use the pond.

*Local conditions*   These will influence the species choice, particularly for a farm or village pond. Note must be taken of aquatic plants occurring elsewhere in the locality and, wherever possible, uncommon varieties and those which do not grow nearby should not be introduced to the new pond in case they spread to other ponds with potentially disastrous results. For instance, if a very invasive and locally uncommon floating-leaved plant is put into a new pond and spreads to another, it could cover the water surface of the second pond, perhaps shading out established submerged plants and cutting out light to other pond life beneath. If the invader is allowed to grow on unchecked and it eventually dominates the pond, it will have totally upset the ecological balance in what might otherwise have been a very stable environment. In preference to this, the use of native species which flourish locally will increase the chances of accomplishing a successful introduction programme, because the common plants will be adapted to local conditions and should therefore thrive in the new pond.

*Water quality*   This will have an influence over which plants are capable of surviving in the pond. Some species are less tolerant than others of acidic conditions. Plants such as amphibious bistort and flowering rush are able to grow only in nutrient rich waters, whereas soft rush, marsh marigold and water forget-me-not will thrive in a wider range of conditions.

Appendix 2 contains a list of plants suitable for ponds, with notes as to their suitability for different conditions.

### Is the Introduction of Aquatic Plants Necessary?

There is no hard and fast rule to state that plants should be introduced into a new pond. Without man's intervention, some species will become established, but the development of a rich diversity of pondlife will almost certainly take many years. A restored pond ought to be left alone for one or, at the most, two growing seasons to allow for the re-establishment of plants which grew in the pond prior to management and whose seeds remain in the soil. Where few plants have re-established after this time, introductions can be made. Where a farm pond is excavated in an isolated position or a garden pond is constructed, limited plant introductions should be made soon after completion, although some plants will be dispersed naturally into new ponds by visiting animals. Charles Darwin noted in 1859 in his work *The Origin of Species by Means of Natural Selection, or the Preservation of Favoured Races in the Struggle for Life* that small, floating plants such as duckweeds are transported from one pond to another by duck, and fragments of submerged plants are transferred in the same way.

### Site Preparation Prior to Planting

Most site preparation involves designing the pond properly. In general, little work is required after construction and prior to planting, assuming that some soil has been placed on top of any clay or flexible liner to act as a rooting medium before the pond is filled with water. If the pond has been filled with tap water it must be allowed to stand for at least 48 hours before any plant introductions are made.

Under most circumstances, bare rooted plants should be introduced to spread within the pond as quickly as possible. If the physical characteristics of the pond are correct (see pond design) this should not cause future management problems because the plants will be confined to specific zones within the water or around the margins.

The exceptions to this rule are:

- Small garden ponds with a surface area of less than 25 m².
- Where highly invasive and difficult to control species such as water lilies are to be used.

In these cases, the plants should be secured in containers to inhibit rapid spread. A combination of bare-rooted and containerised stock can be used to good effect in small ponds where rapid growth together with species diversity is needed. The quick spread of plants is provided by two or three bare-rooted species, with other slower growing plants able to survive against the competition because they are allowed to grow in large containers (usually 300 mm square) which are readily available at garden centres. However, in the warm, nutrient rich conditions typical of garden ponds, careful management is required to prevent excessive spread of the bare-rooted species beyond the planting ledges, especially where the pond is less than 1 m deep.

**Obtaining Plants**

Wherever possible, indigenous stock should be introduced to offer the best environment for pondlife and make the pond look natural. Combinations of native and 'exotic' strains can be very attractive where the visual appearance of the pond is important. Variegated flag iris, coloured lilies and monkey flower all fit well into an otherwise 'native' pond, but the use of these exotic species should be confined to gardens.

There are some exotic plants which should never be introduced into ponds. The Australian stonecrop is gaining a foothold in many ponds and waterways and, once established, it smothers other species, including native water plants. Once this plant is thriving, control is extremely difficult with resultant disastrous effects on wildlife. Canadian pondweed is another very adaptable species and while its use as an oxygenator can be advantageous, it is quite likely to take over a pond, so it should be avoided where a true 'native' pond is desired.

An increasing number of garden centres and specialist retailers now sell indigenous stock but a good alternative (and cheaper) source of plants is an established pond. Routine pond management produces copious amounts of unwanted plants, some of which could easily be used elsewhere. Friends, neighbours or farmers with ponds will probably be only too happy to part with unwanted plants if asked properly! It must be remembered that it is an offence to uproot any plant which is growing in the wild without the landowner's consent, indeed some species are totally protected (see Chapter 8, Ponds, Wildlife and the Law). Apart from the fact that it is illegal to uproot a wild plant, unplanned plant removals may adversely damage a habitat. If in doubt, seek advice from the Nature Conservancy Council or the County Wildlife Trust. One great advantage of obtaining plants from existing ponds is that they are almost certain to bring invertebrates with them, usually clinging to the roots, so pond colonisation receives an early boost.

Once suitable plants have been obtained, the roots must be kept wet until they can be introduced into the pond. If planting is to be delayed, the roots should be immersed in shallow water.

### How Many Plants Should Be Used?

It is not easy to specify exactly how many plants of different species should be introduced to a new pond of any given size. The best answer is to err on the side of caution and not put too many in too early. While a 5 m × 3 m garden pond may look empty after twenty plants (six to ten species) have been introduced, after twelve months the change will be dramatic. Overstocking early in the life of the pond will cause major problems later and advance the time when management is needed. (See plates 4.9 and 4.10.)

As a guide, an established field pond might contain several marginal and emergent species, two floating and two submerged species.

### Planting Technique

A planting programme is best carried out in the spring, to allow the plants a full growing season in which to become established. While this is fine if the planting stock is readily available, if it is being obtained from ponds cleared during the autumn, the planting will have to be done at the end of the season.

#### Marginal plants
These should be planted just above the water line, with the roots or rhizomes pushed gently into the soil. Once the plants are established they will spread very quickly down into the water.

#### Emergent plants
Bare-rooted plants should be introduced to the pond in the same way as marginals, but the roots should be planted in shallow water. It may be necessary to weight the roots by placing bricks or large stones over the soil to hold the plants *in situ* until the roots take a hold; this is a very useful technique to try in ponds with flexible liners where there is only a

little soil. If duck are present on larger ponds, the areas where emergent species are establishing will need to be protected by wire netting, to stop the duck disturbing the root systems as they feed on the bottom of the pond.

Sedges have sharp pointed growing tips to their roots and if they are to be used in ponds with lightweight flexible liners, an additional layer of material should be placed beneath them to prevent the roots penetrating the membrane.

Reeds will establish from cuttings pushed into the ground at or just above water level. They will shoot from the nodes on the stem if 1 m long, green stems are pressed into the soil at an angle of 45° to the vertical. This is an easy way to produce a flourishing reed bed around the banks of large expanses of water.

### Planting in groups

When a variety of different marginal and emergent species are introduced into a pond they will compete against each other and as a result some may be eliminated. A technique successfully used by the Game Conservancy Trust in gravel pit restoration is to use groups of the same plant in specific locations around the water's edge. In this way, each species is able to create its own niche and, as the pool matures, the result is a varied waterside flora supporting a wide range of wildlife which also looks quite natural and very attractive. (See colour plate 16.)

### Submerged rooted plants

These are planted below water level, down to a depth of 450 mm. Normally, introductions are made at around 250–300 mm, another reason for leaving areas of shallow water around the pond margins. Many species will root in much deeper water but because they are being planted within reach of the bankside it is only possible to put them into the shallows and allow them to spread out from there.

### Floating-leaved rooting plants

Species such as water lilies should be planted in containers. The best way to introduce them into the pond is to drop the container into the water, over the point where the plant is required. It is possible to throw the container a couple of metres into a small pond, but on larger waters a boat will be needed to get the lilies out towards the middle.

### Free floating plants

These include many of the best oxygenating species and so it is essential that plants in this category are put into the water at an early stage.

Oxygenators are usually purchased in small bundles, or if taken from another pond a few handfuls will suffice. They should simply be placed in the open water and allowed to disperse. In warm conditions, a few shoots from a species such as hornwort will rapidly multiply. Free floating plants removed from established ponds in early to mid summer will usually have small invertebrates, pond snails and even eggs adhering to them—these will all help with the colonisation of the new water body.

## Introducing Animals to the Pond

Apart from 'accidental' animal introductions such as these, other creatures should not be put into the pond until the plants are well established and providing plenty of oxygen, food and cover. Many small animals will find their own way to the new pond and it will probably become colonised naturally after a few months. Where there are other areas of water nearby, water bugs, beetles and other insects will fly to the new pond, while the movement of larger animals from one wetland habitat to another will result in the dispersal of species which cannot fly but which cling to other creatures.

## MARSHLAND AND TERRESTRIAL PLANTS

The significance of these zones to wildlife has been described in Chapter 3, Pond Design, but unfortunately the vegetation which normally colonises the banks of new or restored ponds is not always that which encourages the development of the best habitat. When excavated soil has been deposited on the banks, typical species of disturbed ground will thrive. These include nettles, thistles, docks and willowherbs. While these have some value for conservation, they also compete with less aggressive and often more attractive plants. This makes it impossible for the establishment of varied (and thus valuable) habitat, as well as hindering access which may adversely affect any proposed use of the pond.

On completion of excavation or desilting, the soil must be spread out, graded and allowed to dry. As soon as it has dried out, grass seed should be sown to create a dense sward and prevent aggressive species from becoming established. A seeds mixture containing 70 per cent turf perennial ryegrass and 30 per cent creeping red fescue, sown at approximately 70 grams per square metre should provide a suitable base for future habitat improvements. If the soil has a pH outside the band 4.5–7.2, some corrective treatment should be applied prior to seeding with this mixture. It is also important to ensure that a genuine turf perennial ryegrass with a dwarf habit is used, as opposed to the more common agricultural ryegrasses, which are unsuitable for this type of project. As an alternative to sowing as soon as the soil is dry, early plant regeneration from dormant seeds could be killed off using a herbicide to leave a clean base into which the seeds can be sown.

It is at this stage that the pond owner has the perfect opportunity to create very attractive and valuable species rich grasslands and wetlands. The loss of these extremely important habitats throughout the country since 1949 has been serious. The Nature Conservancy Council estimates that 95 per cent of lowland neutral grasslands (which include herb rich meadows) now lack significant wildlife interest and that only 3 per cent of these grasslands have been unaffected by agricultural intensification.

The excavation or restoration of a pond, even a small one in a garden, provides an exciting chance to re-introduce wild flowers into the environment, albeit on a modest scale. If every pond scheme included the creation of an area of marshland plus a mini-meadow of terrestrial wild flowers and grasses, there would be a dramatic increase in the total area covered by these species, which although not as ecologically valuable as the old sites which have been damaged or lost, would nevertheless represent a significant gain for wildlife. (See colour plate 17.)

If a saturated marsh has been formed adjacent to the pond, this can either be planted using appropriate species or sown with a specially formulated wetland wild flower seed mixture. These mixtures are now readily available in either large or small quantities from agricultural seed merchants or specialist seedsmen. The wild flower seedsman John Chambers offers a

*Plate 5.2   A well developed garden pond and marsh constructed using a butyl liner. A pair of sedge warblers successfully nested in the clump of sedges (left centre).*

pack containing seeds of popular pond edge plants, providing enough seed to sow 4 m² of marsh. These packs, on sale at many garden centres, are a marvellous low-cost way of developing attractive garden habitats. Larger quantities of seed are also easily available to sow over more extensive areas, for instance around farm or village ponds.

Similar packets of seed can be purchased containing formulations for sowing on drier ground—in this case the mixtures (usually 80–85 per cent wild grasses and 15–20 per cent wild flowers) are prepared for different soil conditions, usually clay, loam, sand or chalk based. Mixtures of this type should always contain seed produced from native strains of plant and be prepared in accordance with the guidelines set out in the Nature Conservancy Council publication *Creating Attractive Grassland Using Native Plant Species*.

As an alternative to using seeds, individual wild plants can be propagated or purchased for introduction to existing grassland. This is a good technique to try around old established ponds where greater diversity is required. Individual wild flower plants, for instance ragged robin or purple loosestrife, are also suitable for a garden and provide excellent habitat and colour adjacent to the pond, growing into very large specimens if kept free from surrounding competition.

### Creating a Marsh or Terrestrial Wild Flower and Grass Area from Seed

*Site preparation*

The majority of the species which are included in seed mixtures grow best in competition with each other in soils of low fertility. Optimum conditions are often present following pond excavation where top soil has been stripped. This is one advantage of good forward planning, because areas earmarked for wild flower seeding can be prepared and left free of topsoil following construction thus saving time and money.

If fertile soil or vegetation covers the area to be sown, some preparatory work will be required. Existing plant growth must be eliminated using a herbicide—with care taken to ensure that any areas identified during the preliminary site survey as being rich in plant life are not damaged. Seeds which have lain dormant in silt dredged out of restored ponds should be allowed to regenerate prior to this herbicide treatment. Once any unwanted plant growth has been killed off, a fine, firm seedbed should be prepared and if further plant regeneration occurs, this too should be eliminated prior to seeding.

*Sowing*

Late spring and early autumn are the best times to sow wild flower and grass seed mixtures. For small schemes, sowing is best done by hand. There are likely to be up to 30 different plant species in each mixture, the seeds all of varying sizes. To ensure an even distribution over the area to be sown, the seeds should be mixed with fine dry sand or sawdust (one part of seed to ten parts of sand or sawdust). This will also help to identify the areas once they are sown if a large scheme is being tackled. Seedsmen's recommended sowing rates (as provided with each mixture) should always be followed. Where a very large wild flower area is to be created, slot seeding using agricultural machinery should be considered.

After sowing, the seedbed should be lightly raked over and watered. An average covering of 5 mm of soil will suit the varying light and depth requirements of most of the species included in the mixtures. Seeds sown in late spring must be kept well watered during the summer.

*Post sowing management*
Following germination, the wild flowers and grasses will look very poor and thin; many land owners have spent time at this stage wondering whether their project is on the way to becoming an expensive failure! Newly sown wild flower meadows do not have a close-knit sward. There are many gaps between the plants in the early stages which will remain until all of the species are well established.

Once plant growth is 150 mm high, the area should be cut and all the clippings removed. Cutting must be repeated throughout the first full growing season and will help to reduce the persistence of annual plants which are not part of the seed mixture, as well as eliminating problem species such as nettles or thistles.

After the first year, the meadow or marsh should be flourishing, but on difficult sites where there was vigorous vegetation cover prior to seeding either a second year of cutting may be needed or spot herbicide treatment of persistent weed patches. Once the wild flowers and grasses are fully established, normal management routines should be followed as described in Chapter 6, Pond Management.

## TREES AND SHRUBS

Trees and shrubs planted near to the pond are important because:

- They will help create shelter and seclusion.
- Trees and shrubs are host plants for many different types of insect.
- Natural food and cover will be provided for birds, mammals, insects and amphibians.
- They will help to landscape the pond and make it visually attractive.

These benefits will be of value no matter how the pond is to be utilised. (See colour plate 18.)

## What Should Be Planted?

As with aquatic plants, indigenous tree and shrub species must be used wherever possible, especially in rural areas. Trees and shrubs which occur naturally in the United Kingdom indisputably support the most wildlife. For example, the common oak is host to hundreds of different kinds of insect, whereas introduced or 'exotic' trees such as southern beech (nothofagus) have very few dependent species. In addition to being the best for conservation, the native trees and shrubs, especially those growing in the locality of the pond, will be the ones best suited to the site and therefore the most likely to thrive.

It is also best to use native species for wildlife gardening in urban areas, but within the garden environment exotic shrubs can be planted to great visual effect while still encouraging plenty of animals.

Appendix 2 provides a list of native species which can be planted as part of pond creation or management schemes.

## Obtaining Native Trees and Shrubs

Some garden centres stock indigenous trees and shrubs, particularly those which might normally be planted in gardens (such as rowan), but the best choice is provided by a forest nursery. Addresses of local nurserymen can be found in the telephone directories.

There is a choice of sizes for planting. Small seedlings or transplants can be used to great advantage in farm conservation schemes, but for amenity value and use in gardens larger specimens are often chosen, although they are more expensive to buy. In fact, given good post planting management, many seedling shrubs and trees will grow very quickly, often catching up with larger plants within a few years, so it is not always necessary to spend large sums of money purchasing big trees.

An important point to remember when planting seedlings is not to be fooled by their appearance. One day they will be big. Too many little plants put into a small area will soon need thinning out and a tiny tree planted in the corner of a garden might one day overshadow the whole neighbourhood!

## Planting and Aftercare

There are plenty of sources of advice and information available. It is well worth ensuring that all planting and aftercare is carried out properly and

*Plate 5.3   Landscaping a newly created farm pond using individually protected shrubs. Note the gently sloping bankside (left) and the land drain feeding water into the pond (centre).*

also that the trees and shrubs are well cared for prior to planting. Many good young trees die on account of poor handling, their roots drying out in storage or exposed to the wind during planting.

A number of simple guidelines should be followed with all planting schemes:

- Decide in advance of planting where the trees and shrubs are to be located and mark this on the management plan.
- Select the species most suited to the site.
- Prepare the ground well.
- Protect all trees and shrubs against damage by hares and rabbits—the use of individual guards is best for farm conservation schemes. If deer are known to be a problem in the locality seek expert on-site advice.
- Fence livestock out of new plantings.
- Water the trees and shrubs regularly during the first growing season.
- Control vegetation in a 1 m diameter circle around each tree or shrub to prevent competition from other plants for light, moisture and nutrient.
- Prune trees lightly four or five years after planting to encourage a single, vigorous leading shoot.
- Remove tree guards, ties and stakes once the trees are large enough to withstand damage from vermin.

## Habitat Boosters

The term 'habitat booster' refers to anything which does not grow on site and which is introduced to the pond or surrounding area with the express purpose of attracting animals.

One of the most obvious aids to wildlife in any situation is the bird nesting box. This theme can be further developed to encompass exciting features such as cliff faces for nesting kingfishers and sand martins, or floating rafts used as nesting platforms and roosts by wildfowl, or on large ponds and lakes possibly even by terns.

Habitats for bats are continually under pressure and simple bat boxes can be constructed and erected in suitable locations. Piles of logs or rotting timber ('ecopiles') stacked in dark, damp places near to ponds provide marvellous homes for wildlife; amphibians use them for hibernation in winter, while birds and small mammals use them as cover and come to feed on the insects living in the decaying wood.

### Artificial Nesting Devices

There are very few sites where it is inappropriate to place a nest box for birds—providing there is an adequate supply of food, birds will

*Plate 5.4    A small garden pond with butyl liner. The log has been used to provide an escape route for amphibians, and refuges have been created under the paving slabs.*

nest. Around any well designed and managed pond, there ought to be an abundant stock of seeds, berries and insects for food, therefore many species of bird could be encouraged. The absence of suitable nest sites is usually the factor determining whether or not birds will breed, so the use of artificial nesting devices is well worthwhile.

Many different types of nesting box can be built and sited in trees and shrubberies near ponds, to cater for birds of all sizes. Boxes with small entrance holes (25 mm diameter) will attract blue tits and coal tits, while a box with a larger hole (28 mm diameter) should encourage great tits, tree sparrows and pied flycatchers. Larger, open fronted nest boxes will attract spotted flycatchers, robins, redstarts, wrens and wagtails, while an adventurous way to attract treecreepers is to fix bark over a hole or depression in a tree trunk so these birds can nest behind it.

The range and precise design of boxes is too great to summarise here adequately, and reference should be made to specialist sources of advice such as the British Trust for Ornithology Guide number 20, *Nest Boxes*.

*Nesting sites for wildfowl*
Traditional picturesque Dutch nesting baskets woven out of willow or cane can be purchased readily and located around pond margins, mounted on a tripod of stakes sufficiently high above maximum water level to avoid flooding. As an alternative, the baskets can be located on floating rafts. Wherever they are placed, the baskets should be tilted slightly backwards to discourage nest predation by rats.

Wigwams are also good nesting sites. Bundles of reeds or conifer branches can be placed 'wigwam' fashion over a shallow depression in the ground and, providing there is plenty of vegetation cover around the wigwam, it stands a good chance of being inhabited.

Mallard will nest in boxes, normally sited on rafts. Boxes should be 300 mm square and 225 mm high (inside dimensions) with horizontal slits cut into the sides so that the mallard can see out while sitting on the nest. The entrance should be 150 mm square and, to prevent predation by corvids, a 300 mm long by 150 mm square funnel should be placed over the entrance hole. A shallow ramp leading up to the funnel entrance is a useful addition, enabling ducklings to return to the nest the first night after hatching.

*Rafts*
A pond where there is no solid island can be improved by using a raft which, if securely anchored, will certainly encourage wildfowl to roost and hopefully breed. Raft building should take place as near to the water as possible to avoid the need to transport the heavy, cumbersome assembly across rough terrain.

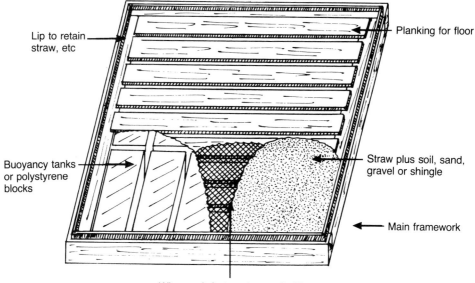

Lip to retain straw, etc

Planking for floor

Buoyancy tanks or polystyrene blocks

Straw plus soil, sand, gravel or shingle

Main framework

Wire mesh fastened over planking

Figure 5.1    Raft construction

The raft should comprise four main timbers bolted together to form the framework, with wooden slats attached across the top to provide a floor. Gaps should be left between the slats to allow plant roots to reach the water. Rabbit netting must be stapled over the slats to prevent ballast or plants falling out should one of the slats decay. As an alternative, the centre of the raft assembly could be made solid to act as a base for gravel or shingle ballast.

Once the main structure is complete, buoyancy should be added. Expanded polystyrene blocks are simple to use, either inserted between the main timbers beneath the floor or sealed inside clean plastic drums. Once the buoyancy tanks are attached to the raft, more wire netting should be fastened around them and fixed to the main frame to stop the tanks breaking free. A gently sloping ramp must be attached to the side of the raft to help the duck enter and leave the water.

After launching, the raft must be ballasted to the correct depth. Gravel or shingle should be placed in the centre and once the slats almost touch the water some plants can be put around the edges to create natural cover. Soft rush establishes well in these conditions but almost any species can be used, including an occasional shrub if enough soil is provided. On large ponds or lakes located near the coast, rafts covered in shingle but with no vegetation cover may attract nesting tern—in this case a 200 mm high lip must be built around the edge of the raft to stop the chicks falling into the water and some form of rough shelter should be provided.

Once the raft is in position it must be anchored securely—the best method is to chain the structure to large masonry blocks placed in position on the pond bed, ensuring that there is enough weight in the anchor to prevent dragging. The anchor chains should be fastened to opposite corners of the raft and laid out parallel to the prevailing wind. Mooring lines which are attached to the bank give easy access on to the raft for rats and should be avoided wherever possible.

*Nesting Cliffs*
Sand martins and kingfishers, which nest in tunnels, can be encouraged by the provision of an artificial cliff-face habitat, particularly in the latter case if fish are present in the water. When site conditions make it impossible to retain a suitable cliff during pond construction, a concrete bank can be created.

A vertical concrete wall should be constructed (using shuttering), and must be a minimum of 5 m long, rising at least 1.5 m above the maximum water level. While the concrete is being poured, clay drainage pipes should be set into the wall, one end flush with the outer face and exiting 1 m above water level. Gaps of 300 mm should be left between each pipe on the outer face of the wall, and the pipes should slope upwards at an angle of 15°, so that the tunnels are free draining.

Once the concrete has cured, the shuttering can be removed and the area between the wall and the pond bank backfilled with stone-free spoil. More clay pipes (or plastic drainage piping), 60 mm in diameter for kingfishers and 100 mm for sand martins, must be linked to the original clay entrance pipe and run back into the spoil at least 700 mm for kingfishers and 1,000 mm for sand martins. After backfilling, the pipes must then be filled with sand to within 25 mm of the entrance hole.

The top of the bank should be planted with overhanging vegetation providing that it does not obscure the holes, but the cliff base must be kept plant free. One or two perches set into the cliff will help to encourage kingfishers. Once the tunnels have been used for nesting, the holes should be refilled with sand each winter to within 25 mm of the entrance.

## Bat Boxes

It is well worth considering bat conservation as a small but very valuable part of the overall pond creation or management programme. Bats frequent a variety of roosting places: holes in trees, disused ground burrows, tunnels, caves, buildings and behind ivy or loose bark on trees. In recent years, habitats for bats have declined as have the mammals' principal source of food—insects. Many ponds lie in close proximity to trees, hedges or woodland and plenty of insects should be present around a well managed pond, providing a convincing case for the erection of bat boxes in sunny, sheltered locations close to the water.

Bat boxes must be constructed using untreated timber—rough sawn softwood is ideal. The box should be firmly attached to a tree, generally at least 4–5 m above ground level, although some species will use boxes which are sited lower down. No branches should be present within 3 m of the bottom or sides of the box and nothing should be closer than 1 m above. In addition, the boxes should face south-east or south-west so that they receive sunlight.

Bats and their habitats are protected by the Wildlife and Countryside Act 1981. If bats are known to roost in any location, for instance in an old tree near to a pond, it could be an offence to damage or remove that tree as part of a pond management scheme. Further information regarding bats and the construction of bat boxes can be found in the Nature Conservancy Council booklet *Focus on Bats: their conservation and the law.*

# Chapter 6

# Pond Management

All ponds require positive management if they are to provide continuing value to wildlife, fulfil the functions for which they were originally created or restored and give pleasure to their owners. Without adequate management, problems can arise such as pollution and a reduction in water quality; loss of water and siltation; and growth of excessive quantities of vegetation.

Ponds have a tendency to become more productive with time. This is quite natural—as life within the water flourishes, more nutrients will be released into the pond, augmented by the breakdown of leaves and other organic matter which finds its way into the water. This process will cause all of the problems cited above to occur, although the rate at which it happens will vary according to the nature of the pond, the surrounding vegetation, the catchment area and the use to which the pond is put.

Water which runs off agricultural land into ponds is likely to be rich in soluble nutrients as a result of the increasing amount of inorganic fertiliser which has been used on farms in recent years. This nutrient rich water will encourage greater growth of plants in ponds and watercourses, thus increasing the need for management.

Given time, natural succession occurs (see Chapter 2, Life in the Water) whereby the pond reverts to dry or marshy ground. While ponds still fulfilled a function on farmland as a source of water either for the farm or for livestock, management was frequently carried out to keep the pond in a desirable condition. Labour was more plentiful and available as necessary to cut back vegetation or desilt the pond, while marginal plants were often checked by livestock trampling round the edges of the water, thus helping to keep natural succession at bay. Sadly, as ponds ceased to play a role as essential components of farm and village life, so management inputs declined, with the resultant losses which have been described in the first chapter.

Any pond which is created or restored today will ultimately suffer the same fate unless the need for positive management is understood and the appropriate work is implemented. This need for management will arise

*Plate 6.1    A neglected village pond. Open water has ceased to exist and the pond is slowly reverting to marshland through natural succession.*

no matter what the pond's use is—whether it exists purely for wildlife conservation or is used for another purpose such as angling. The purpose of management is therefore to halt the process of natural succession and sustain the pond at a given point in its life cycle.

Where there is only one pond to look after, for example in a garden, management decisions are somewhat simplified because the options open to the gardener are relatively straightforward. On the farm, however, pond management can be much more complex because where several ponds exist each could be maintained in a different way to meet varying objectives. This is a good reason for the farmer or landowner to consider having a whole farm countryside management plan prepared, to look not only at nature conservation but also at opportunities for farm diversification—see Chapter 7, Pond Utilisation.

Pond management should not be seen only as an exercise to control vegetation or improve water quality. Desilting with a mechanical excavator offers great opportunity to develop better habitats in the pond. Banksides can be graded and shallow water areas created, while the decision to cut back overhanging trees and scrub to open up a pond could lead to the establishment of a buffer-zone between the water and adjoining cropped land. In fact, the creation of many of the features described in Chapter 3 can be incorporated into a management plant for an existing pond. (See colour plates 19 and 20.)

There is no ideal formula which can be invoked when a pond needs to be managed. No two ponds are the same and even if two ponds are ecologically similar, it is unlikely that the other factors which are of relevance would be identical, for instance the available management resources, ease of access to the water's edge, opportunities for spoil disposal or even the personal preferences of the pond owners or those people responsible for formulating and implementing the plans. For these reasons, every pond must be considered individually and on its own merits.

## MANAGEMENT PLANS

In every instance, the starting point for a pond maintenance programme should be a management plan. Different groups of landowners and managers will have varying criteria for managing ponds arising out of their own particular interests. For example, organisations concerned with nature conservation will seek to promote the management and restoration of those ponds with the greatest ecological value, while an individual landowner might be prepared to restore a pond which would form an attractive visual feature enhancing his property or which might improve the sporting potential of the land.

### Site Appraisal

Some form of assessment of the status of the pond must be made prior to deciding on the best form of management to achieve any given objective. The starting point for the management plan should therefore be an appraisal of the conservation value, the result of which will affect the work which needs to be carried out and influence any proposed post-management utilisation of the water.

Such an assessment is essential where there are several ponds which are considered to be in need of management but where resources are such that only one or even two can be tackled. An appraisal of all the ponds should reveal an order of priority and the limited resources available can then be utilised in the most effective manner. Likewise, to a farmer who wishes to diversify his business for instance by introducing an aquaculture or angling enterprise, the assessment will be vital to ensure that the destruction of a valuable wetland habitat does not occur when good forward planning might have identified a much poorer pond on the same farm which could have been developed with less adverse environmental impact.

Examples of two types of pond assessment form which can be used to help carry out such an appraisal are reproduced in Appendix 3. The first, reproduced with the kind permission of the Norfolk Farming and Wildlife Advisory Group and the Terrestrial Ecology Research Fund, is a guide which is intended primarily for use by farmers. It enables the strengths and the weaknesses of a pond and its surrounding habitat to be identified, thus highlighting possible management options. The FWAG appraisal is quite simple to complete, because it does not require any specialised botanical or zoological knowledge. The criteria used to assess the quality of the pond are based on the number of aquatic plant species present in and around the water. Even if the owner cannot identify the individual plants, it is easy to recognise how many different types are growing.

Ponds which are classed as having high nature conservation value are those with:

- Four or more aquatic plants, including submerged and emergent species.
- Plenty of invertebrates and amphibians present in the water.
- A reasonably stable water level.
- A gently sloping shoreline on at least one side of the pond, together with a variety of depths within the water down to at least 2 m.
- Good light penetration into the water with open areas to the south of the pond and some shading around other banks.
- A variety of marginal vegetation and adjoining terrestrial habitats.
- A buffer zone between the pond and areas of conventional land use, such as cropped fields or roads.

A far more detailed system of appraisal has been developed by the North Hertfordshire Museum's Natural History Department and is reproduced by kind permission of that Department. This much more complex appraisal is better suited for use by conservation advisers, students or those with specialist technical knowledge, because it requires species identifications to be made and recorded. Once the initial appraisal is complete, the information which has been collected must be analysed using a site assessment system developed by the North Hertfordshire Museum's Natural History Department. A copy is reproduced in Appendix 3, also with the kind permission of the Department. The assessment seeks to score the pond according to a number of categories:

- Age or naturalness of the aquatic habitat.
- Management, history and site stability.
- Stability of the wetland habitat.
- Biological interest and diversity.
- Whether the pond is worthy of conservation.

**Colour plate 1**

*An enclosure pond in Clwyd, constructed to supply water to two fields.*

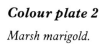
**Colour plate 2**

*Marsh marigold.*

**Colour plate 3**

*Ragged robin.*

**Colour plate 4**

*Purple loosestrife.*

**Colour plate 5**

*Yellow flag iris.*

**Colour plate 6**

*Water mint.*

**Colour plate 7**

*Bogbean.*

**Colour plate 8**

*Branched bur-reed.*

**Colour plate 9**

*Flowering rush.*

**Colour plate 10**

*A well-designed upland pond. Note the shape, islands, marshy areas and new planting set well back from the water's edge.*

**Colour plate 11**

*Common frog.*

**Colour plate 12**

*Common toads.*

**Colour plate 13**

*Great crested newts.*

**Colour plate 14**

*Natterjack toad.*

**Colour plate 15**

*Good cover for wildfowl, allowed to develop within a few metres of the water's edge.*

**Colour plate 16**

*The effect of planting emergent species in groups. Each species finds its own niche with resultant diversity.*

**Colour plate 17**

*A small, shallow pond excavated beside a large lake on the Ford Motor Co. estate at Dagenham. The objective is to create better wildlife habitat, and the surrounds of the pond have been planted with a mixture of native wild flowers, shrubs and trees.*

**Colour plate 18**

*A well-designed large pond in Somerset. A mixture of native shrubs has been planted on land surrounding the pond, guelder rose in the left foreground.*

**Colour plates 19 & 20**

*Attractive and valuable buffer zones such as these can be retained only through good management.*

**Colour plate 21**

*Cutting back overhanging scrub to open up an old pond is best done during winter.*

**Colour plate 22**

*Desilting a derelict farm pond during winter.*

**Colour plate 23**

*This pond is being managed to provide good plant zoning both in and out of the water. Apart from the benefits to wildlife, the visual effect is very pleasing.*

**Colour plate 24**

*This small farm pond was originally constructed to supply water to livestock using the adjacent lane. Following restoration, bankside vegetation management will be important if good quality habitat is to develop and the pond is to remain attractive.*

Ponds assessed under this system can be ranked according to a score, based on the following table:

| Pond score value | class |
|---|---|
| 46 and over | A |
| 36–45 | B |
| 26–35 | C |
| 16–25 | D |
| 0–15 | E |

It must be recognised that the score is related only to the data collected from the appraisal. During the Hertfordshire Pond Survey carried out in 1986, no pond came into the A category and out of 730 surveyed, only 22 ranked as B, with 136 classed as C grade ponds.

The purpose of using an appraisal scheme such as this is that it enables the owner or manager to identify the most important and valuable sites, thus ensuring that the necessary resources can be allocated to those ponds which are most worthy of attention. This type of pond appraisal work can be carried out properly only during the summer months, when there is an abundance of pond life and when plant species can be recognised clearly.

Other variations on the theme of pond appraisal have been produced in the past—a conservation checklist prepared by the Agricultural Development and Advisory Service of the Ministry of Agriculture, Fisheries and Food during the early 1980s suggested that a number of criteria should be considered when assessing the wildlife value of a pond:

- The presence of more than fifteen species of flowering plants occurring below the edge of the pond bank, five of which should be in the water.
- More than 25 per cent of the pond surface to be free of plant cover.
- Less than half the pond perimeter to be trampled by livestock.
- The presence of nesting cover for birds on at least 10 per cent of the ground around the edge of the pond.

It can be seen from all of these systems of appraisal, and by reference to the various assessment forms, the type of information which has to be gleaned from the site prior to producing any targets for management. Although a detailed survey of the pond and its environs is not always practical, some attempt must be made to assess the status of all ponds which are being considered for management. As already described, the timing of such an inspection is vital. A visit to the pond during the winter will not provide all the information which could be gathered from a look at the pond in June or July. In an ideal situation, a number of visits ought to be made during the different seasons so that an overview of the pond can be developed to aid decision making.

## Drawing Up a Management Plan

Assuming that the findings of the site survey are such that pond restoration or management is deemed both necessary and worthwhile, a plan must be prepared. This does not always need to be elaborate. In most cases, a simple document outlining a number of relevant points is enough.

The plan should include a description of the pond together with notes about its history and past use, current use and any information on the plant or animal life found therein. Helpful detail can often be obtained from old Ordnance Survey maps. An assessment of the archaeological significance of the pond or surrounding area is also essential. Where a pond, for instance forming part of an old moated site or fishpond complex, is considered to have some archaeological interest, special considerations will apply to any management; these are outlined on pages 122–23. An indication of the conservation value is important (as obtained from the pond appraisal), plus comments on any factors likely to influence the long term management such as the proximity of a potential source of pollution.

The plan's stated objectives of management and restoration will need to be broadbased, for example: 'to improve the conservation value'; 'to

*Plate 6.2   This pond has been newly restored, with no subsequent bankside management. The value to wildlife is greatly reduced by the dense, rank vegetation.*

develop a new farm business opportunity—angling'; 'to provide water for livestock'; or 'to enhance the appearance of the pond'. It is vital to decide on objectives in advance of carrying out any work. The management of a pond which is to be let for angling will vary from that undertaken where the pond is retained purely for its amenity value. For instance, where fishing is an objective, stretches of the bankside will need to be kept free of emergent species and large areas of open water will have to be cleared of floating-leaved and submerged plants, to allow space for the fish and to prevent interference with fishing lines. This would not be so important in a wildlife pond.

A section on the method of management or restoration must outline the physical work which is required to achieve the objectives, together with an indication of any resources which will be needed, such as capital, machinery and labour. Likely sources of grant aid, specialist advice or assistance should also be noted.

Aftercare is vitally important, otherwise the pond will gradually succumb to problems such as siltation, natural succession or shading of the water, at least one of which may be the reason why management or restoration was required in the first place. The management plan must show how any aftercare treatment is to be carried out and identify what resources will be needed. If adequate provision for follow-up treatment cannot be made, restoration will be largely worthless and time, effort and money will have been wasted.

Finally, the management document should include plans showing:

- The location of the pond including a five figure map reference.
- A sketch of the pond marking any features of interest discovered during the initial assessment, e.g. unusual plants.
- An annotated sketch plan showing the proposed shape of the pond after restoration, particularly if the outline is to be modified. This sketch should also show where any trees or shrubs are to be planted or where plants are to be introduced into the pond itself. Numbers and size of plants should also be specified.
- A cross-sectional diagram showing how any desilting or regrading of banks is to be carried out.

It is important to remember that management of the pond does not just involve keeping the water clean or slowing the rate of natural succession. The surrounding bankside terrestrial habitats are equally significant in terms of the overall value and they therefore need to be taken into account in all management planning. Likewise, human factors such as the need to provide recreational resources must be considered and, if necessary, reconciled with nature conservation so that a balanced approach to management can be devised and sustained.

## The Archaeological Implications of Pond Management

Many ponds have archaeological interest. Agricultural enclosure ponds are not normally of value, but features created for industrial purposes, old moated sites and fishponds may be of significance, depending on past management. It is better from the archaeologist's point of view if the pond is overgrown and damp rather than waterfilled, but in any event, wet and waterlogged features provide extremely good conditions for the preservation of objects made out of organic materials such as wood, leather and bone. The fine sediments at the bottom of ponds are also excellent mediums for the preservation of inorganic materials such as metalwork.

There are three categories of items of interest to the archaeologist:

i   Structural remains—for instance revetments, sluices, jetties and bridges. These are normally made of brick, stone or wood and provide good evidence of the use, method of construction and date of the site.
ii  Rubbish—normally deposited in the pond to fill it in. Household, industrial and building materials might all be discovered, enabling a picture to be built up of how and when the site was used and why it fell into disrepair.
iii Casual losses—these could be of almost any items associated both with the use of the site and those people who used it. Objects found could include tools and even boats in large ponds.

Over and above the discovery of artefacts, silt may preserve pollen, seeds, plant material and shells, which would be of value to the environmental archaeologist.

Advice on the archaeological implications of pond management should be sought from the staff of the County Archaeological Department prior to any work being carried out on a pond which is likely to be of interest. In addition, many historic features are Scheduled Ancient Monuments and as such are protected under the Ancient Monuments and Archaeological Areas Act 1979 (see Chapter 8, Ponds, Wildlife and the Law).

It is essential that any management work carried out in a pond with historical significance should be undertaken in such a way as to minimise the archaeological damage. The following notes should be used for guidance:

• Earth moving machinery should be used very carefully to ensure that the original pond profile is retained and that surrounding earthworks or deposits (especially in and adjacent to moated sites) are not disturbed.
• Silt deposits from restored ponds should not be dumped in the immediate vicinity of the pond because this will alter the shape and appearance of any surrounding earthworks.

- Overhanging trees should be cut and removed, with the stumps left *in situ* to decay. The dragging out of roots will alter the form of any earthworks and may disturb remains in the ground.
- New tree and shrub planting should not be carried out on earthworks or historical features such as moat platforms.

## Amount of Work Which Should Be Done at Any One Time

This depends very much on the circumstances associated with the pond. In an ideal situation, the needs of wildlife should be placed first on all priority lists. Disturbance to the pond ought to be minimised as much as possible, so where the pond has been found (as a result of an appraisal) to have a high nature conservation value, management should be carried out in the most sensitive manner. No more than half the pond should be desilted or cleared of vegetation in any one season, to prevent loss of habitat and adverse effects on wildlife. This is of particular importance when the pond attracts plenty of dragonflies and amphibians. Where any pond is found to be of especially high value in this respect, or if there is any doubt as to its status, an expert opinion should be taken from either the County Wildlife Trust or the Nature Conservancy Council, who will advise on the frequency and scale of management operations.

In reality, it is often not feasible to desilt a pond in two stages in successive years. The cost of hiring excavators is high, as is the expense of actually transporting the machinery on to site. Many farmers will take the opportunity to clean out several ponds on the farm whenever the appropriate machinery is already available, perhaps originally brought in to restore one particular pond or to maintain ditches and water courses.

In these cases, a prior assessment of all the ponds likely to be tackled at any one time is vital to guard against accidental damage to a valuable, previously unrecognised habitat which would otherwise be lost by opportunist pond restoration. Such an assessment could be made as part of the whole farm countryside management plan. The risk with opportunist overall pond clearance schemes is that everything will be lost by emptying the water out of the pond and total desilting. Care is vital to try to retain some of the original silt in the bed of the pond as well as areas of emergent vegetation, to aid recolonisation once the pond has refilled with water.

Many derelict farm ponds have become so neglected, overgrown and heavily silted, scoring so low on a nature conservation assessment, that the only option is a total clearout prior to starting again. In these cases the end result after desilting is similar to a newly created feature, whereby plant introductions may be necessary to accelerate the rate of species colonisation and the development of wildlife habitat.

## Timing of Management Operations In and Out of the Water

From the point of view of nature conservation, the optimum time to undertake management work in and around a pond is late in the year, from September until December, with one or two exceptions. By late summer, the breeding season for animals in the water is over and, in the case of amphibians, the young have left the pond. Aquatic plants will have flowered and died back, while young wildfowl will be independent.

Disturbance to the pond during the early part of the season will (in many instances) destroy breeding sites or remove sources of food, while during the winter, frogs hibernating in the mud at the bottom of the pond will be adversely affected by desilting.

In practical terms, mid summer and early autumn are good times to work, especially where desilting is necessary. Many farm ponds are inaccessible during the early part of the summer because of growing crops, while during the winter months the surrounding ground may be too wet for heavy machinery to operate without causing damage to both soil structure and terrestrial habitats.

In late summer, after harvest, there is often a 'window' when an isolated farm pond can be desilted and the spoil spread easily on to adjoining stubbles or carted off site before the land surrounding the pond is re-drilled or becomes too wet to work during the autumn. Late summer is also a time when suitable machinery may be available on the farm to desilt the pond, following routine ditch maintenance or field drainage.

The exceptions to this timing of management operations are when herbicides are being used or if reed cutting is required. Herbicides are often applied early in the growing season (depending on manufacturers' instructions). At this time, plant biomass is not too great and as the vegetation dies back after treatment there is less risk of serious oxygen depletion within the water. July is reckoned to be the most effective time for cutting reeds, with little regeneration from the base of the plant over the remainder of the growing season, providing that cutting has taken place just below the water level.

Around the perimeter of the pond and on adjoining land, grass cutting, scrub and woodland management should be carried out at normal times to avoid damage to breeding sites, destruction of cover and sources of food. Grasses and herbaceous plants should be managed in the appropriate way during late summer or early autumn (exceptions are when herbicides are to be used which should be applied in accordance with the manufacturers' instructions). Scrub and woodland should be worked during the winter months, so that there is no risk of damage to nesting birds, although the later that scrub cutting can be left during the winter the better, so that birds and mammals have the benefit of seeds and berries on which to feed. (See colour plate 21.)

## Maintenance of Water Quality

One of the reasons for undertaking pond management or restoration is to improve water quality. When water quality is poor, the range of species able to flourish within the pond is strictly limited, normally due to oxygen starvation. The pond is also likely to be visually unattractive, characterised by oil films on the surface, scum, algal blooms and unpleasant smells. This will adversely affect any proposed uses such as the provision of drinking water for livestock or angling.

A polluted pond should be easily recognisable when the management plan assessment is carried out. Other than surface oil films, indications of pollution within the water may be:

- A limited range of plants or animals present in or around the pond. The animals present in a polluted pond which is low in oxygen may consist of species such as red worms and hog lice, whereas healthy ponds should contain mayfly nymphs, freshwater shrimps, water beetles, dragonfly and damselfly larvae, snails, water bugs and leeches.
- Excessive volumes of decaying organic material in the water.
- The growth of 'sewage fungus' on plants or stones within the pond—this occurs as the result of a build-up of bacteria in the water.

Where pollution is identified as a problem, it is essential that the source of the trouble is located and if possible removed or controlled. Contamination may come from external sources:

- Effluent seepage or direct inflow to the pond.
- Livestock excreta.
- Pesticides and inorganic fertilisers used on adjoining land.
- Run-off from roads or concrete yards.
- Drains.
- Fly-tipping—especially where the pond is near a public highway.

More common, however, is pollution originating from within the pond itself. Accumulations of leaf litter (falling from overhanging trees and shrubs or reaching the pond from woodland located too near to the water's edge) will combine with dead and decaying organic matter derived from plants within the pond to over enrich the water during decomposition. This will reduce the depth of water and utilise excessive amounts of oxygen, thus starving pond life of its essential life support.

External sources of pollution can in most cases be prevented. If the pond is stream fed and the contamination originates some distance away, the regional office of the National Rivers Authority should be consulted for advice. Where the pond is located on a farm, try to exclude supplies of water which may pick up silage or slurry effluent further up-stream.

*Plate 6.3  Pollution caused by a lack of management and a pipe discharging farm effluent into a pond.*

*Plate 6.4  Major pollution caused by unrestricted livestock access to a pond. Note the lack of vegetation around the pond margins.*

*Plate 6.5   Trees planted too close to a pond result in massive accumulations of leaf litter in the water. (Dr H. Gracey)*

*Plate 6.6   This pond has been fenced against livestock. Note the growth of marginal and emergent plants.*

An interesting new process is being tested by the Anglian Water Authority to assess whether sewage can be treated by being passed through a bed of common reed. The theory is that the reed roots or rhizomes form a hydraulic pathway through the soil, along which sewage is allowed to seep. As the raw sewage passes through the reedbed, impurities are broken down by bacteria surrounding the rhizomes. The oxygen which is needed by the bacteria is provided by the reeds, which absorb oxygen through their stems. At the present time, large expanses of reedbed are required for this treatment process to work, but the Root Zone Method may have some application in the future for the control of pollution in ponds—see Chapter 3, Pond Design.

Build-up of livestock excreta can be dealt with by restricting livestock access to the margins of the pond. It is best to pump water to a drinking trough rather than letting animals walk into the pond. If this is not possible, create a fenced drinking bay with a hard base, so that livestock movements are restricted and excessive sediments are not stirred up by animals trampling in the pond.

Empty spray containers should never be disposed of in or near ponds and watercourses, and the use of pesticides must be avoided around the perimeter of the pond. A buffer or 'set aside' zone should be established, which is neither cropped nor subjected to chemical treatment. In addition, sprayers should not be flushed out near ponds or watercourses. Agricultural sprayers should never be filled from ponds.

The sources of internal pollution within a pond can also be controlled if most of the overhanging trees and shrubs are cut back, especially to the south of the pond, with one or two retained to provide limited shade and perches for birds. Vegetation management within the water is also essential (see p. 133), to remove some of the emergent plants and introduce submerged oxygenating species, to restore oxygen levels.

It is possible that water quality is affected by different types of leaf litter altering the chemical and physical nature of the pond floor, thus having an impact on the flora present in the pond. A research project started by the Suffolk Farming and Wildlife Advisory Group is seeking to discover which species of tree are best suited for planting near to ponds from the point of view of leaf litter deposition. Species normally associated with terrestrial sites, such as oak and beech, are less suitable than traditional waterside species, for instance alder and willow, whose leaves decompose more rapidly. The planting of conifers near water will certainly have an adverse effect. Water quality could therefore be improved by careful selection of tree species for planting near to ponds. Excessive quantities of leaf litter on the floor of the pond will also prevent the growth of rooting plants, thus affecting the development of a balanced ecosystem. If this is the case, removal of leaf litter will be required.

The control of sources of contamination may not in itself be sufficient to improve water quality. Where pollution from external sources has occurred over a long period of time or where leaf litter accumulations are severe as already mentioned, desilting will be required. This is necessary because although the source of the pollution may be stopped, organic matter already in the pond will continue to breakdown, releasing nutrient and utilising oxygen. Where slurry or toxic substances have reached the pond in previous years, they may contain harmful trace elements which will adversely affect wildlife for a long time into the future and which must also be removed.

## Liming

Where the water in a pond is acidic it is possible to raise the pH by using crushed limestone or chalk (but not pure lime), thus increasing the opportunities for flora development. Champagne chalk, which is being tested for use as an aid to desilting, will also have the same effect. Prior to taking any action to reduce the acidity of a pond, expert on-site advice must be obtained, to prevent the loss of species adapted to survival in acid waters. These may in certain circumstances be more desirable than species suited to eutrophic conditions.

The water chemistry of oligotrophic ponds may also be altered over long periods of time by applications of limestone on to surrounding agricultural land, residues of which will reach the pond through ground water or surface run-off.

## LOSS OF WATER AND SILTATION

The water level in a pond may fall because of an irregularity or cessation of water supply, because of seepage and leaks, or because of siltation. If a pond is losing water, a check must be made on the supply. New farm drainage systems often prevent surface run-off from reaching ponds, while ditches feeding ponds may have been infilled or become blocked, especially if drainage systems have taken their place or if plant growth has been profuse. If an adequate supply of water is to be restored, it is vital to ensure that it is available not only to refill the pond but also to keep it topped up each year.

Puddled clay linings may become punctured after many years, especially where management has been neglected and livestock have trampled the margins of the pond, thus weakening the lining. It is possible to use chemical tracers to pinpoint the approximate location of the hole which can then be repaired, or if in doubt a new layer of clay can be reworked over the bed of the whole pond. Specially formulated sodium bentonite clays can also be used to rectify faults in old clay linings. See Chapter 4, Pond Construction.

In the case of siltation, as sediment accumulates within the pond and the water becomes shallow, natural succession will occur at a faster rate, while at the same time more evaporation takes place in the summer months as the shallow water warms up more quickly than deep water. The only solution is desilting, with action taken to prevent subsequent accumulations of silt, usually by the provision of a silt trap (see Chapter 4, Pond Construction).

### Desilting

This is not easy and success will be determined by the stability of the surrounding soils, methods of silt disposal and the type of pond.

Silt can be moved by excavation, by pushing (using a bulldozer), dragging, pumping or by using explosives. Traditional methods, using two steam engines on opposite banks to drag a large bucket through the pond, can still be used today, but it is more conventional to use a hydraulic tracked excavator or dragline working from the bank, an island or pontoon.

*Plate 6.7   This pond has been desilted very thoughtfully. A few mature trees have been retained on the banks, the pond margins have been profiled and a deep trench cut around a block of reedmace which is to be retained as a habitat.*

(See colour plate 22.) The use of explosives is very limited and is damaging not only for wildlife but also to the surrounding land, because the silt is spread over a very wide area. This technique only has value when the pond is totally inaccessible to machinery.

Silt contains a very high proportion of water (up to 90 per cent) together with sand, clay and organic matter. It is too wet to be deposited in a heap on the side of the pond and, on account of its water volume, moving it off-site in trailers can be a very messy business. Hence the need for stable banks and good access, preferably in dry conditions.

A large surface area is required for silt deposition around the edge of the pond, so that the material can be spread out and allowed to dry. Once it is dry, it can be thinly graded over adjoining land and any foreign objects can be removed. Where spoil disposal in this fashion poses a problem, the pond should be drained and the silt left to dry *in situ* prior to removal so that the volume of material to be taken out is greatly reduced.

Large areas of water can be desilted by pumping, providing that there are not too many objects such as bottles and branches in the pond which will block the pump. The silt removed in this way is very wet and, because the solids need to be allowed to settle out in lagoons or tanks, this technique is not normally cost effective for farm ponds. However, if the pond has a flexible liner, mechanical desilting will be very difficult and in this case pumping may be the only solution.

Where mechanical desilting is being carried out, the opportunity should be taken where appropriate to regrade the pond banks and create a more varied shoreline in the interests of wildlife conservation.

*Champagne chalk*
A recent technique developed in France is now being tested as a means of desilting ponds and waterways. Champagne chalk consists of minute fossils called coccoliths which are small enough to penetrate down into the silt, where they help to create the optimum environment for the action of micro-organisms. These digest the organic matter in the silt, thus releasing water and reducing the volume of silt in the bottom of the pond. The technique works best where the silt has a high organic content, so samples must be tested prior to treatment, to avoid unnecessary expense.

Because the alkalinity of the water is increased by the application of

*Plate 6.8   Applying champagne chalk to a heavily silted moat.*

champagne chalk, its use in acidic ponds should not be considered without careful thought as to the potential impact on pond life. However, this technique could be advantageous where desilting is required but where both access to the pond and spoil disposal are difficult, or where damage to pond surroundings might cause problems, for instance in gardens.

Application rates vary according to the site, but on average 2.5 tonnes of champagne chalk per hectare are applied in the spring, with a further 1.8 tonnes per hectare after six months. Thereafter a third dose may be required during the second year, depending on the rate of success. In any event an additional 150 kilograms per hectare per annum will be needed in subsequent years to try to prevent further silt accumulations.

At present there are a limited number of suppliers of this material in the United Kingdom. Extensive trials are being conducted to assess the long term effects of the technique and its environmental impact. At the current time, it appears to be a product that is certainly worth considering where a high proportion of the silt in a pond is found to be organic in content.

## CONTROL OF AQUATIC PLANTS

Vegetation control is the key to good long term pond management, no matter how the pond is to be utilised. It is ironic that in the early stages following the creation of a pond, one of the routes to success is ensuring that a wide variety of plants either colonise or are introduced, not only into the water but also around the perimeter. In later years much effort is expended either in pulling their descendants out of the water or cutting back the growth around the banks! Vegetation control falls into two categories: control of aquatic plants, and control of plants growing on the banks of the pond.

By controlling the aquatic plants, the pond can be maintained at a pre-determined stage in its succession. The management objectives will specify precisely what stage this should be, but, in general, control will provide for the zonation outlined in Chapter 2, Life in the Water. When the pond is maintained at this precise stage, a greater diversity of species can flourish. Vegetation control can then be used to prevent aggressive emergent species, for instance reedmace, common reed and reed sweet-grass, establishing dominance to the detriment of less competitive plants. Submerged species such as Canadian pondweed and hornwort can also be kept in check, otherwise they are likely to cause large scale problems, dominating the open water and preventing other submerged species from gaining a foothold. In addition to the conservation benefits, the pond will look more attractive if there is more diversity in terms of different species of plants and a wider range of conditions for wildlife. (See colour plate 23.)

Ponds which are overgrown with aquatic plants will not provide good angling, while open, sheltered water on larger ponds is essential for roosting wildfowl, especially for over-wintering duck, which will feed at night on the adjoining farmland. Areas of open water must also be retained if you wish to encourage amphibians such as the great crested newt.

Control of aquatic plants in onstream ponds may reduce the risk of flooding because water can flow through the pond, reaching the outflow unimpeded by large quantities of plant material. This flow will also help to reduce the rate of siltation.

A major problem with aquatic plant control usually occurs around the margins of the pond, as the shallow ledges and slopes leading into the water become overrun by emergent species. The shallow edges of the pond are usually quite accessible from the bankside, which should simplify management, but because this zone is the most significant for wildlife, great care is needed to minimise disturbance.

It is also worth remembering that while the visible problem within the pond may be copious growth of plants, there will be a reason why this is happening. Perhaps an excessive volume of nutrient is present within the water, which will quickly cause a recurrence of the problem. It may be more cost effective in the long term, and less damaging to wildlife, to try to rectify the cause of the problem rather than repetitively control the results.

The frequency of this type of management depends on the physical characteristics of the pond and the type of species requiring control. In a small, shallow garden pond, where there is plenty of nutrient coupled with high temperatures, emergent species can very quickly spread and occupy too much space. In this case control will be needed at intervals of three or four years. One way to slow the rate of growth is to plant some species into containers to restrict root development (see Chapter 5, Supplementary Habitat Creation). The rate of natural succession in a large pond with much deeper water (1.2–3 m) will be correspondingly slower, because the emergent plants are restricted to the shallows round the edge and the water temperature is lower. If the range of plants growing in marginal areas is limited to the more aggressive species, management will need to be undertaken at more regular intervals than if a greater variety of plants is present.

Results obtained from the Countryside Commission Demonstration Farms Project have shown that height above sea level and exposure play an important role in determining the rate of plant growth in ponds. Lowland ponds are more productive and therefore require management at more regular intervals than exposed ponds on higher ground, where colonisation is somewhat slower. There is no rule to state that vegetation control in lowland ponds should take place every four, six or eight years, or that in the uplands the interval should be ten, twelve or fourteen years. Because

*Plate 6.9   Copious growth of water fern on the surface of a garden pond is cutting out light to plants in the water. Management is essential.*

every pond is different, the frequency of management must of necessity be varied, but as a guide, once pond vegetation is well established some degree of management should be anticipated at 6–10 year intervals in the lowlands and 10–15 year intervals in the uplands.

A basic principle of aquatic vegetation control is to work wherever possible in localised areas within and around the pond. Localised treatment costs less than total control and less damage is caused to wildlife within the pond—habitats are always retained despite management operations. There is also less risk of a total 'invasion' by aggressive, undesirable species such as algae, which will quickly recolonise a cleared pond, thus reducing diversity and probably rendering the effort and cost of clearance worthless. Working this way also reduces the chance of oxygen starvation in the water. This is due partly to the removal of oxygenating plants and partly on account of the uptake of oxygen by decomposing plant tissues which remain in the pond, for instance after cutting or chemical control.

Three main types of management may be adopted:

- Manual.
- Mechanical.
- Chemical.

Biological and shading methods are also described, on pp. 141–44.

## Manual Vegetation Control

This takes the form of digging out, cutting or raking. Manual control is probably the least harmful to wildlife and is the easiest approach towards the management of small garden ponds. It is also extremely selective, so problem species or very localised areas can be tackled. In ponds with flexible liners, where digging would damage the liner and cause leaks, cutting is often the only practical way to manage plant growth (though in some circumstances chemical control is possible). Digging, cutting and raking are very slow, tedious tasks, but on sites with a high conservation value, the extra effort which is required can often be justified, especially if volunteer assistance is available to help keep costs to a reasonable level.

*Digging* is an excellent way to remove rooted species from the margins of the pond, because cutting will induce vigorous regrowth and thus necessitate further work at a later date. Wherever possible, all unwanted vegetation should be removed by digging, with the additional advantage that the removal of the entire root system will immediately increase the depth of water in the pond by about 150 mm. In a small garden pond this could be extremely desirable, extending the opportunities for amphibians by creating a larger expanse of open, shallow water.

Digging is more awkward towards the middle of the pond, once the water is more than waist deep. At this point it becomes difficult to work effectively and to remove root systems thoroughly, especially once the silt on the floor of the pond is stirred up, adversely affecting the visibility. Two additional disadvantages are that the increased turbidity will reduce photosynthesis and lower the oxygen levels, while stored nutrient will be released from the pond floor into the water.

Rooted aquatic plants grow from rhizomes which spread and form a thick fibrous mat of roots in the bottom mud of the pond. If the plants are being controlled by digging, it is important that all rhizomes in the area to be managed are removed, otherwise the roots will rapidly shoot again. Providing that entire root systems are cleared over localised areas, the spread of the plants can be controlled fairly easily on future occasions, simply by cutting round the edges of the remaining blocks of vegetation on the periphery of the previously worked areas.

*Cutting* is far quicker than digging but, because the plant roots are left behind, re-growth has to be controlled more regularly. In deeper water, hoeing can be used to cut and drag out non-rhizomatous submerged plants; but, again, long term control over a localised area is not really possible because only the growing parts of the plant are removed and the submerged and buried roots are left behind.

Cutting can be carried out using hand tools or a chain scythe. This has a cutting edge which is dragged through the water by operators working either from boats or from the banks of the pond. All the cut plant material floats to the surface, where it can be collected easily. Chain scything is a useful method of large scale control but it is non-selective; every plant growing in the path of the scythe is cut.

*Raking* will control free floating plants, together with surface species such as duckweeds, water fern or frogbit. These plants must be controlled, in order to let light reach submerged species so that they can photosynthesise and put oxygen back into the water. Raking is an effective short term solution to the problem of excessive surface cover, but because the free floating plants reproduce so readily, if any number are left behind (which is almost inevitable) the work will have to be repeated on several occasions throughout the growing season, especially on small ponds which provide ideal conditions for these species.

A large garden rake can be used under most circumstances, to drag free floating plants from the water, but a boom is easier to pull over the surface for collecting duckweeds etc. A simple wooden lath or a thick rope will serve as a boom; when it is pulled across the pond, the plants are gathered in front of it and can be taken out at the water's edge.

*Removal of debris*    Once vegetation has been dug, cut or raked up, it must be cleared from the pond. Otherwise, oxygen depletion and a build-up

*Plate 6.10   Plant growth removed from a pond should be allowed to dry out on the banks. Pondlife will then have time to return to the water.*

of nutrient from decaying tissue will accelerate regrowth and cause water quality problems. Cut and raked material should be deposited temporarily on the sides of the pond. The debris should be turned daily, to encourage it to dry out and provide an opportunity for animals collected along with the plants to return to the water. Likewise, plants which have been dug out should be left on the banks for two to three days. Disposal of the rubbish off site will be easier once it has dried out.

## Mechanical Control

Mechanical excavation or cutting can be done either from the bank or by using weed cutting boats. Boats are normally useful only on flowing water or large lakes on account of the cost and the difficulties of manoeuvring the equipment on to site. For routine pond management, the landowner is mainly concerned with mechanical clearance working from the bank.

Most farmers will have access to some item of machinery which can be used for localised vegetation control—for instance a tractor with a rear mounted bucket excavator. This can be positioned on the pond bank and used to dig out blocks of plants, including the roots. The limiting factors will be the reach of the machine over the water and the need to have a solid bankside surface from which the machine can work safely.

Where work is required towards the centre of a large pond, or where the bankside is either inaccessible or should not be disturbed, more sophisticated equipment with a much longer reach, such as a hydraulic tracked excavator or dragline, will be needed. The size of these machines and the operating costs will make the treatment much less selective but, for large projects, this is often the only way to proceed, bearing in mind that the pond may also be desilted at the same time. Excavators are very useful for reedbed management, because they are able to cut deep trenches round areas of emergent plants, preventing them from encroaching across shallow ponds.

Tractors with cutting bars or flails can be used to trim pond margins, assuming that the ground is firm enough to support the weight. Limited cutting of emergent vegetation can be done this way, with the proviso that cut material is removed wherever possible.

## Chemical Vegetation Control

The use of herbicides in pond management may appear to be wrong when one of the objectives is nature conservation. On balance however, because of the very strict rules governing the screening, use and application of herbicides, they can, if correctly applied, be a valuable aid to water management. However, herbicide usage in and around garden ponds is not recommended, partly because most garden ponds are too small to justify the cost and partly because appropriate herbicides are more generally available to farmers. Manual control methods are more suitable for small ponds.

The use of pesticides (which includes herbicides) is regulated by the Food and Environment Protection Act 1985, under the terms of the Control of Pesticides Regulations 1986 (COPR). Prior to this, the safety aspects of pesticide usage were governed by clearances issued under the Pesticides Safety Precautions Scheme (PSPS). It is now illegal to sell, supply, store, advertise or use an unapproved chemical and all users of pesticides must comply with the conditions of approval for each chemical or product.

Chemical manufacturers are obliged to test their products extremely thoroughly prior to approval being granted and particular attention is given to ascertaining the side effects of pesticide usage. As an example, although a chemical may be intended to control one specific plant species, tests will be carried out to discover what the effect of the chemical on other plants or wildlife will be, not just directly but also through food chains and any long term residual effects.

Under the PSPS, herbicides which could be used in or near water received special clearance, and they are specially treated by the new regulations. A limited range of chemicals and products is approved for use and in every case the 'Guidelines for the Use of Herbicides on Weeds in or near Watercourses and Lakes', published by the Ministry of Agriculture, Fisheries and Food, must be followed and only a herbicide approved for use in or near water should be used. In addition, if there is any chance that a chemical could reach a watercourse, consent must be obtained from the regional office of the National Rivers Authority before it is used.

Approved products can be used with great effect to cover a large area when little labour is available but a quick solution to a problem is required. This is often the case on a farm where countryside conservation of necessity has to be integrated with farm management routines and all tasks must be carried out quickly and cost effectively. If farm employees are properly trained in the safe handling and use of pesticides, herbicide usage in and around water should not be a problem, assuming that a number of basic requirements are met.

The plant species which requires control must be correctly identified, and the correct herbicide selected to deal with the target species. This requires some care, because while one species may be selected for control, the herbicide which is deemed appropriate may also control a number of other plants which are growing in the area. For instance, a herbicide used to control Canadian pondweed will probably also eradicate other submerged or floating pondweeds. For this reason, selection must be carried out with caution and with full knowledge of the wider effects of the herbicides available.

Correct timing and method of herbicide applications are important. Failure to accomplish these will lead to poor results, wasting time and money. In all cases, applications must be made in accordance with the manufacturer's instructions, as shown either on the label or in the leaflet accompanying the product.

Despite such stringent precautions, there are a number of situations where herbicides should not be used in or around water:

- Where the pond forms part of a Site of Special Scientific Interest, notified by the Nature Conservancy Council under the Wildlife and Countryside Act 1981. In this case the NCC should be consulted prior to any management operations being carried out.
- Where the initial site appraisal has revealed that the pond has above average nature conservation interest. In this case the use of a herbicide could be potentially disastrous, for instance by removing vegetation which is essential as egg-laying cover for amphibians and invertebrates; by causing oxygen depletion or by reducing the quantity of plant growth which is available as food for animals in the water. Even where the pond does not have a particularly high wildlife value, the use of a herbicide may reduce the volume of plant growth available as cover for fish, together with the loss of spawning sites.
- Where the pond is home for a protected species such as the great crested newt.
- Where there is any doubt as to the management problem. If an owner is uncertain as to whether the use of an approved herbicide is appropriate for pond management, expert advice must be taken.

Notwithstanding these precautionary comments, the use of herbicides does have very positive advantages in certain situations. Some species, such as hornwort or Canadian pondweed, will grow from vegetative fragments and rapidly recolonise a pond following cutting or raking, because it will be impossible to remove all the pieces. Herbicide treatment would overcome this. Using herbicides, very selective control is possible. For instance, where a pond is dominated by a submerged species, areas of open water can be created in precise locations as an aid to fisheries management. At the same time, disturbance to the pond can be kept to a minimum.

Treatment with a herbicide approved for use late in the season is least damaging to the ecosystem. There will be little detectable difference between die-off following treatment and end of season die-back, apart from the fact that treated plants will not grow again the next year. This is most advantageous for the management of emergent species.

Two final points regarding herbicide usage must not be overlooked.

First, with the exception of emergent species, plants killed by herbicides should be removed from the water wherever possible. Failure to do this could result in deoxygenation, with potential destruction of fish stocks. In any event, the decaying plants will steadily add to the nutrient and silt build-up within the pond—which if not the original cause of the problem, will certainly not discourage further growth. Second, removal of a submerged plant using a chemical may enable another species, perhaps blanket weed, to become established in the newly created space and thrive on the nutrient released into the water by the dead plant tissue. The new 'weed problem' may be even harder to control than the initial one.

Appendix 4 contains a list of approved herbicides.

## Shading

Any structure or fabric covering part of the water surface will prevent light reaching the pond, either stopping the growth of aquatic plants or killing off any already present. The use of black polythene sheeting to control plant growth is a technique sometimes applied in fisheries management and is of value in a pond. Sheets measuring 16 × 8 m are the largest which can be handled easily. These should be carefully unfolded at the water's edge and totally submerged so that they are not damaged by the wind. Once the sheets are in the right place, the corners should be weighted down to anchor them over the plants which are to be controlled. Small holes should be made at regular intervals in the sheeting, to allow gases generated in the mud on the floor of the pond to escape, unless a gas permeable material is used. After about a month, sheeting can be removed, the plant growth beneath having died back; at this stage the roots will still be alive and regeneration will occur. To achieve total kill, the sheets will have to be left for longer, over three months in the case of some emergent species.

The use of trees to control plant growth is an accepted technique in watercourse management, but it needs very careful planning around ponds. Many old and neglected ponds have trees growing close to the water's edge. These are often removed as part of a restoration programme to allow light to reach the water surface. In some cases it may be advisable to retain limited tree cover around the southern perimeter to help prevent rapid growth of algae while the pond ecosystem develops. The same principle would apply where trees are growing around the site of a new pond. (See also pp. 44–45.)

Trees could also be advantageous where the source of water for a pond is known to be rich in nutrient. The shade cast over the water by trees on the southern bank would help to prevent vigorous growth of plants in response to the nutrient.

These benefits must be offset against the inevitable accumulations of leaf litter which build up on the floor of the pond beneath the trees. In a river, the flowing water will help to disperse the leaves and also sustain oxygen levels, but in a small pond, serious deoxygenation could occur. Another problem is the potential loss of water which could result. The most suitable bankside trees, alders and willows, will draw large volumes of water from the pond and if too many are growing around a small pond, this could lead to significant water loss.

## Biological Control

*Grass carp* The use of fish to control aquatic plant growth is not common in the United Kingdom, but research has demonstrated that it is possible to introduce grass carp (*Ctenopharyngodon idella Val*) to stillwaters to feed on plant growth and effectively control vegetation. If stocked at correct levels and managed properly, grass carp have advantages over more conventional aquatic vegetation control methods such as cutting. In the long term, costs of control can be reduced, although instant control is not possible, while the control which the fish exercise is persistent throughout the growing season as opposed to intermittent. The grass carp themselves are a valuable source of protein, are highly regarded as table fish, and could be a valuable fish to stock as part of an angling enterprise.

Experiments have shown that grass carp have a number of preferred food plants in ponds: duckweeds, stoneworts, starworts, small leaved pondweeds and Canadian pondweed. Hornwort, milfoils, mares-tails and large leaved pondweeds are not so popular. The fish dislike water lilies and water crowfoot. Grass carp require warm water if they are to feed at high levels. Optimum temperatures are 23°–25°C, and where these are achieved in a pond the fish will grow well, consuming large amounts of plant biomass. In fact, at 25°C, each fish is capable of consuming its own body weight in vegetation per day, although as they are inefficient food processors, around 50 per cent of the food which they eat is undigested and returned to the water. At the other end of the scale, the fish will not feed at all if the water temperature is less than 16°C.

Effective control appears to depend on the total weight of fish in the water, i.e. stocking density. This in turn depends on the growth rates of the fish after initial stocking plus any subsequent fish losses, for instance from predation. A large number of small fish will grow rapidly and the subsequent weight of fish in the water may need to be reduced in the interests of good management. Other species such as pike or perch can decimate populations of juvenile grass carp, thus rendering the initial stocking not only worthless in terms of vegetation control but also expensive on account of the high cost of the fish. It would seem that introducing 200 kg of 100 g fish per hectare could give good long term vegetation control as the fish grow. As with any form of intensive fish management, there will be accumulations of nutrient derived from excreta which may cause problems with water quality over a long period.

The grass carp is native to Siberia and China, but in recent years has been introduced to more than fifty other countries. Because of the feeding habits of the grass carp, its introduction into ponds and waterways in the United Kingdom has aroused much debate, not least because of concern that this species could establish in the wild and eventually populations might become out of control. It is most unlikely that the grass carp could breed in the United Kingdom, because the fish require very specific conditions including high temperatures, together with precise waterflow rates in rivers for larvae survival. Most of the grass carp reared today are produced by artificially induced spawning and so the development of a self-supporting population of fish in ponds and waterways is highly unlikely.

As the fish are an exotic species, the stocking of any area of water with grass carp must be licensed under the terms of the Wildlife and Countryside Act 1981. Also, the regional unit of the National Rivers Authority would need to license the use of this species—see Chapter 8, Ponds, Wildlife and the Law.

Anyone considering the use of grass carp for aquatic vegetation management should in the first instance seek advice from the National Rivers Authority. Until more data is available on stocking densities and management of this species in the United Kingdom, together with the long term effect on the aquatic environment, it is highly unlikely that the use of these fish will become widespread. However, plant control using grass carp is being practised in certain parts of the country and it is possible in the future that the use of these fish in conjunction with other control methods may become possible. One option would be to use conventional management to clear plant growth and subsequently stock ponds with grass carp at low densities to control the regeneration.

*Crayfish*  Information on the stocking of ponds with crayfish can be found in Chapter 7, Pond Utilisation. It is possible that if crayfish are stocked at a high enough density, an element of plant control may be achieved, particularly with regard to submerged species.

*Coarse fish*  Where a pond is stocked with coarse fish there is likely to be a reduction in the volume of plant growth for a number of reasons. Common carp (including mirror carp) are bottom feeders, searching the mud on the floor of the pond for food. This activity results in plants being uprooted and therefore unable to flourish. Because the carp are omnivorous they will also graze on the young shoots of submerged plants and have been known to control marginal species by uprooting them.

Bottom feeding fish cause turbidity in the water on account of their feeding behaviour, stirring up sediments from the bed of the pond. This in turn prevents light percolation and so further reduces plant growth but it also releases nutrient into the water, encouraging algal growth and giving stocked ponds their characteristic green appearance.

Other fish, such as roach, feed on plants in the pond. Where they are heavily stocked, grazing pressure will prevent many plants becoming established with knock-on effects for the smaller animals which find food and shelter amongst aquatic vegetation.

## Control of Algae

The characteristics of algae are described in Chapter 2, Life in the Water. These are primitive plants which are bound to appear in ponds and which, under adverse circumstances, can cause severe problems. The prevention of undesirable algal growth is better than control, which will remove the algae but probably not stop the recurrence of excessive growth.

Algal growth occurs in ponds in the spring and early summer. Light is very intense at this time of year and the algae are able to grow and utilise nutrients which have accumulated in the water. They flourish at lower temperatures than other plants and so a long, cold winter followed by a cold spring could increase algal problems in a pond, because the algae 'get away' faster than higher plants and suppress them. The reverse applies when early spring is warm, as the higher plants can grow faster and earlier, thus avoiding the competition.

The problems caused by algae manifest themselves in a number of ways:

- Unsightly algal 'blooms' occur.
- Oxygen supplies within the water are depleted as the algae die and decompose.
- Water movement through the pond is hampered.
- Water may be rendered toxic by blue-green algae. This could pose a hazard to livestock if sufficient quantities of water contaminated with high concentrations of algae are ingested.
- The growth of other plants is restricted because the algae prevent light penetration into the water.

When a new pond is excavated it often suffers from algal blooms during early summer for the first few years. The soil on the floor of the pond slowly releases nutrient into the water during the early years and because life within the pond has not had time to develop, there are neither enough broadleaved plants in the water competing for the nutrient and shading out the algae, nor sufficient numbers of animals to consume the excessive growth. For this reason, fish should never be put into a newly created or restored pond until the pondlife is sufficiently developed; otherwise the higher plants will have little chance to establish and the algae will persist as a problem and require regular chemical treatment. Once the pond becomes established, the natural production of algae should decrease unless other factors interfere.

The main reason why algae become a problem in established ponds is that too much nutrient is made available in the water over and above that which is produced under normal circumstances. This nutrient, chiefly in the form of nitrates and phosphates (availability of phosphate is usually the limiting factor for growth) can accumulate for a number of reasons. In some cases nutrients reach ponds in surface run-off, drainage water, as a result of seepage from roads and yards on farms or by direct pollution. Excess nutrient may also be caused by the presence of too much decaying organic matter in the water. Finally, livestock fouling the edge of the ponds cause nutrient to be released from the mud and add to the problem by excreting in the water. These sources of enrichment must be identified and stopped. Better still, they should be prevented from occurring in the first place (see pp. 125–29).

If severe algal blooms do occur, they can be treated chemically using an approved algicide although this may adversely affect other, more desirable plants within the water. Many species of algae can also be treated with copper compounds. These are not cleared for general use in the United Kingdom and are available for legal use only in garden ponds in the form of pond blocks, which can be obtained at many garden centres. Filamentous algae can be raked off ponds, but this usually provides only a temporary respite as the underlying cause of the problem will remain. After raking, the cleared algae must be removed from the pond to prevent deoxygenation.

The Root Zone Method of sewage treatment using reedbeds (described on p. 128) has been shown to be effective in reducing the phosphorate levels in effluent and may thus be of value in helping to prevent algal growth where ponds are fed by nutrient rich waters. Experimental work is also being carried out to assess whether straw can be used in water to immobilise phosphate. Loose straw (barley straw is best because it contains the least amount of phosphate compared to other straws) can be applied to the pond in early spring, before algal growth starts. Ten conventional straw bales per 4,000 m² of pond surface area appears to be an optimum application rate, although this is still very much an experimental technique. As the straw decomposes, phosphate is 'locked up' and is unavailable to the algae.

In addition to preventing algal growth, there is a valuable extra benefit to be derived from this technique because the straw provides an excellent source of food for animals within the pond, with a resultant increase in the productivity of the water. This has been shown to be of considerable importance where the pond is being managed for wildfowl, although as described in Chapter 3, much higher application rates must be used where wildfowl management is an objective.

## BANKSIDE VEGETATION MANAGEMENT

Control of vegetation on the wetland and terrestrial features adjacent to the pond is essential to ensure that the pond and surrounding area is maintained at a given stage in the succession. This means that scrub invasion must be prevented and grasses or broadleaved plants cut at regular intervals. Control of vegetation will also provide a diverse range of bankside nesting sites and cover for the birds and animals which either visit the pond or live in proximity to it.

Cutting back trees and shrubs will prevent excessive shade, allowing sunlight to reach the water surface. It will also reduce the rate of accumulation of leaf litter in the water caused by overhanging trees and shrubs. Coppicing or pollarding will help to sustain the vigour of trees growing on the bank.

Control of bankside vegetation can protect flexible liners. Debris from

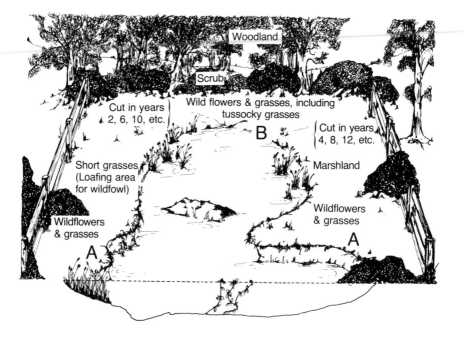

Figure 6.1　Bankside vegetation management

surrounding areas, branches falling off trees or even trees which are uprooted may puncture the liner with resultant loss of water. Regular clearance of weak or broken wood can help prevent this type of damage.

General control of surrounding vegetation may be necessary to maintain or improve the appearance of the pond. More specific measures will be required to sustain recreational or other non-conservation activities, for instance to provide access to a pond for anglers or to guarantee the ability of the pond to serve as a reservoir for fire fighting. (See colour plate 24.)

There are five acceptable forms of control for bankside vegetation:

- Manual.
- Mechanical.
- Chemical.
- Grazing.
- Burning.

Manual and mechanical operations are less easily separated on the bankside than in the water, and so are treated for convenience under one heading.

## Manual and Mechanical Control on the Bankside

Three zones must be considered:

1. Marshland, short grassland, tall or tussocky grasses and broadleaved plants.
2. Scrub.
3. Woodland.

*Marshland and grassland, etc.*
This zone extends from the water's edge to the start of the scrub belt, or in the case of a garden pond, as far as individual shrubs planted to provide cover or a source of food for wildlife. The basic management principle is to follow a cutting regime. Scrub colonisation or regeneration must be discouraged in this zone otherwise it will, within a few years, become covered in bushes which will spread towards the water's edge and ultimately shade the water. The frequency of cutting will vary according to the type of plants which are growing. Likewise, the pattern of cutting will depend on how the zone is structured. The following information is for guidance—where doubt exists as to how zonation should be interpreted on a particular site, advice must be taken locally.

*Marshland*  Cut in late summer once all the plants have flowered and set their seed. Rake off all cuttings.

*Short grasses (loafing area for wildfowl)*  Cut several times during the growing season to retain a short sward, removing the cuttings if possible.

*Wild flowers and grasses, including tussocky grasses*  This should be divided into two sections:

(*a*) adjacent to the loafing area.

(*b*) abutting the scrub zone.

Section (*a*) should be cut late in the summer. August and September are ideal months, because by then the majority of the plants will have flowered and set seed, thus ensuring continuity of species diversity. All of the cuttings should be collected to prevent soil enrichment or mulching. If there is a late flush of autumn growth, a light cut should be made early the following spring before the start of the next growing season.

Section (*b*) should be subdivided, with each half of the area linked to the scrub zone cut every four years, but with some management every two years. In this way, there will always be some tall, herbaceous plants and tussocky grasses present throughout the winter and spring offering nesting cover for wildfowl and seeds for other birds and mammals. There is bound to be some scrub growth but it will be kept in check by the irregular cutting.

Under no circumstances should any cutting be undertaken during spring and early summer, to avoid disturbance to ground nesting birds.

### Scrub

This zone encompasses any broadleaved shrubs planted on the banks of the pond, together with those sited away from the water's edge and adjoining woodland or groups of trees. In a simplified form, the management guidelines also apply to individual or small groups of shrubs planted to enhance a garden pond.

Maintenance work generally consists of cutting back or coppicing shrubs (cutting to ground level), to encourage different growth stages thus improving the quality of the habitat. A rotational system of cutting is best, whereby blocks of scrub are coppiced in different years. This way there is always some tall, mature cover, some which has been newly cut and plenty in intermediate growth stages. Where there are large blocks of scrub, some of these could be allowed to grow on indefinitely, especially where there are no nearby trees. In these instances, the taller 'shrub' trees, such as hawthorn, alder and willow will provide extremely valuable additional habitat as well as improving the overall appearance of the pond.

### Woodland

This zone includes individual trees as well as copses and larger parcels of woodland.

Basic principles of woodland management apply to the treatment of copses and large plantations. Near to the pond, unless they are being used as an aid to vegetation management, trees should be kept clear of the southern perimeter to reduce the problems caused by shading and leaf deposition. If the scrub zone adjoins woodland, an irregular boundary should be created, whereby there is no instantly recognisable dividing line between scrub and trees.

Alders and willows growing on the bank of the pond should be maintained by pollarding or coppicing, with very large specimens treated before they become top heavy, die back and shed limbs into the water. In this way they will be sustained as trees and will contribute towards the appearance of the pond and the landscape.

Many old ponds on farmland are overshadowed by large oak or ash trees. Good specimens should not be felled; providing any surrounding scrub is cut back to allow light to reach the pond, one or two trees can be retained to add diversity both to the habitat and the landscape. In some agricultural areas, the contribution made to the landscape by these groups of trees is very significant, particularly when there is no woodland nearby.

The felling of trees is subject to licensing under the Forestry Act 1967, see Chapter 8, Ponds, Wildlife and the Law.

*Tools*
The equipment available to the pond manager will vary according to whether the pond is located in a garden, on a farm or on some other site, for instance a park or nature reserve.

For the garden owner, most small tasks will have to be undertaken using conventional hand tools, although the use of a powered strimmer or brush cutter would be advantageous for the management of herbaceous vegetation and grasses. On larger sites, mechanical scythes are very useful, providing there is easy access around shrubs and the ground is not too wet.

Brush cutters are also excellent for use around ponds on farmland. If used correctly, they are able to cope with quite tough vegetation in any location where the operator can move. Where a large expanse of grass free from obstructions such as trees or bushes requires cutting, tractor mounted equipment can be used, providing damage to the ground can be avoided. In these situations, a jungle buster or flail is very effective providing it is used properly.

Wherever possible, cuttings should be raked up and collected.

## Bankside Vegetation Management Using Chemicals

Farmers and landowners are more accustomed to using herbicides in terrestrial situations than in and around water. But in control of bankside vegetation, as with aquatic vegetation, there is a place for herbicides, providing use is in strict accordance with manufacturers' guidelines and the correct chemical is selected to tackle the problem.

Most herbicides will, however, eliminate many of the wild flowers and grasses which are so desirable around ponds. Where these plants are being encouraged, herbicide treatment must be avoided in close proximity to these areas. It must also be remembered that any herbicide used for the management of a terrestrial site adjacent to a pond or watercourse must be approved for use near water.

## Grazing

Livestock are useful aids to management. However, as with other forms of vegetation control, if overdone, grazing can harm the habitat rather than enhance it.

The grazing of cattle is not advisable because, being heavy animals, they are liable to poach the ground by excessive trampling and if they obtain access to the water they will foul it and possibly damage lining materials. Sheep are far better because of their lighter weight and they should be used to graze selected areas of the bankside late each year. Young trees and shrubs will need to be protected against damage by grazing livestock.

## Burning

The burning of vegetation is a valuable form of management if it is undertaken with care. Small areas of herbaceous vegetation can be burnt off during the winter months, either as control in its own right, or as a prelude to scrub cutting or woodland management. In the latter case, care is essential to avoid damage to living trees.

## Supplementary Habitat Creation and Bankside Management

An opportunity to create a new habitat or retain an existing valuable one often arises during pond management. A good example of this is the treatment of dead or dying trees. Leaving a dead or dying tree *in situ* (unless it is dangerous), to rot down and provide a wealth of food for wildlife, nesting holes for birds and homes for plants such as fungi and lichens is a very simple way to improve habitat quality. When scrub or trees are cut, stacks of small timber can be retained as ecopiles, see Chapter 5, Supplementary Habitat Creation.

## AUTUMN AND WINTER MAINTENANCE

*Leaves*

The problems caused by leaves falling into a pond have already been described, but garden pond owners may be able to prevent excessive autumn leaf deposition. A net may be stretched over the pond, attached to stakes driven into the ground beyond the outer edge of any lining membrane. The net should encircle the banks of the pond and be lifted high enough over it to prevent interference with tall emergent plants.

*Ice*

It is not often that ice becomes a serious problem, but where there is no regular flow of water through the pond, in a severe winter an ice sheet may form and cover the surface for several days. If this happens, there will be a build-up of toxic gases in the water, produced by the decomposition of organic matter. To prevent this harming pondlife, part of the water surface needs to be kept clear of ice, which will also be of value to birds and mammals which need drinking water during freezing weather. Sheets of ice pushing against steep sided ponds could also puncture waterproof membranes, so the presence of at least one gently graded bank for the ice to ride up will be an advantage.

Holes should not be made by smashing thick ice—shock waves could kill pondlife—melting the ice or lifting sheets out are preferable techniques. Floating a ball, piece of wood, decoy duck or even a plastic duck on the pond during the winter should help to keep a small area of water open in all but the most severe conditions.

# Chapter 7

# Pond Utilisation

The long tradition of pond construction and management in the United Kingdom has not grown out of a simple desire to conserve wildlife, but rather because ponds have been created for functional reasons. Notwithstanding the fact that many of these reasons are now consigned to the archives, ponds are still valuable in their own right and are probably one of the most underutilised and undervalued resources on farms today.

Management of ponds to provide drinking water for livestock, attract wildfowl and act as reserves of water for firefighting has already been described, see Chapter 3, Pond Design. These three reasons are often the standard answers given when a farmer is asked to justify pond creation or management (as opposed to reservoir construction) for purposes other than nature conservation. In these days when attractive farms are priced at a premium, a well kept pond is also seen as adding value to property.

In today's changing farming climate, the management of ponds for angling, fish or shellfish production and the possibility of including water in the development of a farm-based leisure enterprise are opportunities which no-one can afford to dismiss. With increasing pressure being placed on farmers to cut back on conventional agricultural production, the need to find new sources of income is becoming vital and while a pond is not necessarily an underwater goldmine, there may be some possibilities for raising a modest income. This income, when aggregated with revenue from other farm resources such as woodlands, could start to make 'diversification' an attractive proposition.

## Farm Plans

The starting point for any farmer or landowner who wishes to diversify his business should be an appraisal of the resources which are available on the farm, as well as any relevant external factors. The farm resources will include land, buildings, access, woodlands, water, labour availability and capability, plus the desires and abilities of the farmer and his family. The external factors will include the availability and size of markets (local or otherwise) for new services and products. Once the existing resources are identified and the potential for new features is evaluated—in the latter instance the creation of woodland or water are good examples—it will be possible to see what (if any) new enterprises can be developed.

The farm plan must take into account the ecological value of the various resources and, in the same way that buildings of outstanding architectural significance need to be safeguarded against unsympathetic development, so too must many ponds and other farmland habitats. Where a pond is found to be of above average value to wildlife or is less valuable but significant for some other reason—perhaps ponds are locally scarce—it must not be subjected to any management changes which would have a detrimental effect on wildlife. Such management changes could be: the introduction of fish where previously no fish were present; increasing access and therefore disturbance round the pond; feeding wildfowl. If in doubt as to the value of the pond for nature conservation, take professional advice.

The next stage is to decide what options are available for water utilisation and conduct a feasibility study. The extent of this will depend on the scale of the project; a simple scheme to increase the opportunities for wildfowling will require less close scrutiny than a proposal to start rearing fish for sale. A detailed feasibility study will need to show:

- What resources are needed to establish the new enterprise.
- The estimated cost of the project and any likely sources of grant aid.
- Whether existing labour can be used and if so whether any training is required.
- The expected level of income and the length of time before income is produced.
- Anticipated running costs.
- Whether there are any legal constraints.
- How the service or product is to be marketed.
- Whether the financial return is going to be satisfactory.
- A recommendation as to whether or not to proceed with the project.

The options open to farmers fall into two categories, those which utilise the water alone and those where the pond is part of a scheme which includes other resources. In some cases the two categories overlap.

## UTILISING THE WATER

### Angling

Stocking a pond with fish and letting the angling is probably the most popular way of deriving income from water. The greater the area of water the better, and the opportunities for developing a profitable enterprise will be increased if 2–3 ha of water are available rather than a 0.4 ha pond, but nevertheless small areas of water can be utilised very effectively.

The design of a pond which is to be stocked with fish does not need to vary very much from the guidelines set out in Chapter 3, Pond Design. The longer the length of bankside, the more space there is for anglers. If the shape of the pond is too regular and cannot easily be modified, jetties or platforms should be constructed to allow for more freedom of movement. The finished appearance of the pond is very important—an exposed site is less likely to be popular with anglers than one which looks attractive and provides a certain amount of shelter. The 'conservation' input to a fishery can never be underdone and will prove to be a great asset when the resource is being marketed. Landscaping of both new and existing ponds needs to take this into account. Some of the best stillwater fisheries in the country are very attractive places where the fishermen can enjoy their surroundings as well as their sport.

The biggest variation from the conventional design criteria for ponds is to be found in the water depths which are required for fish. Salmonids (trout and salmon) thrive in water temperatures which do not exceed 20°C, while cyprinids (members of the carp family) do best when the water is warmer and therefore fairly shallow. Cold, deep water retains more oxygen than warm, shallow water, and because the cyprinids can tolerate lower oxygen levels than salmonids, they will flourish in ponds with an average depth of around 1.2 m. However, it is important that the surface does not become completely icebound during the winter and there are one or two deep holes in the pond floor into which the fish can retreat during the cold weather.

Salmonids—in the case of ponds, trout—require much more oxygen and so unless the pond is large, approaching 0.4 ha in area, stocking with these fish is only really feasible if there is a flow of water within the pond or artificial aeration is available. This is particularly important during warm summer nights, when oxygen depletion is at its greatest and often leads to fish mortality. To help retain oxygen and regulate water temperature, an average depth of 3 m is necessary for trout.

In addition to these specific depth requirements, the gradient of the pond banks needs careful consideration. A heron will be able to catch fish in the shallow margins of the pond and if these predators are given easy access into the water—they walk in from the bank—fish losses could be high. A steep drop into the water will deter heron but will be less attractive to other wildlife, so the farmer must decide what level of interference with fish stocks can be tolerated in the interests of nature conservation.

*Game fisheries*
Game fish include brown and rainbow trout, migratory trout and salmon. The pond owner is only concerned with the first two. Salmonids rarely

breed successfully in still waters and so most ponds and lakes managed as game fisheries are run on a 'put and take' basis.

The introduced rainbow trout is more tolerant than the native brown trout of warmer water and lower oxygen concentrations, so the rainbow trout tends to do better in ponds. Rainbow trout have a shorter lifespan than brown trout and are less hardy during the winter but, despite this, the recapture rates for rainbow trout are greater than for brown trout in relation to the initial stocking density, so many game fisheries stock both species.

The fish are best introduced to a well established pond during the spring. Assuming that the water is highly productive in terms of generating natural food for the trout (they eat moving prey, mainly small invertebrates found in and around aquatic vegetation), a weight of fish equivalent to 40–80 kg per ha (pro rata) could be stocked each year. The exact weight will depend on the size and quality of the pond and the number of fish which are caught during the season.

*Coarse fisheries*
The most common species of coarse fish found in ponds are cyprinids. They include common or mirror carp, roach, rudd, bream and tench. Carp tend to move in shoals and are bottom feeders, stirring up the silt on the floor of the pond in their search for food. They feed on zooplankton (mostly small crustacea), consuming large numbers of water fleas (daphnia) as well as chironomid larvae which are present in the mud. This feeding behaviour accounts for the turbidity of ponds which are stocked with cyprinids.

Coarse fish are able to breed successfully in warm, shallow water and so many old, unmanaged farm ponds contain large numbers of small fish, particularly roach and rudd, all competing for limited amounts of food and consequently never achieving good growth rates. Prior to establishing a coarse fishery, these old ponds should be drained and cleared of existing fish stocks, some of which may be saleable to a dealer. The pond should then be left for a season to encourage plant growth and a build-up in productivity before re-stocking. Much of the productivity will occur in the plant rich areas of the pond and so it is vital that these have a chance to establish before fish are introduced. For the same reason, a newly created pond should be left until it has developed over at least one, or preferably two, seasons.

The choice of fish for stocking will depend on local conditions and markets. In some areas it may be worthwhile specialising in carp and excluding other species, whereas elsewhere it could be lucrative to stock and manage a pond to produce large roach. A feasibility study carried out during the farm planning stage will help to highlight the demand for a certain type of angling in a particular locality.

Where the natural productivity of the pond is high, a weight of fish equivalent to 150–250 kg/ha (pro rata) should be introduced. The actual number of fish will be determined by individual sizes and weights. Regular control of stock density will be required in future years to check that numbers do not increase too rapidly, especially in the case of roach.

### Facilities for anglers

In addition to well managed and attractive ponds, it is worthwhile providing easy access to the water, preferably with nearby car parking. Where anglers have to walk over fields or cross ditches and fences, routes must be clearly marked and maintained with good stiles and bridges. A path round the perimeter of the pond is essential, with steps leading down to fishing platforms on the water's edge. This will help to prevent bankside erosion and reduce damage to plants. The opportunity to provide access to suitable ponds for disabled anglers should not be overlooked.

The area around the pond needs to be kept tidy and a regularly emptied litter bin should be clearly marked and located near to the path. For game fisheries, a secure hut is needed, where anglers can weigh and record their catches. A simple shelter will suffice for a coarse fishery. If children are likely to visit the pond, a lifebelt should also be provided.

### Income and marketing

Income from fishing can be derived in a number of ways.

Many farmers are approached by angling clubs which offer to pay rent for a pond, the scale of which will depend on the type and quality of the fishing and the apportioning of responsibility for payment of rates, stocking and management.

The farmer himself could set up a syndicate, sell fishing to individuals, or market the angling on a day ticket basis; assuming in the latter instance that a convenient and reliable outlet for ticket sales is available. Fishing might also be offered as an attraction for visitors to farm holiday accommodation or caravan sites. In this case direct income could be obtained or, as an alternative, the availability of fishing might encourage higher occupancy of the holiday accommodation with income indirectly obtained via the charges for the accommodation. Some hotels and country clubs are interested in providing recreational pursuits for their guests and it is worthwhile investigating this type of outlet where it exists locally.

A good coarse fishery near to an urban conurbation is more likely to be successful than one in an isolated rural area, again stressing the need for forward planning. There are fewer costs incurred with a coarse fishery. Once stocking is complete, the annual costs will be associated with routine management. In a game fishery, annual management costs will be supplemented by the expense of restocking.

The number of anglers who can be accommodated round a pond

will vary according to whether the water is managed for game or coarse fish. As a guide, one rod per 60–100 m of bank is an average density for trout fishing and for coarse fishing one rod per 25 m of bank is possible, depending on whether the shallows around the pond margin can be fished. On this basis, a circular pond with an area of 0.4 ha could support 12 coarse or 3 game fishermen, the numbers rising if the length of bankside can be extended, for instance by creating bays and spits. The number of syndicate members could be higher than this, because not every member will fish daily. So depending on how the angling is controlled, the syndicate and thus the return could be considerably larger.

*Fisheries and the law*
The stocking of an area of water is subject to approval by the National Rivers Authority, see Chapter 8, Ponds, Wildlife and the Law. In every case where it is proposed to set up a fishery it is advisable to seek assistance from the local fisheries officer of the National Rivers Authority.

The close season for trout is 1st October–last day of February. The close season for coarse fish is 15th March–15th June.

Where fishing rights are separated from the occupation of the land they will be rateable.

## Extensive Fish Rearing in Non-Drainable Ponds

The letting of water for angling may not be an attractive proposition for landowners who do not wish to administer the scheme or who fear an invasion of privacy. Waters which are suitable for angling can also be used to grow on coarse fish, which will be harvested from the pond at regular intervals. Income will be forthcoming where the fish are sold to restock angling waters or as 'cold water ornamentals'.

To be suitable for this type of enterprise, the pond must be capable of being netted so that the fish can be harvested. This means that the water must be free from obstructions in the form of both natural debris and man made items—many odd things find their way into the bottom of ponds! It has been estimated that 30 per cent of enclosed waters are incapable of being netted on account of obstacles. Prior to stocking, it is often worth-while desilting the pond and at the same time taking the opportunity to level out major irregularities in the pond floor where the fish will hide in winter and thus avoid the nets.

For extensive fish rearing, water quality must be high with no accumulation of pollutants within the pond. The pond should not be too deep, an average of 1.2–2.0 m is ideal, and the pond needs to be accessible so that equipment can be moved to the pond and the fish transported away. As most netting is done during the winter months when ground conditions are poor, isolated field ponds will probably be unsuitable. Overhanging scrub should be cut back to reduce shading and allow working access around the pond.

Assuming that the pond is suitable, existing fish stocks should be removed before re-stocking. The services of a specialist dealer should be engaged and he will also be able to supply the fish for restocking. Typical species grown on in this manner include common or mirror carp, green tench, golden orfe and goldfish, although any of the cyprinids are suitable. Artificial feeding is not required because the fish feed on natural food produced within the water and, on average, the pond is harvested (by a specialist dealer) at three yearly intervals.

*Yields and stocking densities*
The yield of a pond is measured in terms of its productivity, described as the liveweight gain per annum of the fish which are stocked. Pond productivity varies according to the biomass of zooplankton present in the water, which in turn varies according to the location of the pond, the amount of sunlight and available nutrient, water temperature and pH, which should be in the range 7–8.5.

The location of the pond is important, because it determines the volume of nutrient which runs off adjoining land into the water. A pond situated in the middle of an area of intensively managed grassland will receive more nutrient than a pond located on the edge of woodland and, assuming other factors are similar, the grassland pond will be more productive. Temperature is also significant because, as already described, water productivity is higher in warmer water and the fish themselves grow best when the temperature is over 20° C. The growing season in the South of England generally lasts from May–September when the water is at its warmest, but in a cold summer yields will be poor. The natural yield from a farm pond will vary between 10–100 kg/ha (pro-rata) per year, depending on the above factors.

Stocking density is directly related to the productive capacity of the pond. For example, if the pond is reckoned to be capable of producing 50 kg/ha of liveweight gain per year, 200 fish of 250 g weight introduced in the spring should each put on 250 g during the growing season, assuming a 100 per cent survival rate which is unlikely. If more fish are stocked, the weight gains will be individually lower as the total pond production will have to be more widely distributed. The best way to proceed, is to stock a pond and assess its productive capacity over a period of time.

*Marketing*
The harvesting and sale of fish is best carried out through an experienced dealer.

*Extensive fish rearing and the law*

As with angling, the stocking of ponds requires the consent of the National Rivers Authority. In addition, the farmer needs to be aware of the provisions of the Diseases of Fish Act 1937 and 1983. Fish rearing will be subject to rating when the fish are not being produced for the table.

## Extensive Fish Rearing in Drainable Ponds

This is better described as aquaculture and requires considerably more technical knowledge and commitment on the part of the farmer and his employees than the use of non-drainable ponds. However, there are many advantages of this method over the system previously described. Stocking densities can be precisely controlled, and harvesting is easier, with less risk of damage or stress to the fish. When the pond is empty, the drying out and weathering of the mud on the pond floor helps to increase productivity, which can be further increased by manuring the pond floor and applying fertiliser to the pond at regular intervals during the season. Then, because productivity is higher, yields are better. Disease can be controlled because parasites are eliminated when the pond floor dries out. If a serious problem persists, lime can be applied.

Against these advantages, a farmer contemplating this type of enterprise should consider the following facts. The pond must be capable of being emptied; a disposal point must be available for water draining out of the pond; and there must be an adequate source of high quality water which can be used to refill the pond. Unless a second pond is available all the fish may have to be sold when the main pond is emptied in the autumn, or in the spring in the case of cold water ornamentals. In the latter case, losses could be severe in a long, cold winter. Finally, holding facilities may be required for batching up the fish ready for market.

In addition to the physical requirements of the enterprise, a high level of expertise is necessary. If management is not good, fish mortality may be high. A 70 per cent survival rate is reckoned to be good. Good marketing is essential and the pond will have minimal value to wildlife.

*Pond design*

Large ponds are best suited to this kind of system, because the bigger the pond the more fish can be stocked and the potential returns are therefore greater. Purpose built ponds are usually regular in shape, often rectangular, the sides twice as long as the ends. An average depth of 1.2 m is ideal and the sides should slope steeply to deter predators.

The floor of the pond should fall towards a catch pit where the fish can gather and be harvested as the water is drained off. The catch pit is best situated adjacent to the monk or outlet pipe. Where it is not possible to

*Plate 7.1   Fish pond in Bavaria. The pond has been drained, allowed to dry out, cultivated and fertilised. Note the perimeter drainage channel and the monk.*

drain the pond, water can be pumped out, the hose drawing water from the catch pit. A trench excavated around the edge of the pond floor will help drainage and encourage the mud to dry out, which is of value in increasing productivity. If the pond cannot be emptied by drainage, the overall returns will be lower on account of pumping costs and the fish may be adversely affected by oxygen starvation if the pond is emptied slowly prior to being harvested.

### Yields and stocking density

Yields will vary according to pond productivity and can be raised if manure or fertiliser is applied to the pond. Yields of mirror carp in excess of 300 kg/ha per annum have been achieved in drainable ponds with no manuring, while over 600 kg/ha have been obtained following applications of specific quantities of organic manure.

Stocking can be at a high density. If it is intended to produce carp of 1 kg or larger over a period of three summers (assuming an overwintering pond is available), as many as 5,000 fingerlings per ha (pro rata) can be stocked initially. Surplus fish can be sold off in years two and three as the fish grow, and stocking densities reduce each season.

Interested readers should refer to Appendix 7 to find sources of further information.

*Marketing*

Good marketing is crucial to the success of an aquaculture enterprise. There is a constant demand for coarse fish for restocking angling waters and most species can be produced under this system. The market is growing for cold water ornamentals such as goldfish, golden orfe, koi carp, green and golden tench and golden rudd. In the case of koi carp, production is best left in the hands of experienced fish farmers, but the other species can be grown on successfully in ponds and sold in spring when the demand is greatest.

Carp for the table are popular in European countries and with ethnic groups in the United Kingdom. However, consumer resistance to carp needs to be broken down if the UK market for table carp of 1–1.5 kg is to develop further. A concerted marketing campaign is required, together with an exploration of the possibilities for adding value through processing. If successful, this could encourage both the production of more fish and the utilisation of suitable ponds, with great benefit to the development of alternative farm incomes and the rural economy.

*Aquaculture and the law*

Any farmer wishing to diversify in this way should register the business as a fish farm, see Chapter 8, Ponds, Wildlife and the Law. Planning consent may be required where fish are not produced for the table. Advice should also be taken from the local fisheries officer of the National Rivers Authority. The production of fish for food is not rateable but where the fish are sold as ornamentals or for restocking angling waters, the business will be rated.

## Intensive Aquaculture in Drainable Ponds

Intensive aquaculture is highly specialised and requires a very great level of expertise and day to day management. In addition to manuring the ponds, supplementary feeding will be necessary to boost yields. The risks are considerable, as are the potential rewards, especially where high value ornamental fish are produced. Any farmer interested in diversifying his business in this way should seek professional guidance, in the first instance approaching the local fisheries officer of the National Rivers Authority.

## Shellfish Production

There has been considerable interest and publicity in recent years concerned with the stocking of ponds with crayfish. Many landowners have found to their cost that a seemingly easy way to generate revenue from ponds, at the same time producing a table delicacy, is not quite as simple as it seems. Crayfish production has a number of pitfalls and the problems must be weighed very carefully against the benefits before any pond is stocked with them.

The indigenous freshwater crayfish of the United Kingdom is the Atlantic stream crayfish, *Austropotamobius pallipes*. Unfortunately, this species has disappeared from many freshwater habitats, probably eliminated by the crayfish plague, *Aphanomyces astaci*, which has also depleted the population of the European crayfish (*Astacus astacus*) in mainland Europe. Because of this reduction in crayfish numbers, North American signal crayfish (*Pacifastacus leniusculus*), which are more resistant to the disease, have been introduced into Europe and have become very popular with pond owners.

This crayfish has faster growth, earlier sexual maturity and greater prolificacy than the native species, features which have made its introduction understandably attractive where there is a commercial interest. There is now concern in scientific circles that as more and more American signal crayfish are stocked and self-supporting communities build up in enclosed ponds, so there will be more and more 'escapees' into the wild. Indeed, many rivers and waterways already have resident populations. While there is little evidence to demonstrate that the surviving native crayfish stocks will be displaced by the newcomers, there is always a risk with a new species that the effect of it 'getting into the wrong place' could be detrimental to other wildlife. In the face of this concern, extreme caution is essential when seeking suitable sites for crayfish production. Well managed, enclosed waters can be used for this purpose, providing native crayfish are not already present, but casual stocking of ponds 'just to see what happens' must be avoided.

*Crayfish husbandry*

Crayfish do not swim, they walk about on the bed of the pond in search of food and lie up either in holes excavated in the pond banks or in artificial hides, for instance old drainage pipes. These hides are very important for crayfish survival. As a crayfish grows it has to moult and shed its hard carapace many times during the two years that it takes to reach sexual maturity. After each moult, the crayfish is unprotected until its new shell hardens. It is thus extremely vulnerable to predation, especially by eels, which can wriggle into the hides. Where stocking densities are high there may also be predation by other crayfish if insufficient hides are available.

The best ponds for crayfish production are those which are unpolluted—high water quality is vital. To encourage carapace development, pH should be at least 6.5. The best ponds are enclosed, to prevent crayfish dispersal,

*Plate 7.2   Adult American signal crayfish.*

*Plate 7.3   A Bavarian crayfish pond. The pond is a very attractive landscape feature and habitat despite the intensity of management.*

and predator free; apart from eels, major predators include mink and perch. If possible the pond should have plenty of natural food. Crayfish are omnivorous and will eat most animal or vegetable matter which they find as they scavenge in the pond. The floor should be hard. Crayfish cannot walk in silt, so newly created or desilted ponds with a clay base are excellent, as are flooded gravel pits.

## Stocking

Because crayfish do not move far from their hides in the pond banks, the length of bankside is more relevant than the area of water when stocking rates are assessed. Where juvenile American signal crayfish are being introduced to a pond, it is normal to stock seven per metre length of shoreline over a two year period. Four juveniles are put in during the first summer and three in the second. It will take fifteen months (two summers) for the crayfish to reach sexual maturity and so in the third summer harvesting can begin, albeit with care not to remove too many females. Yields will be low until a strong, self-sustaining population has been built up by the fifth year. Harvestable crayfish are those over 11 cm long.

If adult crayfish are introduced, two per metre of bankside is acceptable, with females outnumbering males 2:1. Before putting the crayfish into the pond it is essential to acclimatise them to the water temperature. The best way is to wet the adults thoroughly with pond water and let them enter the pond in their own time.

## Yields

Various figures have been quoted for crayfish yields. An intensively managed enterprise, using stew ponds or gravel pits, could produce up to 1 kg per metre of shoreline per year, with eighteen crayfish per kg. This is normally achieved in the fifth year after first stocking with juveniles. It would be safer to work on a figure of 0.5 kg per metre per year for a conventional pond, still a respectable figure.

The trapping season runs from July until October or November. During this period the crayfish are sold live, necessitating some holding facilities on the farm where the crayfish can be batched up and packed prior to despatch to the market.

## Marketing

Most crayfish are sold to good restaurants and hotels. The British Crayfish Marketing Association (a co-operative) has been very successful in developing markets and providing support services for producers. While membership of the BCMA is not obligatory for producers and would-be producers, it is certainly advisable.

In the future, as more and more ponds are stocked and production comes 'on-line', so the marketing may become more difficult and a greater number of outlets will be required. There is considerable scope for individual producers to use their own initiative and seek out local markets.

*Crayfish production and the law*
This is a complex and somewhat 'grey' area. Because shellfish are not subject to the provisions of the Salmon and Freshwater Fisheries Act 1975, no stocking licence is required. However, consent is necessary from the Ministry of Agriculture, Fisheries and Food under the Wildlife and Countryside Act 1981 before American signal crayfish can be introduced to a pond, see Chapter 8, Ponds, Wildlife and the Law.

## Aquatic Plants

The boom in wildlife gardening, which has led to more garden pond creation, has resulted in an increase in demand for indigenous aquatic plants. Shallow areas of water can be used to produce emergent species and also in some cases the true aquatics. The plants can be sold either bare rooted or containerised. Sales are made either direct to the customer through a farm shop or by supplying a wholesaler or local garden centre.

## UTILISING THE POND AND ITS SURROUNDINGS

### Ornamental Wildfowl

This requires some land use around the perimeter of the pond. Many landowners are keen to put ornamental wildfowl on to their ponds and lakes, often as a hobby or to provide attractive visual interest. It is quite possible to generate income through the sale of surplus stock following a good breeding season. However, a pond which supports ornamental wildfowl will not be a valuable habitat for wildlife. In an established pond, fauna and flora will be disturbed and colonisation of a new pond by native species will be seriously impeded.

Ornamental wildfowl are normally kept on a pond close to a house so that they can be seen, enjoyed and protected from predators. The birds are pinioned when they are one day old and, as this is a permanent operation, no further treatment is necessary. Because they cannot fly, the wildfowl are defenceless and cannot escape from predators. For this reason, the pond and surrounding land must be adequately protected with foxproof wire or electric fencing.

Around the pond, the wildfowl will need areas of close mown grasses, together with scrub and taller grasses to act as cover. Shelter for part of

*Plate 7.4　Russian red breasted geese resting on grassland adjacent to a pond. Note the protective fencing and individual tree guards.*

the area should be provided by a hedgerow. In the absence of good cover, successful breeding is unlikely, even if nesting boxes are available.

To people with no experience of ornamental wildfowl, the thought of keeping these birds implies muddy pond banks, damaged grass and dirty water. In fact, these only happen when the pond is overstocked and undermanaged. Hardwearing grasses such as fescues should be sown together with timothy, to provide resting areas; white clover should be mixed in where geese are to be kept, as they find clover very palatable. Clumps of emergent plants growing around the pond margins should be protected using chicken netting, so that they are not disturbed and the visual appearance of the pond can be retained.

The wildfowl will feed in and around the pond, their natural diet supplemented by wheat scattered in the water where it cannot be taken by sparrows and starlings. If necessary, pellet foods can be trough fed.

*Stocking*

A pond approximately 20 m across will support 15–18 pairs of ornamental wildfowl and even very small ponds can be stocked, using species such as ringed teal. For the beginner, it is best to start with common species, for instance tufted duck, red crested pochard, European pintail and shoveller, introducing more variety at a later date. Highly colourful species such as Carolina, mandarin duck and shelduck are also fairly easy to keep. As interest and experience grow, there are many different species for the enthusiast to choose from.

### Income and marketing

Surplus wildfowl can be sold either through advertisement or more often by selling back to the supplier of the original breeding stock. The prices realised will depend on the species; common wildfowl such as mallard and tufted duck are not as valuable as European eider duck or goldeneye, which are more difficult to breed and keep.

Income can also be generated by exploiting the visual attraction as part of a farm-based recreational facility.

### Ornamental wildfowl and the law

It is illegal under the Wildlife and Countryside Act 1981 to allow a non-indigenous species to escape into the wild. Where pinioned birds are kept in a secure enclosure no licence is required, however a licence will be necessary before any ornamental wildfowl can be sold.


## Recreational Use of Water

Activities such as sailing, windsurfing, rowing and, to a lesser degree, canoeing are restricted to large expanses of water such as lakes or reservoirs, because a pond, even of 0.4 ha in area, is simply not big enough. These large scale participative sports generally require plenty of manoeuvring space which is unlikely to be found on waters less than 1.5 ha in extent. A smaller pond is, however, quite capable of forming an integral part of a farm-based recreational enterprise—the most obvious use being fishing. More and more farmers are looking to tourism as a potential source of income and in addition to developing holiday cottages, caravan and camp sites are seeking to create facilities for use in conjunction with these, such as ponds for angling. The marketing of accommodation may be improved if farm-based attractions are available.

The scope for tourist enterprises does not end with residential visitors. Large numbers of people visit the countryside at weekends throughout the year, and during holiday periods many rural areas are inundated with holidaymakers, often looking for interesting places to visit and things to do. Farm parks, trails and interpretation centres developed for educational and recreational purposes are becoming very popular. All are enhanced by the presence of a well managed and attractive pond, especially one which can be 'dipped' by parties of children or students. Where several ponds exist on the farm and a tourism enterprise is being considered, some ponds

*Plate 7.5    This pond is used for angling and forms part of a diversification enterprise on a Somerset farm. The other facilities include pick-your-own fruit (foreground), cricket pitch (rear left) and tea room.*

could be managed purely for nature conservation (with at least one kept free from disturbance) and others stocked with fish or ornamental wildfowl.

School visits to farms are becoming very popular and, while they should not be regarded as a means of directly earning income, the facilities necessary to attract school parties can be used for other purposes. Many schoolchildren encourage their parents to make a visit to a farm trail or centre and income can be derived from admissions, sales of refreshments and souvenirs. The Greenmount Trail at the Greenmount College of Agriculture and Horticulture in County Antrim, Northern Ireland, was established in 1979 and attracts 8,000–10,000 schoolchildren each year. The children are able to look at agriculture, horticulture and countryside management (including a lake and pond) with the aid of a comprehensive guide and workbook. Examples such as this demonstrate the potential which exists when a project is tackled properly and enthusiastically.

In many cases, the development of an alternative farm enterprise which utilises or includes water may be eligible for grant aid. A list of advisory agencies and grant aiding authorities can be found in Appendices 1 and 6.

# Chapter 8

# Ponds, Wildlife and the Law

Pond creation and management may in some cases be constrained by legal requirements. The following resumé of legislation is not exhaustive, but is designed to provide guidance for landowners and managers as to which authorities have a role to play in the management of freshwater and its surroundings. Should there be any doubt as to whether any particular operation requires consent or is affected by legislation, on site advice must be taken from the relevant authority. A list of addresses can be found in Appendix 6.

## Pond Creation

*Conservation*

The creation of a small garden pond is not subject to any constraints.

The position with regard to farmland is less clear. The use of land for agriculture is not classed as development in the Town and Country Planning Act 1971 and therefore planning permission is not required to carry out agricultural operations. However, engineering operations on agricultural land may require planning permission, unless they are classed as 'permitted development' under Schedule 2 Part VI of the Town and Country Planning General Development Order 1988.

In this case, certain building and engineering operations can be carried out without planning approval provided they occur on agricultural land with an area in excess of 0.4 ha which is part of an agricultural holding. These operations must also be 'requisite' to the use of the land for agricultural purposes. These operations usually refer to the construction of farm buildings, but could also be taken to mean any engineering operation necessary to create a pond.

Farmers now receive considerable encouragement to undertake work of value to the environment as part of conventional farming practice. It would, therefore, seem reasonable to assume that the creation of a farm pond for wildlife conservation would be a permitted engineering operation. However, in some areas, local planning authorities are adopting a restrictive approach to pond creation, especially where large areas of water are concerned and nature conservation is not the sole purpose behind the project. The creation of an irrigation reservoir has been deemed to be an engineering operation and not 'permitted development', while the excavation of a large pond where substantial quantities of sand or gravel are to be won would also require planning consent. In the same way, the building of an embankment using soil excavated from a pond could also be classified as an engineering operation, requiring planning consent.

In general, the situation regarding conservation ponds and planning consent is unclear. As a guide, if the pond can be created using machinery normally available on the farm and the pond can be shown to be exclusively for wildlife conservation, it will probably be classed as 'agricultural' and therefore not require planning permission. It should not however be excavated within 25 m of the metalled surface of a trunk or classified road.

Should heavy machinery be required and the pond is to cover a large area, 0.25 ha or greater, it would be advisable to seek an informal opinion from the local planning authority as to whether planning consent is required. The situation in National Parks is different (see p. 175).

### Pond utilisation

While the use of land for agricultural purposes does not require planning consent, any change of use would constitute development and planning permission would be needed. Agricultural uses of water include: the supply of water for livestock; the storage of water for fire fighting; and fish farming (rearing fish for food). Any proposed use of water other than these would be a change of use and therefore subject to planning procedures. The creation of an area of water for a non-agricultural use would also be covered by this requirement.

### Land Drainage Act 1976

The National Rivers Authority must be consulted if it is intended to create a pond on the floodplain of, or close to, a watercourse. The Authority will wish to ensure that soil disposal from the pond is not likely to affect adversely the flood storage capacity of the surrounding land.

## Water Supply and Abstraction

Unless a pond is to be filled by ground water or surface run-off, it will be subject to the Water Resources Act 1963. A licence must be obtained from the National Rivers Authority, either before a watercourse is impounded or prior to an off-stream pond being filled by abstraction from (for instance by pumping) or diversion of a nearby watercourse. A licence will also be required to abstract water from a well, borehole or surface excavation.

This procedure will apply to any size of pond. However, a licence is not needed where the abstraction of water is for an agricultural purpose, for instance farming fish for food. Where a small pond on a farm is to be created purely for nature conservation this might also be construed as being an agricultural purpose and therefore water abstraction to fill the pond would not require a licence. In both instances, the advice of the National Rivers Authority should be obtained.

## Fish Farming

The construction of ponds for the rearing of fish or shellfish for food is exempted from planning controls under the Town and Country Planning General Development (Amendment No 2) Order 1985. The business must be registered with the Ministry of Agriculture, Fisheries and Food under the provisions of the Diseases of Fish Act 1983 and the Registration of Fish Farming and Shellfish Farming Businesses Order 1985. The following constraints apply to the creation of ponds for this purpose: the site area where the operations are to be carried out must not exceed 2 ha; no works must be carried out within 25 m of the metalled part of a trunk or classified road; if minerals (for instance sand or gravel) are to be obtained during working, no excavation must be deeper than 2.5 m and the area of the excavation (including other excavations on the land during the preceding two years) must not be greater than 0.2 ha.

Under the provisions of the Salmon Act 1986 it is no longer necessary for fish farmers to obtain the consent of the National Rivers Authority prior to stocking ponds (see below), once the original stocking of the fish farm is completed.

## Stocking Ponds

The Salmon and Freshwater Fisheries Act 1975 requires any person wishing to introduce spawn or fish to a pond to obtain consent (a stocking licence) from the National Rivers Authority. This includes fish to be reared for food as well as the production of ornamental species such as goldfish and koi carp.

A licence will also be required from MAFF to introduce into the wild any fish or eggs of fish not ordinarily resident in Great Britain or listed in Schedule 9 of the Wildlife and Countryside Act 1981. This includes the grass carp and the American signal crayfish.

Shellfish are not covered by the Salmon and Freshwater Fisheries Act

1975, but prior to the introduction into any pond of species such as the American signal crayfish, a licence must be obtained from MAFF.

## Rod Licences

The Salmon and Freshwater Fisheries Act 1975 specifies that any person letting angling should ensure that all fishermen possess a rod licence issued by the National Rivers Authority. In some cases it may be simpler for a landowner to purchase a general rod licence to cover all visitors.

## Reservoirs Act 1975

This Act strengthens the legislation relating to the safety of large areas of above ground water storage, capable of holding 25,000 $m^3$ of water. The Act does not apply to ponds, because to hold such a large volume of water, a reservoir would need to be greater than 1 ha in area and more than 2 m deep.

## Control of Pollution Act 1974

It is an offence to permit a noxious substance to enter a watercourse, lake or pond. Slurry, dairy washings, silage effluent, sheep dip and rainwater run-off from yards are all pollutants and must be collected and stored in secure tanks on a farm.

## Wildlife and Countryside Act 1981

This is in force in England, Wales and Scotland. The following information does not apply in Northern Ireland where the Nature Conservation and Amenity Lands (NI) Order 1985 and Wildlife (NI) Order 1985 are the two most important pieces of legislation conferring protection on plants and animals.

The Wildlife and Countryside Act is of particular importance to pond owners and land managers because of its emphasis on species protection. Section 1, Part 1, states that it is an offence to take, damage or destroy the nest of any wild bird while the nest is either in use or being built. This is relevant to any management operations around ponds during the nesting season, because although it is a legitimate defence to say that destruction occurred during management that was part of a lawful operation, i.e. normal agricultural practice, a landowner has been prosecuted successfully for destroying a nest while hedge trimming, having previously been warned that the nest was in use.

A number of birds are specifically protected in this section (for instance the barn owl, which may nest in holes in large trees near ponds). It is an offence intentionally to disturb these birds in or near the nest.

Section 2 permits the killing or taking of birds included in Part 1 of Schedule 2 to the Act, outside the close season for that species. The following birds are amongst those included in Schedule 2: coot; tufted duck; gadwall; goldeneye; Canada goose; greylag goose; pink-footed goose; white-fronted goose (England and Wales only); mallard; moorhen; pintail; golden plover; pochard; shoveler; common snipe; teal; wigeon.

Unless a separate order is made by the Secretary of State, the close seasons are:

| Snipe | 1 February–11 August |
| All others in the Schedule | 1 February–31 August |

These dates apply to wild birds in all areas other than below the high-water mark of ordinary spring tides.

Section 9 makes it an offence for a person intentionally to take, kill or injure any wild animal listed in Schedule 5 of the Act. It is also an offence to damage, destroy or obstruct access to any place used by a Schedule 5 animal for shelter, or to disturb the animal in that place. As with Section 1, a defence of 'normal agricultural practice' could be made.

It is also an offence under Section 9 (5) for a person to sell or possess, deal, transport and advertise for the purpose of sale any of the Scheduled species. Of relevance are: bats (all species); Atlantic stream crayfish**; common frog*; great crested newt; palmate newt*; smooth newt*; grass snake*; common toad*; natterjack toad; Norfolk aeshna dragonfly.

Under Section 13, a person commits an offence if he or she: 'intentionally picks, uproots or destroys any wild plant included in Schedule 8; or, not being an authorised person, intentionally uproots any wild plant not included in that schedule'. This means that no wild plant may be dug up, for instance to be moved to another pond, without the landowner's permission; and even the landowner may not uproot one of the very rare species included in Schedule 8, if it grows on his or her land.

It is an offence under Section 14 to release or allow to escape into the wild any animal not ordinarily resident or a regular visitor to Great Britain in the wild state. The species scheduled include: African clawed toad; American mink; Canada goose; Carolina wood duck; coypu; edible frog; European cat fish; European pond terrapin; European tree frog; mandarin duck; marsh frog; midwife toad; pond perch (pumpkinseed); ruddy duck; yellow-bellied toad; zander. Section A also makes it an offence to plant or

---

* Scheduled for the purposes of section 9 (5) only.
** It is an offence to take and sell this species.

cause the following species to grow in the wild, all of which will become established near ponds and waterways: giant hogweed; giant kelp; Japanese knotweed; Japanese seaweed. All reasonable steps must be taken to ensure that these plants and animals do not escape into the wild.

## Ancient Monuments and Archaeological Areas Act 1979

Some areas of water which are considered to be ponds but which are technically moats and medieval fish ponds may be scheduled as Ancient Monuments. Prior to any work being carried out which may affect such a site, Scheduled Monument Consent must be obtained from the Secretary of State for the Environment or the appropriate Secretary of State for Wales or Scotland.

The Ancient Monuments (Class Consents) Order 1987 grants permission for certain works to be carried out in England and Wales without Scheduled Monument Consent. The Ancient Monuments (Class Consents) (Scotland) Order 1981 provides similar permission in Scotland.

Permitted works are:

*Class I* 'Agricultural, horticultural or forestry works, being works of the same kind as works previously executed in the same field or location during the period of five years immediately preceding the coming into operation of this order; but not including subsoiling, drainage works, the planting or uprooting of trees, hedges or shrubs or any other works likely to disturb the soil below the maximum depth affected by normal ploughing'.

*Class V* 'Works which are essential for the purposes of health or safety'.

In the latter instance, the relevant Secretary of State should be advised in writing prior to the commencement of any work. If in any doubt as to whether work is covered by the various class consents, on-site advice must be taken.

The situation in Northern Ireland is different. Ancient Monuments are protected by the Historic Monuments Act (NI) 1971. Where a landowner wishes to carry out work on a Scheduled Ancient Monument he must give at least six months notice to the Department of the Environment (Northern Ireland).

## Sites of Special Scientific Interest

Where a pond forms part of a Site of Special Scientific Interest notified under the Wildlife and Countryside Act 1981, the Nature Conservancy Council will have provided the landowners and occupiers with a list of potentially damaging operations. Prior to any of these operations being carried out, the NCC must be notified in writing so that it can assess the likely effect on the scientific interest and if appropriate enter into a management agreement.

## National Parks

A landowner wishing to create a new pond on land within a National Park should consult with the appropriate planning authority prior to commencing work.

## Health and Safety at Work etc Act 1974

Every employer must ensure, insofar as is possible, the health, safety and welfare at work of him or herself and all employees.

## Occupiers Liability Act 1957

The occupier of premises must take care to ensure the safety of visitors using the premises for the purpose of their visit. Warning notices and or fencing may be needed near ponds where visitors are anticipated.

## Felling Consents for Trees and Woodland

The felling of trees in Great Britain (excluding Northern Ireland) is controlled by the Forestry Commission under the Forestry Act 1967. It is possible that extensive woodland management operations as part of a pond restoration programme may require licensing. A licence from the Forestry Commission is normally required to fell growing trees, but in any calendar quarter up to 5 m³ of timber may be felled by a land occupier without a licence, providing that no more than 2 m³ of timber are sold.

There are a number of further exemptions from the licensing provisions which could apply in the case of a pond: where the tree felling is part of an approved plan of operations under one of the Forestry Commission's grant schemes; where the trees are growing in a garden, orchard, churchyard or public open space; where the trees are all below 8 cm in diameter, measured 1.3 m from the ground, or in the case of thinnings below 10 cm diameter, or in the case of coppice or underwood, below 15 cm diameter; where the trees are dead, dangerous, causing a nuisance or are badly affected by Dutch elm disease.

Where the trees are growing on a Site of Special Scientific Interest, in a Conservation Area or are subject to a Tree Preservation Order, special considerations apply. In the former case the Nature Conservancy Council must be notified and in the latter instances the appropriate District Council must be consulted prior to any work being carried out.

# Chapter 9

# Pond Conservation and the Future

Growing community awareness of conservation issues in recent years has resulted in a surge of constructive action to manage the countryside. This has been particularly noticeable in the agricultural sector, where increasing concern over the impact of modern farming practices on the environment has given rise to much positive and practical effort by farmers on behalf of wildlife and the landscape. Outside the farming industry, major countryside organisations such as the Royal Society for the Protection of Birds report increasing numbers of members, reflecting the mounting interest amongst the population as a whole over environmental topics.

In the light of these changing attitudes towards the countryside, it is a great pity that pond creation and management is not always given the attention and encouragement that is so vital. The demise of the country's ponds has never been highlighted in the way that hedgerow losses were avidly reported in the media over a considerable period of time. Notwithstanding, some progress is being made. Farmers and members of the public are slowly becoming aware of the problems and are taking more advice about freshwater conservation in general. Given time and support, remedial action may start to turn the tide in favour of ponds, so that this fascinating and unique part of the nation's heritage can be safeguarded.

The Farming and Wildlife Advisory Group (FWAG), which has full time advisers in most parts of the United Kingdom, reports rising numbers of requests for assistance from farmers who want to create or rejuvenate ponds. In the 12 months preceding March 1985, some 500 visits were made to farms to advise on ponds. During the following year, 1,161 visits were carried out on the same subject although it must be noted that more advisers were present on the ground. During the 12 months up to March 1988, 924 visits by FWAG advisers to farmers in England and Wales specifically related to ponds, and 88 visits regarding ponds took place in Scotland. While there are no figures to demonstrate whether the advice given was acted upon or, in the event that it was, the end results achieved the desired effect, the statistics are quite encouraging.

Staff at the Royal Society for the Protection of Birds and the County

Wildlife Trusts are often asked for advice by farmers and members of the public—in the latter case, mainly with regard to garden ponds. In conjunction with this, the spate of books written about wildlife gardening together with environmental features in the media have generated further interest. As a result of all these varied sources of information, the success of the common frog in establishing strongholds around urban areas provides good evidence of the enthusiasm with which town and city dwellers have responded to the need to make and manage ponds.

Advice is not the only resource which is needed by potential pond creators and managers. Money for pond conservation is in short supply. In England and Wales, the Countryside Commission provides grant aid via the County Councils to help cover the costs of countryside conservation. Similar assistance is available in Scotland from the Countryside Commission for Scotland. These grants are targeted at landscape conservation and the type of work which is typically assisted includes tree and hedgerow planting to enhance the countryside. Pond conservation has never been considered to have the same level of visual impact as trees and hedgerows. As a result of this, unless a pond is clearly visible from surrounding higher ground or it lies adjacent to a road or public right of way, it is not regarded as making a significant contribution to the landscape from the point of view of eligibility for grant. In lowland areas, many ponds are not easily visible except at close quarters, and those that are adjacent to well used rights of way suffer from disturbance which adversely affects wildlife. In the latter case, management (with grant aid) is of course still well worthwhile, but it is regrettable that the availability of grant aid is limited to those few ponds with deemed landscape or community value.

The Nature Conservancy Council (in Northern Ireland, the Department of the Environment, NI) can provide grant aid for ponds, normally for a specific project to improve the management of a site with importance to nature conservation. Set against a background of limited funds, these grants are not automatically awarded for pond conservation. Unless it can be shown that the proposed management work will offer some positive benefit to wildlife over and above general habitat improvement, a project might not be eligible for support. Nevertheless, these grants are valuable, helping to safeguard the best sites.

Some hope for the future may be provided by the Environmentally Sensitive Areas Scheme launched by the Ministry of Agriculture, Fisheries and Food. By the beginning of 1989 there were 18 designated ESAs around the United Kingdom, covering areas such as the Norfolk Broads, Suffolk River Valleys, Somerset Levels and Moors, Shropshire Borders, Pennine Dales, Lleyn Peninsula, Loch Lomond and Mourne and Slieve Cobb in Northern Ireland. An Environmentally Sensitive Area is one where traditional farming methods have played an important role in the development of an exceptionally attractive landscape which provides plenty of valuable habitats for wildlife. Farmers can voluntarily enter into management agreements with MAFF (or the appropriate departments in Wales, Scotland and Northern Ireland) whereby they agree to adopt or maintain practices which will help to conserve and sustain the area. In return, the farmer receives a grant or an annual payment relating to eligible land or projects on land within the scheme.

The practices which must be adopted vary from one ESA to another, depending on the characteristics and traditions of each locality; but where ponds are features occurring within an ESA they may be highlighted in the obligatory farm management plans. For instance, in the Stewartry ESA in Scotland, ponds occurring on eligible land would have to be fenced to exclude livestock and prevent damage to pond banks and vegetation. This work would automatically attract grant aid. In England, the system of payments to farmers in ESAs is based upon an annual sum in return for farming according to agreed methods. In this case, while ponds may be present on the land, detailed management prescriptions are not compulsory but maintenance must be carried out, for instance to keep overhanging trees or scrub cut back around the pond. The payment to the farmer is not itemised to include an element specifically for pond management, but there should be sufficient money available within the financial incentives to encourage some positive action on ponds and other features of value to wildlife conservation.

By its nature, the Environmentally Sensitive Areas Scheme protects some of the best farmed landscapes in the country. However, with some 80 per cent of land subject to agricultural use, the great majority of ponds which require management lie in areas which are currently subject to no special designations. Unless the ESAs are extended, this will probably remain the case. Farmers who own and occupy 'ordinary' land are already suffering from falling incomes and calls to reduce production. The effect of this will be to force cutbacks in non-essential expenditure and, to many farmers, this non-essential work will include conservation. Basic maintenance of hedges, woodlands, grassland and to some extent ponds and their environs will probably continue as before, using existing labour and resources; but major capital works such as pond desilting or even creation will be hit. If it was made easier for farmers in this position to claim grant aid for major 'pondworks', for instance under the Countryside Commission scheme, this would certainly help to encourage better pond management. However, it can still be argued that, if grant aid is offered at the rate of 40 per cent towards one (relatively modest) desilting operation costing £1,000, the same amount of grant might suffice to cover four amenity tree planting schemes, with greater landscape benefit. While this is certainly a valid point in a country which has lost many millions of trees as a result of

Dutch elm disease and the hurricane of October 1987, the matter should not simply be allowed to rest there. In the absence of some improvement in the availability of grant aid for pond conservation, there seems to be little chance that many of the ponds which are now neglected and declining in value on farms around the country can be properly rejuvenated. The losses to wildlife will be severe. It must surely be in the public interest to promote the management of these historic features for the benefit of the community as a whole.

Further hope for ponds may come with the need to reduce production of cereal crops within the European Economic Community and the introduction of 'set-aside'. Under this scheme, which was introduced in 1988, farmers can voluntarily elect to take a proportion of their cropped land out of production for five years and receive annual payments in lieu. Currently a minimum of 20 per cent of the land growing crops such as wheat, barley, oats, sugar beet and oilseed rape is eligible for the scheme.

While set-aside is designed to help reduce agricultural surpluses, there should be environmental benefits. Some of the land removed from production is being planted with trees to create large new blocks of woodland, while other areas will either be sown to grass or allowed to lie fallow. This

*Plate 9.1    An isolated field pond formerly used to provide water for livestock. Will the introduction of 'set-aside' for agricultural land encourage the restoration of this feature?*

land, which will not be subjected to chemical treatments, will provide new habitats for wildlife and, where ponds are present, extensive buffer zones will automatically be created. Under the rules of the scheme, ponds, ditches or wetland features which lie within the area of land which is set-aside (or are adjacent to it) must be maintained, for instance by cutting back overhanging vegetation, removing debris and keeping outfalls open. Isolated ponds located in the centre of fields could be linked to other features if landowners opt for set-aside on the relevant land, which will encourage better species dispersal around farmland habitats.

One result of set-aside should be that the overall area of land available to wildlife will inevitably increase, with benefits to most of the species which are dependent on ponds, plus many others such as the barn owl. There may also be a negative side. If farmers who opt for set-aside reduce their labour and sell machinery, there will inevitably be fewer resources available to manage farmland ponds.

Both the Environmentally Sensitive Areas Scheme and set-aside offer payments to farmers either in lieu of intensive land management or as incentives to reduce production. These payments are essential not only to protect income but also, as already described, to provide some inducement to conserve valuable habitats or landscapes. Many traditional features of the countryside can be adequately sustained in this way as part of routine management, for instance hedge trimming or meadow cutting. Ponds are different; where they are no longer in use, routine management ceases and so additional effort and capital needs to be expended in restoration and subsequent maintenance.

A scheme which could have the potential to help ponds, if the Government is willing, is the European Commission's draft Directive entitled 'Proposal for a Council Directive on the Protection of Natural and Semi-Natural Habitats and of Wild Flora and Fauna'. The Fauna, Flora and Habitats Directive would, if accepted by the Member States, be used to confer special protection on areas of great wildlife interest and landscape features of significance to wildlife. These may, in some cases, include hedgerows or ponds where these are deemed to be specially important. Of course, protection in the form of Sites of Special Scientific Interest or Nature Reserves is already in existence for extremely valuable features. The new Directive could enable other important features which are not of SSSI status to receive some level of protection, if not from neglect then at least from undesirable development or destruction.

Many ponds lie in areas of the country which are not specially designated or protected. These areas form the backbone of the wider countryside which supports the infrastructure of habitats and landscape features on which wildlife depends for its survival. Any opportunity to safeguard some of the ponds in these areas needs careful examination. Finance would undoubtedly be needed to ensure that adequate levels of management are undertaken. Landowners should not be expected automatically to pay for habitat improvement and maintenance over and above that which might reasonably be practised, on account of special protection being conferred on any site. If this enterprising new European Directive can be taken further than the proposal stage, it may present a means whereby valuable, unique and threatened features can be safeguarded for the future.

The changing face of agriculture is heralding new ideas in countryside management and it would be marvellous if ponds could now receive the attention which they richly deserve through both direct and indirect support. But it is not only protection, advice and financial assistance which is needed. Many of the techniques of pond creation and maintenance are not familiar to farmers. Over the past few years, tree and hedge planting on farms have become more commonplace. Training has been available in establishment and aftercare methods, so that the majority of farmers and their employees are now well able to undertake this kind of work. If increasing emphasis is to be given to pond conservation, training in the appropriate skills will be fundamental so that the work which is necessary can be carried out effectively. With this in mind, the Agricultural Training Board has recently devised courses on pond creation and management which are generally available to farmers throughout the country. Insofar as pond utilisation is concerned, farmers also have access to courses such as those in fish husbandry offered by Sparsholt College in Hampshire. One day courses on crayfish farming, establishing fisheries and many other aspects of freshwater management are now on offer to help farmers make better use of their resources in these changing times.

It is not only the ponds on land owned and occupied by farmers which require management. Large areas of land are owned by institutions or other organisations and it is imperative that management for conservation (including the restoration or creation of ponds) becomes accepted as standard practice. As an example, the Forestry Commission, which is responsible for large tracts of land across the country, has acknowledged that pond and wetland management is an important factor contributing to diversity in the forest. The Forestry Commission has undertaken many significant pond projects in the past and part of its policy is to ensure that, wherever possible, simple techniques such as deepening wet hollows to form viable ponds become integral parts of its forest planting and management programmes.

Many village ponds require maintenance or restoration and in these cases groups such as the British Trust for Conservation Volunteers can play a major role. As already described, vegetation management carried out manually can be very effective, albeit time consuming and expensive. The BTCV is able to organise work parties of volunteers which, under the

*Plate 9.2    Essex farmers attending a training course on pond management.*

*Plate 9.3    The attractively managed village pond at Old Buckenham, Norfolk.*

leadership of skilled supervisors, are well able to undertake many tasks which would otherwise never be done and which are of great benefit to the countryside. Regrettably, as with any voluntary group, resources tend to be limited and there is often more work to be done than people to do it; but if help can be obtained from the BTCV it is well worth having. The benefits of this type of voluntary approach to pond management can be clearly seen in the achievements of the Nutfield and Merstham Pond Restoration Group from Surrey. This group has very successfully attracted support from both individuals and industry, to restore the Marsh Pond on Nutfield Marsh, in the process winning a 'Best of Better Britain Award' from the Shell Better Britain campaign in 1989.

To supplement the advice, training and assistance which is on offer to pond owners, further information must be forthcoming and made available in usable form to the people who need it most—the land managers. Research carried out in recent years has enabled farmers to take great steps forward in conserving wildlife on their land. The Game Conservancy Trust's Cereals and Gamebirds Project has been of immense importance in developing techniques for the management of field margins, while the same organisation's work on gravel pit restoration for wildfowl has already been described.

There is plenty of scope for further research on pond management and as well as the Game Conservancy Trust, other agencies are active in this respect. The Suffolk Farming and Wildlife Advisory Group is producing material as a result of studying 150 Suffolk ponds to look at problems caused by algae and leaf deposition into water. Pond Action, based at Oxford Polytechnic, is co-ordinating research and gathering data on a national basis, to help provide information for use in classifying and managing ponds. To progress one stage further, the establishment of a Freshwater Conservation Society would be a tremendous step forward in the future. This would help to expand the level of knowledge of freshwater habitats as a whole and create a better awareness of the need for pond and wetland conservation, not only in rural areas but also in villages, towns and cities.

There is no doubt that old established ponds are, if adequately managed, of more significance to wildlife than new ponds; but today, the opportunity to create a new pond is open to almost everyone, not just farmers and country landowners. The general availability of flexible pond liners, coupled with the fact that even a pond of 3–4 m$^2$ can support several forms of pondlife, means that freshwater habitat creation and conservation is now within the grasp of most garden owners. The potential which exists for pond creation and management in urban areas is vast and garden owners should not be deterred by thinking that the making and management of small ponds is difficult. It is not. By following the guidelines set out in

*Plate 9.4    A new pond created on industrial waste ground in London.*

the preceding chapters, creation can be carried out step by step and if the pond is maintained properly, it should give many years of pleasure plus the knowledge that something really worthwhile has been done for wildlife.

Notwithstanding the opportunities which exist for the creation of new ponds in both urban and rural areas, the greatest threats to those old ponds which survive on agricultural land are neglect and eutrophication. Neglect can only be overcome by more positive management. The changing attitudes of farmers towards conservation in recent years will unquestionably help, as will good advice and, wherever possible, easily accessible financial assistance. Co-ordinated survey work over the whole country similar to that carried out in Hertfordshire during the preparation of the Hertfordshire Pond Report would be of great value. If the best examples of ponds can be identified, area by area, the owners can be encouraged to manage them properly with financial assistance allocated to the most deserving cases.

If every farmer who has ponds on his land could be persuaded to manage one for nature conservation, taking the appropriate advice and receiving the necessary training, this would represent a significant boost for wildlife. Many farmers are already doing this, but there is still a great deal of room for improvement in the level of pond management on the country's farms. 'Adopt-a-pond' schemes might be one way to increase this level of management without imposing additional burdens on overstretched farm businesses. Links between schools and farms are well established in most parts of the country and if groups of children or students could be encouraged to adopt ponds and carry out simple monitoring of wildlife and basic maintenance tasks, this too would help to reduce the neglect.

This type of scheme need not be restricted to schools and colleges. Individuals or voluntary groups such as Watch, the junior arm of the Royal Society for Nature Conservation, could also participate. If the response to the scheme was high enough, involvement could be one key towards securing grant aid for major restoration projects. Organisations such as the National Farmers' Union and Country Landowners' Association are well placed to promote such initiatives to encourage the better management of rural resources. Watch is also involved in Pondwatch, a national campaign aimed at promoting the conservation of ponds and run jointly with the Wildfowl and Wetlands Trust (based at Slimbridge) and the Shell Better Britain campaign.

Improved utilisation of farm ponds will also help to stave off neglect. Even if ponds managed with a commercial motive are less attractive to wildlife, utilisation will keep the ponds as ponds, holding natural

*Plate 9.5   A pearl in the landscape. This newly restored farm pond is on the edge of woodland in Clwyd.*

succession or deliberate infilling at bay, as well as making a contribution to the rural economy.

Eutrophication is a harder problem to solve. The way in which agricultural land is managed on a day to day basis influences the amount of applied chemicals which reach water, but a lot of the nitrate which finds its way into ponds and watercourses is produced naturally and further research is required into ways of reducing or utilising this. In association with research on nitrate leaching into water, the role which buffer zones can play must be more fully explored. Pollution of water is a major national problem—effluent from agriculture and industry must be prevented from reaching ponds, ditches, streams and rivers. The Farm and Conservation Grant Scheme introduced by the Ministry of Agriculture, Fisheries and Food in February 1989 should go some way towards improving the situation, but still better controls are needed to prevent unnecessary and destructive incidents. It is a pity that this new Grant scheme, with its emphasis on conservation—providing grants for, amongst other things, effluent and waste handling, enclosure of grazed woodland and the repair or re-instatement of traditional buildings—could not have also included some provision for the restoration of farm ponds.

At the end of the day, however, the drastic decline in the number of old ponds throughout the country, and the lack of maintenance which afflicts the surviving examples, cannot be allowed to continue. These small but traditional features of the countryside are exciting and important wildlife habitats requiring careful management; at the same time they are extremely vulnerable to neglect or sudden change, either of which can be catastrophic. These pearls in the landscape are a legacy from the past and they must be sustained for future generations. There is no great mystery surrounding pond management. Those people who have successfully created or looked after a pond will testify to the pleasure they have derived, because if one thing is certain in the changing countryside, if conservation is fun, making and managing ponds is super fun!

*Appendix 1*

# Sources of Grant Aid

The following information is a brief summary of the grants which may be available to farmers and other individuals or groups, to help cover the costs of pond creation or management. As exact scheme details vary from time to time, advice should be taken from the relevant agency when planning a project which may be eligible for grant.

### COUNTRYSIDE COMMISSION

**Landscape Conservation**

Discretionary grants of up to 50 per cent may be available for the restoration or creation of ponds where the site is accessible to the general public or is visible from a road or public right of way. Eligible costs include digging out and removing spoil from a pond. The maximum level of grant aid is £500 per pond. Tree or shrub planting as part of a pond creation or restoration project may also be eligible.

Prior approval of plans is required before any work is undertaken. Application forms and explanatory leaflets can be obtained from local County Councils, usually via the planning department, or from the Countryside Commission (see Appendix 6).

**Recreation**

The provision or improvement of facilities for informal recreation, especially walking or picnicking, may qualify for grant. The development of areas of water for use by the public could be included as an eligible recreational project. Provision of interpretive materials also qualifies for grant.

Prior approval of plans is necessary before any work is undertaken. Application forms and explanatory leaflets can be obtained from the Regional office of the Countryside Commission (see Appendix 6).

## NATURE CONSERVANCY COUNCIL

Three types of discretionary grant are available:

### Small Grants

These are made to private individuals for small conservation projects and are designed to cover the cost of items of equipment costing between £200 and £1,000. These grants enable voluntary bodies, other organisations and private individuals to receive funding for small conservation projects.

Grants (normally up to 50 per cent of acceptable costs) are given to:

- Improve the management of sites of importance to nature conservation.
- Purchase equipment to carry out nature conservation.
- Promote practical species conservation.
- Increase awareness and understanding of nature conservation.
- Other new projects promoting practical nature conservation.

Prior approval is required before any work is undertaken. Application forms and explanatory leaflets can be obtained from regional offices of the Nature Conservancy Council (see Appendix 6).

### Project Grants

These are for practical projects of value to nature conservation and which cost in excess of £1,000. Preference is given to projects carried out in areas of nature conservation importance such as nature reserves, although work on other sites is also eligible. Qualifying activities include the purchase or hire of equipment; management such as fencing or water level control; and the creation of scrape ponds.

Prior approval is required before any work is undertaken. Application forms and explanatory leaflets can be obtained from regional offices of the Nature Conservancy Council (see Appendix 6).

### School Grants

These are designed to help school groups start nature conservation area projects. Prior approval is required before any work is undertaken. Application forms and explanatory leaflets can be obtained from regional offices of the Nature Conservancy Council (see Appendix 6).

## MINISTRY OF AGRICULTURE, FISHERIES AND FOOD

### Farm Diversification Scheme

This is intended to offer assistance to farmers who are seeking to diversify into non-agricultural, profit making activities on the farm. Grants are available towards enterprise feasibility studies, capital costs and initial marketing costs.

*Enterprise feasibility studies*
Grants of 50 per cent of the cost of a feasibility study are available, up to £3,000 maximum for individuals and £10,000 for groups. The feasibility study must be specific and relate to an eligible business activity.

*Capital costs*
Capital grants at a rate of 25 per cent are available on investments up to a maximum of £35,000, for projects which will produce a viable new business or improve the profit potential of the total business. Young farmers who satisfy certain criteria may qualify for additional grants.

Eligible works include the provision of facilities for sport, recreation and education. Ponds for angling are included in this category, as are nature trails or similar activities.

*Initial marketing costs*
Grant will be paid on marketing costs relating to an eligible farm business activity. A three year marketing plan is required. The rate of grant is 40 per cent in year 1, decreasing to 30 per cent in year 2 and 20 per cent in year 3. Applications will not be accepted where they will result in grant payments of less than £250 per year.

There are strict rules for all three grants which must be satisfied, relating to the eligibility of individual farmers. In all cases, prior approval is required before any work is undertaken. Further information and application forms can be obtained from local offices of the Agricultural Development and Advisory Service or appropriate departments in Wales, Scotland and Northern Ireland (see Appendix 6).

## SHELL BETTER BRITAIN CAMPAIGN

This campaign aims to support practical action by voluntary groups working to improve their local environment. Any group can apply providing the project is a practical environmental or conservation project that benefits the wider community. The work for which grant is requested must be carried out by volunteers and not paid workers.

Grants of up to £500 may be made, but are not intended to cover the whole cost of the project. Prior approval is needed before work commences. Application forms and further information can be obtained from the Shell Better Britain Campaign—see Appendix 6.

*Appendix 2*

# Species to Plant In and Around Ponds

PLANT SPECIES

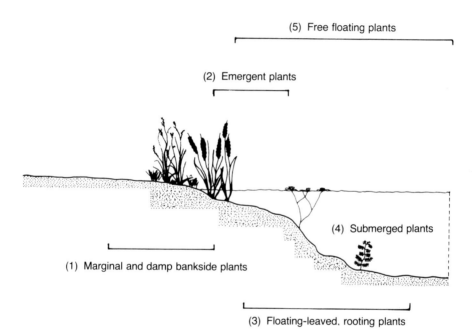

(5) Free floating plants

(2) Emergent plants

(4) Submerged plants

(1) Marginal and damp bankside plants

(3) Floating-leaved, rooting plants

The following lists are not exhaustive. Names of common species are provided together with indications of the type of water in which they flourish, notes on their value to wildfowl and management. Plants are divided into groups according to the parts of the pond or its environs where they are most likely to occur.

## (1) Marginal and Damp Bankside Plants

| PLANT NAME | SCIENTIFIC NAME | NUTRIENT STATUS OF WATER<br>O = oligotrophic (poor)<br>M = mesotrophic (moderate)<br>E = eutrophic (rich) | DISTRIBUTION<br>E = England<br>W = Wales<br>S = Scotland<br>NI = Northern Ireland | WILDFOWL VALUE | NOTES |
|---|---|---|---|---|---|
| Marsh marigold | Caltha palustris | O – E | E, W, S, NI | | Very common, early flowering species. Attractive yellow flowers will enhance any pond or marshland area. |
| Marsh cinquefoil | Potentilla palustris | O – M | E, W, S | | Purple flowering marshland plant less common in southern areas. |
| Bogbean | Menyanthes trifoliata | O | E, W, S, NI | | Attractive foliage and flowers. Can form dense mats covering the water surface. Less common in East Anglia, parts of the Midlands and South West England. Suitable for garden ponds. |
| Water forget-me-not | Myosotis scorpioides | O – E | E, W, S, NI | | Pretty, shade tolerant plant, with small flowers varying between blue, pink and white. Grows in dense clumps. Good for garden ponds. |

| PLANT NAME | SCIENTIFIC NAME | NUTRIENT STATUS OF WATER | DISTRIBUTION | WILDFOWL VALUE | NOTES |
|---|---|---|---|---|---|
| Water mint | Mentha aquatica | M – E | E, W, S, NI | | Very common, found around the edge of ponds. One of the species which helps to improve water quality. Suitable for garden ponds. |
| Soft rush | Juncus effusus | O – E | E, W, S, NI | Good nesting cover. | Useful species around the banks of the pond. On large sites it can be planted to help prevent erosion. One of the species which helps to improve water quality. |
| Meadowsweet | Filipendula ulmaria | — | E, W, S, NI | | A tall plant of damp areas. Has dense clusters of creamy flowers which are attractive to insects. |
| Purple loosestrife | Lythrum salicaria | — | E, W, S, NI | | Tall, very attractive plant with purple flowers. Grows individually or in small groups. |
| Ragged robin | Lychnis flos-cuculi | — | E, W, S, NI | | Typical wetland species with bright pink flowers. |
| Creeping jenny | Lysimachia nummularia | — | E, W, S, NI | | Creeping plant with yellow flowers forming good ground cover. Useful round the edge of ponds to disguise liners. |
| Yellow flag iris | Iris pseudacorus | O – E | E, W, S, NI | Provides cover for invertebrates. | Very common, attractive species. Spreads rapidly. Will need careful management in garden ponds. Of value to amphibians. |
| Common spike rush | Eleocharis palustris | M | E, W, S, NI | Very good. Teal like the seeds. Excellent cover for invertebrates and good shelter. | Can dominate the banks of a pond. |

| PLANT NAME | SCIENTIFIC NAME | NUTRIENT STATUS OF WATER | DISTRIBUTION | WILDFOWL VALUE | NOTES |
|---|---|---|---|---|---|
| Common sedge | Carex nigra | O – E | E, W, S, NI | Very good. Seeds and associated invertebrates are taken as food. Nesting cover. | Sedges are commonly found round the margins of ponds. Apart from C. nigra, many other species occur in localised areas and offer similar benefits to wildlife. |
| Creeping buttercup | Ranunculus repens | — | E, W, S, NI | Useful. | Typical bankside species. Provides good cover for amphibians. |
| Greater willowherb | Epilobium hirsutum | — | E, W, S, NI | Useful cover plant for nesting areas. | Common in damp locations. Great crested newts lay eggs in dead leaves. |
| Redshank | Polygonum persicaria | — | E, W, S, NI | Seeds are valuable as food. | Colonises disturbed ground around new or restored ponds. |

## (2) Emergent Plants

| PLANT NAME | SCIENTIFIC NAME | NUTRIENT STATUS OF WATER | DISTRIBUTION | WILDFOWL VALUE | NOTES |
|---|---|---|---|---|---|
| Water horsetail | Equisetum fluviatile | O – E | E, W, S, NI | Good. Provides cover for invertebrates and also shelters duck. | Very invasive. Will take over shallow areas which are less than 150 mm deep. Requires regular control. |
| Amphibious bistort | Polygonum amphibium | M – E | E, W, S, NI | Excellent source of food. | Showy pink flowers and shiny green leaves make this plant more attractive than its relative, redshank. |
| Water plantain | Alisma plantago-aquatica | M – E | E, W, S, NI | | Grows singly or in clumps. Large broad leaves with flower stems rising clear of the remainder of the plant. Attracts blackfly. One of the species which helps to improve water quality. |

| PLANT NAME | SCIENTIFIC NAME | NUTRIENT STATUS OF WATER | DISTRIBUTION | WILDFOWL VALUE | NOTES |
|---|---|---|---|---|---|
| Flowering rush | Butomus umbellatus | M – E | E, W | | Common in southern areas. A spectacular plant growing singly with a tall stem and very attractive pink flower heads. An ideal species for a garden pond. |
| Arrowhead | Sagittaria sagittifolia | M – E | E | Excellent cover for invertebrates and ducklings. Leaves are also eaten. | Very characteristic arrow shaped leaves with spikes of flowers growing up out of the water. Can be used in garden ponds. |
| Reed grass or reed sweet-grass | Glyceria maxima | E | E, W, S, NI | | Very invasive, growing in dense stands in up to 700 mm of water. Must be controlled or it will dominate a pond. |
| Reed canary grass | Phalaris arundinacea | M – E | E, W, S, NI | | Only grows in very shallow water so rarely encroaches into ponds, preferring the marginal areas. Occurs in small clumps or as a fringe to the pond. |
| Brooklime | Veronica beccabunga | M – E | E, W, S, NI | | Small plant occurring singly or in clumps. Very pretty blue or pink flowers. Not invasive, good for garden ponds. |
| Branched bur-reed | Sparganium erectum | M – E | E, W, S, NI | Good food plant and provides cover for invertebrates. | Very invasive, common species. Needs careful management. |
| Greater reedmace or bulrush | Typha latifolia | M – E | E, W, S, NI | Useful food plant. | Very invasive but attractive species. Will grow in a wide range of water depths. Often dominates the fringes of the pond. Needs careful management. Of value to amphibians, dragonflies and damselflies. |

| PLANT NAME | SCIENTIFIC NAME | NUTRIENT STATUS OF WATER | DISTRIBUTION | WILDFOWL VALUE | NOTES |
|---|---|---|---|---|---|
| Common clubrush | Scirpus lacustris (schoenoplectus) | O – E | E, W, S (lowlands) | Useful. | Tall plant growing in up to 500 mm of water. Less common in Southwest. |
| Common or Norfolk reed | Phragmites communis | O – E | E, W, S, NI | Provides good cover for invertebrates and wildfowl. | Typical species of reed swamp. Very invasive and will spread across shallow as well as deep water. Excellent habitat for birds where dense stands occur. Has a role to play in water quality control. |

## (3) Floating-Leaved, Rooting Plants

| PLANT NAME | SCIENTIFIC NAME | NUTRIENT STATUS OF WATER | DISTRIBUTION | WILDFOWL VALUE | NOTES |
|---|---|---|---|---|---|
| White water lily | Nymphaea alba | M – E | E, W, S | | Invasive over a period of many years. Large leaves and attractive white flowers. Less common in North-east England. Can be a problem for fishery managers. Grow in a container in a garden pond. |
| Yellow water lily | Nuphar lutea | M – E | E, W, S, NI | | Very common, more so than white water lily. Also more invasive, especially in shallow water. Can be a problem for fishery managers. |
| Broadleaved pond weed | Potamogeton natans | O – E | E, W, S, NI | Good cover for invertebrates. Seeds are eaten. | Very aggressive species. Should be introduced only to ponds over 2 m deep. Causes problems for fishery managers. |

## (4) Submerged Plants

| PLANT NAME | SCIENTIFIC NAME | NUTRIENT STATUS OF WATER | DISTRIBUTION | WILDFOWL VALUE | NOTES |
| --- | --- | --- | --- | --- | --- |
| Common water crowfoot | Ranunculus aquatilis | M – E | E, W, S, NI | Very good. Provides cover for invertebrates. Seeds are a valuable source of food and leaves are sometimes eaten. | Attractive plant. Buttercup type flowers appear in early summer with long trailing stems across surface of water. Can cause problems for fishery managers. Of value to palmate and common newts. |
| Spiked water milfoil | Myriophyllum spicatum | O – E | E, W (not common) S, NI | Excellent cover for invertebrates. | Grows profusely in nutrient rich ponds. Good in garden ponds. |
| Starwort | Callitriche spp. | O – E | E, W, S, NI | Good cover for invertebrates. | Very delicate plants with both submerged and floating leaves. Tiny yellow flowers appear throughout the summer. Good oxygenator. Can be a problem for fishery managers. |
| Mare's tail | Hippuris vulgaris | M – E | E, W (rare) S, NI | Good cover for invertebrates. Seeds are eaten and cover is provided for ducklings. | Underwater stems can grow up to 1.5 m long with the emergent part of the plant rising 300 mm above the water surface. Will grow in quite deep water and can be a problem for fishery managers. |
| Canadian pondweed | Elodea canadensis | M – E | E, W, S, NI | Good cover for invertebrates. | Not a 'native' plant but is now common in ponds. Grows at a wide range of depths and is a good oxygenator. Very invasive and can easily take over a pond if allowed to grow unchecked. |

| PLANT NAME | SCIENTIFIC NAME | NUTRIENT STATUS OF WATER | DISTRIBUTION | WILDFOWL VALUE | NOTES |
|---|---|---|---|---|---|
| Small pondweed | Potamogeton berchtoldii | M – E | E, W, S, NI | | Grows in up to 1 m of water. |
| Fennel leaved pondweed | Potamogeton pectinatus | E | E, W, S, NI | Good cover for invertebrates. | Will grow in heavily polluted or turbid water. Can cause problems for fishery managers. |
| Curled pondweed | Potamogeton crispus | M – E | E, S, NI | | Not as aggressive as some of the other pondweeds. Less common in South-west and Wales. Can cause problems for fishery managers. |
| Stoneworts | Chara spp. | O – E | E, W, S | Good cover for invertebrates. Eaten by pochard. | These are algae and are fast growing early colonisers of new or restored ponds. Good oxygenators. |
| Rigid hornwort | Ceratophyllum demersum | M – E | E | Useful cover for invertebrates. | Most common in South-east. Grows very rapidly and requires regular management. Can cause problems for fishery managers. Can be used in garden ponds. |

## (5) Free Floating Plants

| PLANT NAME | SCIENTIFIC NAME | NUTRIENT STATUS OF WATER | DISTRIBUTION | WILDFOWL VALUE | NOTES |
|---|---|---|---|---|---|
| Algae | | O – E | E, W, S, NI | | Inevitably occur in ponds – no need to introduce these! See Chapter 6, Pond Management. |
| Water fern | Azolla filiculoides | M – E | E (South), elsewhere as an escapee from garden ponds | | Forms very dense surface cover and requires regular control. Attractive plant with vivid red colouring in autumn. |

| PLANT NAME | SCIENTIFIC NAME | NUTRIENT STATUS OF WATER | DISTRIBUTION | WILDFOWL VALUE | NOTES |
| --- | --- | --- | --- | --- | --- |
| Frogbit | Hydrocharis morsus-ranae | E | E (South-east) | | Small, lily-like leaves and foul smelling white flowers. Attractive, visual plant in a small pond. Can form large mats of vegetation requiring management. Most common in South-east. Of value to palmate and common newts. |
| Common duckweed | Lemna minor | M – E | E, W, S, NI | Eaten by duck. | Can easily choke the surface of a pond without careful management. |

# TREES AND SHRUBS

The following list is not exhaustive. Names of common and especially attractive species are provided, together with indications of preferred site conditions, wildlife value and management notes.

| SPECIES | PREFERRED SOIL CONDITIONS | DISTRIBUTION | HEIGHT RANGE | WILDLIFE VALUE | NOTES |
| --- | --- | --- | --- | --- | --- |
| | 1 = wet<br>2 = light soils<br>3 = heavy soils<br>4 = acid conditions<br>5 = alkaline conditions | E = England<br>W = Wales<br>S = Scotland<br>NI = Northern Ireland | | | |
| Alder (alnus glutinosa) | 1, 5 | E, W, S, NI | 15–20 m | Good. 141 associated invertebrates. Siskins often feed on seeds. Mallard find this species attractive. | Very common, fast growing waterside species. Tolerant of cutting, it coppices well. |

| SPECIES | PREFERRED SOIL CONDITIONS | DISTRIBUTION | HEIGHT RANGE | WILDLIFE VALUE | NOTES |
|---|---|---|---|---|---|
| Crack willow (Salix fragilis) | 1 | E, W Occurs only as an introduction in North Scotland and Northern Ireland. | 20 m + | Willow spp. have over 250 associated invertebrates. | Tall, bankside tree. |
| Goat willow (Salix caprea) | 1 | E, W, S, NI | 3–10 m | Good. | Grows as a bushy shrub. Good, quick growing cover round ponds. |
| Common sallow or grey willow (Salix cinerea) | 1 | E, W, S, NI | 2–10 m | Good. | Grows as a bushy shrub. Good, quick growing cover round ponds. |
| Purple willow (Salix purpurea) | 1 | E, W, S, NI | 1–3 m | Good. | Much less widely distributed. Grows as low shrub cover. |
| Hawthorn (Crataegus monogyna) | 2, 3, 4, 5 | E, W, S, NI | 0.5–5 m | Excellent for wildlife. Over 200 associated invertebrates. Berries are taken by birds and small mammals. Teal eat seeds. | Common hedging species. Establishes quickly and provides good shelter. Coppices well. |
| Blackthorn (Prunus spinosa) | 2, 3, 4, 5 | E, W, S, NI | 0.5–5 m | Over 150 associated invertebrates. Good, dense nesting cover for small birds. | A very invasive species. This will quickly spread over unmanaged land. |
| Hazel (Corylus avellana) | 3, 5 | E, W, S, NI | 5–15 m | Over 100 associated invertebrates. | Quick growing traditional coppice species. Provides good shelter. |
| Dogwood (Cornus sanguinea) | 2, 3, 5 | E, W | 0.5–5 m | Birds feed on the seeds. | More common in the South of England. When cut regularly the stems have a very attractive red colour in autumn and winter. |

| SPECIES | PREFERRED SOIL CONDITIONS | DISTRIBUTION | HEIGHT RANGE | WILDLIFE VALUE | NOTES |
|---|---|---|---|---|---|
| Guelder rose (Viburnum opulus) | 1, 3, 5 | E, W, S, NI | 0.5–5 m | Good. | A very attractive shrub less widespread in Scotland and Northern Ireland. Pretty flowers in summer with distinctive foliage and large clusters of berries in autumn. |
| Dog rose (Rosa canina) | 2, 3 | E, W, S, NI | 0.5–5 m | Useful for birds. | Good species to plant in scrub areas. Tolerates wet but not waterlogging. |
| Field maple (Acer campestre) | 3, 5 | E, W | 5–15 m | Over 50 associated invertebrates. | Common in South and East England. Will sometimes grow into a tree. Attractive autumn colours. |
| Alder buckthorn (Frangula alnus) | 1, 5 | E, W, NI (extremely rare and now a protected species) | 5–15 m | Food plant of the larvae of brimstone butterfly. | Occurs locally in England and Wales. A useful addition to a 'conservation' planting scheme. |
| Purging buckthorn (Rhamnus catharticus) | 3, 5 | E, W, NI | 0.5–5 m | Food plant of the larvae of brimstone butterfly. | More common in England. |
| Bramble (Rubus fruticosus) | 1, 2, 3, 4, 5 | E, W, S, NI | 0.5–5 m | Excellent. Provides cover and food for wildfowl. Other birds also derive benefit. Good habitat for invertebrates, amphibians and mammals. | Very invasive. Useful in scrub areas around pond if properly managed. |
| Holly (Ilex aquifolium) | 2, 3, 4, 5 | E, W, S, NI | 5–15 m | 96 associated invertebrates. Attractive to birds. | Useful provider of evergreen cover and shelter. |

| SPECIES | PREFERRED SOIL CONDITIONS | DISTRIBUTION | HEIGHT RANGE | WILDLIFE VALUE | NOTES |
|---|---|---|---|---|---|
| Common oak (Quercus robur) | 3, 5 | E, W, S, NI | 20 m+ | The best species to plant for wildlife. 423 associated invertebrates. Plenty of nesting sites in older trees. Mallard eat acorns. | Oak should be used (on suitable soils) as a component of all tree planting schemes. It should never be planted within 20 m of the water's edge. |
| Wild cherry or gean (Prunus avium) | 3, 4 | E, W, S, NI | 20 m+ | Good. | Attractive species to plant individually or as part of a wood. Less common in Northern Ireland. Do not plant within 20 m of water. Secondary host to aphids, so care is needed when planning a scheme adjacent to arable land. |
| Ash (Fraxinus excelsior) | 1, 2, 3 | E, W, S, NI | 20 m+ | 68 associated invertebrates. | Should not be planted within 20 m of pond. Will grow in damp conditions and can tolerate seasonal waterlogging. |
| Silver birch (Betula pendula) | 2, 4 | E, W, S, NI (not widespread in NI) | 15 m+ | 334 associated invertebrate species. Mallard feed on seeds. | Quick growing attractive tree. |
| Downy birch (Betula pubescens) | 1, 4 | E, W, S, NI | 15 m+ | Excellent. | Attractive tree, better suited to wet conditions than silver birch. |
| Rowan or mountain ash (Sorbus aucuparia) | 2, 4 | E, W, S, NI | 5–15 m | 58 associated invertebrates. Birds find berries very palatable. | Attractive species. Not so common in South-east England. Useful addition to the edge of a tree planting scheme or use individually. |
| Crab apple (Malus sylvestris) | 2, 3, 5 | E, W, S (South), NI | 5–15 m | 116 associated invertebrate species. High value to birds. | Not easy to obtain true crab-apple. Attractive tree to include on edge of new planting or individually. |

# Appendix 3 Examples of Pond Assessment Forms

NORFOLK FWAG & TERRESTRIAL ECOLOGY RESEARCH FUND (Sponsored by Agriculture Division of Hoechst)

## POND SITE SURVEY

**Part 1.** This form sets out the important factors that should be considered on the farm as a first stage in assessing the wildlife potential of a pond. See overleaf for the next stage.

To be used in conjunction with booklet 'FARM POND MANAGEMENT' (produced by Norfolk FWAG/TERF 1987)

Farmer's Name:

Address:

Farm Address:
(if different)

| Pond name or field location: | Grid ref: | Total number of ponds on farm: | Date of survey: 1. 2. 3. 4. |
|---|---|---|---|
| Size of whole site (incl surrounds): | Adjacent land use: | Surrounding habitat: | O/H wires or other obstructions: |
| Depth of sediment: | Pollution: | Soil type and bottom sealing: | Seasonal variation in water levels: / Evidence of land drains: |

| Water source: | Area of water: | % Open water: | Depths of water: |
|---|---|---|---|

Aquatic plant species:

Identified:                     Unidentified:

Animal species (incl fish and birds):

Archaeological interest (origin of pond):

Use of pond (e.g. nature conservation, fishing):

Farmer's ideas for the site:

Present management adopted:

Profile of Pond:

Additional notes:

North   Plan of pond and surrounds

Recorder's Name:

See overleaf for Part 2

FWAG Farm Conservation Advisers can assist with site surveys, assessments and the preparation of management plans. Further copies of this form can be obtained from county Farming and Wildlife Advisory Groups.

203

## WILDLIFE POTENTIAL

### Part 2. This form provides a convenient method of assessing the wildlife potential of a pond having completed stage 1 overleaf

To be used in conjunction with booklet 'FARM POND MANAGEMENT' (produced by Norfolk FWAG/TERF 1987). Tick appropriate boxes

| FACTOR | HIGHER VALUE | ✓ | INTERMEDIATE | ✓ | LOWER VALUE | ✓ |
|---|---|---|---|---|---|---|
| **WATER QUALITY** (Check for plant/animal life) NB – Water quality may be masked by excessive shading. | 4 or more aquatic plants including both submerged and emergent species. Teeming with a variety of invertebrates/amphibians. | ☐ | Less than 4 aquatic plant species. A few invertebrates/amphibians. | ☐ | Little plant/animal life. Overgrown eg common reed, reed mace (*Typha latifolia*), willow. Leaf litter problem. | ☐ |
| **POLLUTION** | Few or no algae. Clear water, no discolouration. No dumped rubbish. | ☐ | Probably some algae. Slight discolouration of water. Slight leaf litter. | ☐ | Algae abundant. Severe discolouration of water. Possibly dumped rubbish. Leaf litter serious. | ☐ |
| **WATER LEVEL** | Reasonably stable. Little or no fluctuation. | ☐ | Fluctuation occurs but at least 0.3 to 0.6 metres (1 to 2 feet) at all times. | ☐ | Severe fluctuations. May dry out completely. | ☐ |
| **PROFILE AND DEPTH** | Gently shelving shore on at least one edge. Range of depths to 2 metres or more. | ☐ | Shelving edge but little range in depths. | ☐ | Steep bank all round. Shallow water severely silted up possibly with leaf litter. | ☐ |
| **LIGHT ACCESS TO WATER SURFACE** | Open to south but with some shaded areas. | ☐ | More shaded than open. | ☐ | Completely enclosed by surrounding or overhead growth. Little light access. | ☐ |
| **SURROUNDINGS AND LINKS** | Marginal vegetation with a range of native trees/shrubs but not causing too much shading over water nor producing undue leaf litter. Preferably linked with other habitat eg grassland, hedge, woodland edge. Buffered from spray, fertiliser, livestock, road run-off, rubbish and effluents. | ☐ | Marginal vegetation minimal. Linking with other habitats rather limited. Some buffering from sources of pollution. | ☐ | Trees/shrubs causing problem of light access and leaf litter or completely open eg mid-field arable with no protection from chemicals. Open to other sources of pollution. Few or no useful links with other habitats. | ☐ |
| **RARE SPECIES** | Presence of any rare plant/animal species. | ☐ | If rare species present consult the local Nature Conservation Trust or the Nature Conservancy Council who will advise on management provided the landowner agrees. | | | |

See overleaf for Part 1          RECORDER _____          DATE _____

**FWAG Farm Conservation Advisers can assist with site surveys, assessments and the preparation of management plans.**
**Further copies of this form can be obtained from county Farming and Wildlife Advisory Groups.**

204

## HERTFORDSHIRE POND SURVEY: 1986

| Site name | | Map No. | Grid ref. | Site no. |
|---|---|---|---|---|
| Owner | | Status | Photo frame no. | |
| Surveyor | | Date | | |

MANAGEMENT

| Unmanaged | | Fishing | | Stock watering | | Wildfowling | | General recreation | |
|---|---|---|---|---|---|---|---|---|---|
| Nature conservation | | Ornamental | | Other (specify): | | | | | |

INDICATORS, COMMENTS

## HABITAT DETAILS

**1. Origin**

| Spring-fed pool | | Drainage pond | | Dew pond | | Moat | |
|---|---|---|---|---|---|---|---|
| Natural flood-hollow | | Gravel pit | | Artificial dam | | Bog pool | |

Other (specify):

**2. Habitat features**

| Open water present | | % area: | | pH: | |
|---|---|---|---|---|---|
| Marginal marsh present | | Main species: | | Extent: | |
| Floating aquatics present | | Main species: | | | |

| Gravel bottom | | Clay bottom | | Silt bottom | | Depth | | Detritus bottom | | Depth |
|---|---|---|---|---|---|---|---|---|---|---|

| Other substrate: | | Estimated depth: | |
|---|---|---|---|

| Steep banks present | | % length: | | Concrete banks | | % length: | |
|---|---|---|---|---|---|---|---|
| Trampled margins | | % length: | | Wooden structures in/by water | | | |

**3. Neighbouring land-use**

| | Woodland | | Scrub | | Common land/village green | |
|---|---|---|---|---|---|---|
| Pasture | | Kind of stock present: | | Access open to pond:   Yes / No | | |
| Arable | | Separated from pond by barrier? (type): | | | | |
| Housing | | Road | | Other (specify): | | |

*Reproduced by kind permission of Hertfordshire County Council and North Hertfordshire Museums Natural History Department.

## PLANT COMMUNITIES & ZOOLOGICAL SAMPLE

| Weather conditions: | | Air temp. | |
|---|---|---|---|

| **AREAS SAMPLED** | Open water | Marginal veg. & mud | Emergent veg. & mud |
|---|---|---|---|

### HABITATS SAMPLED

| Bottom deposits | Silt | Gravel | Large stones | Plant detritus | Other |
|---|---|---|---|---|---|

| Vegetation | Marginal (type?) | | Emergent (type?) | |
|---|---|---|---|---|
| | Floating (type?) | | Submerged (type?) | |

| Other (state) | |
|---|---|

### INVERTEBRATE SAMPLE

| Group | Genus/species | Abundance | Group | Genus/species | Abundance |
|---|---|---|---|---|---|
| Sponges | Euspongilla | | Plecoptera | Nymphs/adults | |
| Platyhelminthes | | | Ephemeroptera | Nymphs/adults | |
| Oligochaeta | Tubifex | | Odonata (adults) | Aeshna grandis | |
| | Others | | | A. cyanea | |
| Hirudinea | All genera | | | Libelluia depressa | |
| Gastropod molluscs | Valvata spp. | | | Enallagma/Coenagrion | |
| | Potamopyrgus | | | Ischnura elegans | |
| | Bithynia spp. | | | Others | |
| | Physa spp. | | | | |
| | Lymnaea truncatula | | | Nymphs | |
| | L. Palustris | | Hemiptera | Notonecta spp. | |
| | L. stagnalis | | | Corixa etc. | |
| | L. Auricularia | | | Gerris spp. | |
| | L. peregra | | | Hydrometra | |
| | Planorbis (type) | | | Velia etc. | |
| | Planorbarius corneus | | | Nepa cinerea | |
| | Acroloxus lacustris | | | Ranatra linearis | |
| | Succinec/Oxyloma spp. | | | Ilyocoris | |
| | Deroceras laeve | | | Plea leachi | |
| Bivalve molluscs | Unio spp. | | Megaloptera | Sialis (ad./larvae) | |
| | Anodonta cygnea | | Trichoptera | All genera | |
| | A. Anatina | | Coleoptera | Dytiscus marginalis | |
| | Sphaerium spp. | | | Other dytiscids | |
| | Pisidium spp. | | | Dytiscid larvae | |
| Cladocera | | | | Hygrobia herrmanni | |
| Ostracoda | | | | Gyrinus spp. | |
| Copepoda | | | | Others | |
| Isopoda | Asellus | | | | |
| Amphipoda | Gammarus etc. | | Diptera | Culicid larvae | |
| Hydracharina | | | | Chironomid larvae | |
| Araneae | Argyroneta | | | Syrphid larvae | |

Other invertebrates of note:

## PLANT ABUNDANCE CODES: RARE (R); OCCASIONAL (O); FREQUENT (F); ABUNDANT (A)

### PLANT COMMUNITIES

(*: denotes reference specimen should be collected)

| Marginal species | | Emergent species | | Floating/submergent species | |
|---|---|---|---|---|---|
| Alisma spp. | | Apium nodiflorum | | Azolla filiculoides | |
| Bidens spp. | | *Ceratophyllum spp. | | Callitriche spp. | |
| Cardamine pratensis | | Hippuris vulgaris | | Elodea spp. | |
| Carex acutiformis | | *Myriophyllum spp. | | Lemna minor | |
| C. riparia | | Nasturtium spp. | | Lemna trisulca | |
| C. pendula | | Phragmites australis | | *Lemna gibba | |
| Carex (others) | | Potamogeton natans | | *Lemna polyrhiza | |
| *Catabrosa aquatica | | *Potamogeton (others) | | Nuphar lutea | |
| Eleocharis palustris | | Ranunculus spp. (crowfoots) | | Nymphaea alba | |
| Epilobium hirsutum | | Rorippa spp. | | Nymphoides peltata | |
| Epilobium (others) | | Stratiotes aloides | | *Utricularia spp. | |
| Filipendula ulmaria | | Typha latifolia | | Other species: | |
| Glyceria maxima | | Veronica beccabunga | | | |
| Glyceria (others) | | V. anagallis-aquatica | | | |
| Iris pseudacorus | | Veronica (others) | | | |
| Juncus inflexus | | *Zannichellia palustris | | | |
| J. articulatus | | Other species: | | | |
| J. effusus | | | | | |
| Juncus (non-det.) | | | | | |
| Lychnis flos-cuculi | | | | | |
| Mentha aquatica | | | | | |
| Myosotis spp. | | | | | |
| Phalaris arundinacea | | | | | |
| Ranunculus flammula | | | | | |
| Ranunculus sceleratus | | | | | |
| Scrophularia aquatica | | | | | |
| Sparganium erectum | | | | | |

### VERTEBRATE SPECIES NOTED

| Group | Species | Notes | Group | Species | Notes |
|---|---|---|---|---|---|
| Fish | Three-spined Stickleback | | Birds | Moorhen | |
| | Nine-spined Stickleback | | | Mallard | |
| | Roach | | | Dabchick | |
| | Perch | | | Reed Bunting | |
| | Carp spp. | | | Sedge Warbler | |
| | Tench | | | Other species: | |
| | Pike | | | | |
| | Others: | | | | |
| Amphibians | Smooth Newt | | Mammals | Water Vole | |
| | Crested Newt | | | Water Shrew | |
| | Common Frog | | | | |
| | Common Toad | | | | |
| Reptiles | Grass Snake | | | | |

### GENERAL COMMENTS:

207

| **4. Habitat condition** | Is the pond influenced by any of the following? | | | | | | |
|---|---|---|---|---|---|---|---|

| Isolated from other wetlands | | Within 400m of other wetlands | | Part of a linked series | |
|---|---|---|---|---|---|

| Evidently silted | | Affected by rubbish dumping | | Polluted | | Source: |
|---|---|---|---|---|---|---|

| Adverseley affected by neighbouring land use | | How? | | Deliberately infilled. Part / all |
|---|---|---|---|---|

| Water level acceptable for time of year/weather | | Evidently low | | Dried out (cause?) | |
|---|---|---|---|---|---|

| Invaded by scrub/carr | | Main species: |
|---|---|---|

| Overgrown by marsh (i.e. little/no open water) | | Species causing problem: |
|---|---|---|

| Damaged by excessive human use (e.g. over-trampled, over-fished) | | State activities noted: |
|---|---|---|

| Over-shaded by adjacent trees | | Species: | | Extent (%) |
|---|---|---|---|---|

| Seriously eutrophied (e.g. with algal bloom) | | State evidence: |
|---|---|---|

| Water clarity | Turbid | | Stained (e.g. peat) | | Average | | Very clear | |
|---|---|---|---|---|---|---|---|---|

## SITE LOCATION MAP(S)

Complete rough site plan and location map (Highlighting any important/unusual features)

# ASSESSMENT CARD

Site _____  Grid. ref. _____  Tetrad _____

BIOLOGICAL SITES ASSESSMENT CARD: OPEN WATERS          Hertfordshire

This assessment is intended for use with rivers, streams, lakes and ponds.

## A) Age or naturalness of the aquatic habitat.

1. Is the wetland known to be or likely to be a more or less natural feature of long-standing?

2. Even if the wetland has been constructed or modified severely by man, is it known or likely to have been in existence for at least 100 years?

3. Does the wetland have any special archaeological or historical importance or show evidence of early water management (e.g. a moat or a decoy)?

## B) Management history and stability of the site.

4. Does the wetland have a stable/reliable water supply?

5. Are there no signs that the wetland, including its banks or margins, has been seriously disturbed within about the last ten years?

6. Is the present management of the site in accordance with its traditional use? (e.g. fishing stock lake, cattle pond).

7. Is the present management of the site conducive to the survival of a characteristic wetland community?

## C) Stability of the wetland habitat.

8. Is the wetland large enough and/or stable enough for its character-istic communities to be relatively unaffected by neighbouring land use? (If yes, score: Ponds: 1 for ponds 200 sq. yds. - ½ acre; 2 for ponds ½-1 acre; 3 for ponds 1-3 acre; 4 for lakes over 1 acre. Rivers/streams: 1 for small streams; 2 for small rivers under 10 ft. wide; 3 for rivers 10-30 ft. wide, 4 for large rivers over 30 ft.)

9. Is the wetland free from significant pollution or eutrophication (i.e. such that its natural flora or fauna is permanently impaired)?

10. Is the wetland relatively unaffected by human activities, other than traditional management (i.e. any disturbance which might cause permanent or serious damage to either the aquatic communities or to a significant part of the wetland margin)?

11. Is the wetland free from the effects of accelerated dessication?

12. Is the wetland protected from any adverse effects of neighbouring land use by some kind of effective barrier (e.g. scrub, grassland, wall)?

13. Is the wetland free from the excessive overgrowth of marginal scrub or trees (ie. such as to shade most of the water or to impede the course of a river)?

14. Is the wetland relatively free from excessive deposition of organic silt/peat?

15. Is the wetland linked to or reasonably close (within 200 yds) to another natural or semi-natural wetland site?

## D) Biological interest and diversity.

16. Does the wetland have a good associated marginal flora? (Score 1 for 10-20 spp.; 2 for 21-30 spp.; 3 for 31-40 spp.; 4 for more than 40 spp. N.B. Only those species of plants found directly associated with the wetland margin are to be recorded here)

17. Does the watercourse have a good representative aquatic flora (Submerged or floating species including Chara spp.)? (Score 1 for 2-3 spp.; 2 for 4-5 spp.; 3 for more than 5 spp.)

18. Is the site known to support a wide range of aquatic invertebrates? (Score 1 for the presence of each of the following groups: Mollusca, Crustacea, Platyhelminthes, Coleoptera, Odonata, Hemiptera Trichoptera, Neuroptera, Ephemeroptera, Annelida, Plecoptera)

19. Does the wetland support a good range of fish and amphibians (apart from obviously introduced species)? (Score 1 for 1-4 spp.; 2 for 5-7 spp.; 3 for more than 7 spp.)

20. Does the site support a good range of resident/breeding aquatic birds and mammals? (Score 1 for the presence of each of the following: Coot, Moorhen, Mallard, Kingfisher, Sand Martin, Sedge Warbler, Reed Warbler, Reed Bunting, Little Grebe, Great Crested Grebe, Water Vole, Water Shrew, Otter, Daubenton's Bat).

21. Is the wetland otherwise important for migrant or wintering birds?

22. Does the wetland support any nationally or regionally rare species of plant or animal? (Defined as occurring in less than 10 ten-km grid squares in East Anglia).

23. Does the wetland support any locally scarce species of plant or animal (for plants: those occurring in less than 50 two-km squares in Herts. For animals: those known to be of local occurrence in Herts.)? (Score 1 for 1 sp.; 2 for 2-5 spp.; 3 for 6 or more spp.)

24. Is the wetland a diverse habitat? Score 1 for each of the following sub-habitats represented:
    deep water, greater than 4 ft.
    bottom deposits of stones, bare rock or stony shoals.
    submerged shoals of mud or silt.
    Open banks or margins.
    Marginal stands of reeds, sedges, rushes, reedmace, etc., if these do not threaten the rest of the site.
    occasional overhanging trees or rootstocks partly in the water, if these do not form a dense cover.
    islands
    marginal earth cliffs or very steep banks.
    margins of stonework, concrete, brick, etc.. or bridge structures.

## E) Conservability

25. Is the wetland reasonably unaffected by factors which might prevent its conservation for its characteristic fauna and flora, other than temporary factors, easily remedied?

Notes for the completion of the Open Waters Assessment Card.

Answer 'yes' or 'no' to each question except for those requiring a score. Estimation of wetland size should include marginal vegetation. Assessment of threat to habitat by overhanging vegetation should take into account possible benefits, such as the presence of otters.

© North Hertfordshire Museums Natural History Department.

209

*Appendix 4*

# Herbicides Approved For Use In and Around Ponds and Watercourses

HERBICIDES FOR AQUATIC USE

The following table correlates the main weed groups with the particular herbicides suitable for their control or suppression. Where a choice of more than one chemical exists, select the one which will affect the fewest number of non-target plants.

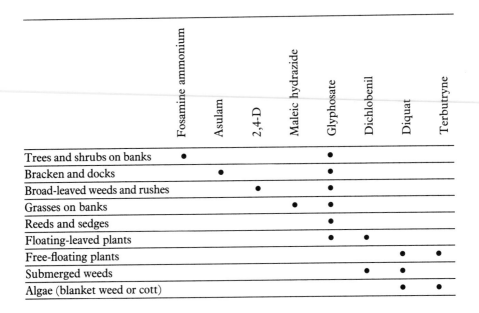

| | Fosamine ammonium | Asulam | 2,4-D | Maleic hydrazide | Glyphosate | Dichlobenil | Diquat | Terbutryne |
|---|---|---|---|---|---|---|---|---|
| Trees and shrubs on banks | • | | | | • | | | |
| Bracken and docks | | • | | | • | | | |
| Broad-leaved weeds and rushes | | | • | | • | | | |
| Grasses on banks | | | | • | • | | | |
| Reeds and sedges | | | | | • | | | |
| Floating-leaved plants | | | | | • | • | | |
| Free-floating plants | | | | | | | • | • |
| Submerged weeds | | | | | | • | • | |
| Algae (blanket weed or cott) | | | | | | | • | • |

## PRODUCTS APPROVED FOR USE IN OR NEAR WATER AS AT 1 FEBRUARY 1989

| Chemical | Safety interval before irrigation | Approved products | For control of |
|---|---|---|---|
| asulam | nil | Asulox | Bracken and docks on banks beside water |
| 2,4-D | 3 weeks | Atlas 2,4-D Dormone | Emergent broad-leaved weeds and weeds on banks |
| dichlobenil | 2 weeks | Casoron G Casoron GSR | Some floating submerged weeds |
| diquat | 10 days | Reglone | Some floating and submerged weeds and algae |
| | | Midstream | Submerged weeds |
| fosamine ammonium | nil | Krenite | Deciduous trees and shrubs on banks beside water |
| glyphosate | nil | Mascot Sonic Roundup Spasor | Water lilies, reeds and emergent weeds |
| maleic hydrazide | 3 weeks | Regulox-K Bos MH 180 | Suppression of grass growth on banks beside water |
| terbutryne | 7 days | Clarosan | Some floating and submerged weeds and algae |
| dalapon* | 5 weeks | BH Dalapon | Bulrushes, reeds, grass weeds on banks |

* Although still approved, this is no longer manufactured, so availability will be limited.

Taken with thanks from Ministry of Agriculture, Fisheries and Food Booklet 2078, *Guidelines for the Use of Herbicides on Weeds in or near Watercourses and Lakes*, © Crown Copyright 1989.

*Appendix 5*

# Scientific Names of Species*

## Birds

| | |
|---|---|
| Barn owl | *Tyto alba* |
| Blackbird | *Turdus merula* |
| Blackcap | *Sylvia atricapilla* |
| Blue tit | *Parus caeruleus* |
| Carolina duck | *Aix sponsa* |
| Coal tit | *Parus ater* |
| Corvids-crows | *Corvus spp.* |
| Eider duck | *Somateria mollissima* |
| European pintail | *Anas acuta* |
| Goldfinch | *Carduelis carduelis* |
| Goldeneye | *Bucephala clangula* |
| Great tit | *Parus major* |
| Grey heron | *Ardea cinerea* |
| Grey wagtail | *Motacilla cinerea* |
| Hawfinch | *Coccothraustes coccothraustes* |
| Kingfisher | *Alcedo atthis* |
| Mallard | *Anas platyrhynchos* |
| Mandarin duck | *Aix galericulata* |
| Moorhen | *Gallinula chloropus* |
| Pied flycatcher | *Ficedula hypoleuca* |
| Pied wagtail | *Motacilla alba* |
| Pochard | *Aythya ferina* |
| Red-crested pochard | *Netta rufina* |
| Redstart | *Phoenicurus phoenicurus* |
| Reed bunting | *Emberiza schoeniclus* |
| Reed warbler | *Acrocephalus scirpaceus* |
| Ringed teal | *Calonetta leucophrys* |
| Robin | *Erithacus rubecula* |
| Russian red-breasted goose | *Branta ruficollis* |
| Sand martin | *Riparia riparia* |

*This includes all species mentioned in the main text except for Chapter 8.

212

| Shelduck | *Tadorna tadorna* |
| Shoveller | *Anas clypeata* |
| Snipe | *Gallinago gallinago* |
| Song thrush | *Turdus philomelos* |
| Spotted flycatcher | *Muscicapa striata* |
| Stock dove | *Columba oenas* |
| Swallow | *Hirundo rustica* |
| Teal | *Anas crecca* |
| Tern | *Sterna spp.* |
| Treecreeper | *Certhia familiaris* |
| Tree sparrow | *Passer montanus* |
| Tufted duck | *Aythya fuligula* |
| Wren | *Troglodytes troglodytes* |
| Wood pigeon | *Columba palumbus* |

## Mammals

| Bats (various) | *family — Vespertilionidae* |
| Brown hare | *Lepus capensis* |
| Common or brown rat | *Rattus norvegicus* |
| Fox | *Vulpes vulpes* |
| Hedgehog | *Erinaceus europaeus* |
| Mink | *Mustela vison* |
| Rabbit | *Oryctolagus cuniculus* |
| Stoat | *Mustela erminea* |
| Weasel | *Mustela nivalis* |

## Amphibians and Reptiles

| Common frog | *Rana temporaria* |
| Common or smooth newt | *Triturus vulgaris* |
| Common toad | *Bufo bufo* |
| Grass snake | *Natrix natrix* |
| Natterjack toad | *Bufo calamita* |
| Palmate newt | *Triturus helveticus* |
| Warty or great crested newt | *Triturus cristatus* |

## Fish

| Bream | *Abramis brama* |
| Brown trout | *Salmo trutta fario* |
| Common or mirror carp | *Cyprinus carpio* |
| Eel | *Anguilla anguilla* |
| Goldfish | *Carassius auratus* |
| Golden orfe | *Leuciscus idus* |
| Grass carp | *Ctenopharyngodon idella Val* |

| Green and golden tench | *Tinca tinca* |
| Koi carp | *Cyprinus carpio* |
| Perch | *Perca fluviatilis* |
| Pike | *Esox lucius* |
| Rainbow trout | *Salmo gairdneri* |
| Roach | *Rutilus rutilus* |
| Rudd | *Scardinius erythrophthalmus* |
| Salmon | *Salmo salar* |

## Shellfish

| American signal crayfish | *Pacifastacus leniusculus* |
| Atlantic stream crayfish | *Austropotamobius pallipes* |
| European crayfish | *Astacus astacus* |

## Plants

| Alder | *Alnus glutinosa* |
| Amphibious bistort | *Polygonum amphibium* |
| Arrowhead | *Sagittaria sagittifolia* |
| Australian stonecrop | *Crassula helmsii* |
| Barley | *Hordeum distichon* |
| Bramble or blackberry | *Rubus fruticosus* |
| Beech | *Fagus sylvatica* |
| Bogbean | *Menyanthes trifoliata* |
| Brooklime | *Veronica beccabunga* |
| Bur reed | *Sparganium erectum* |
| Canadian pondweed | *Elodea canadensis* |
| Common or Norfolk reed | *Phragmites communis* |
| Creeping bent | *Agrostis stolonifera* |
| Creeping buttercup | *Ranunculus repens* |
| Creeping red fescue | *Festuca rubra* |
| Docks | *Rumex spp.* |
| Duckweed | *Lemna spp.* |
| Flax | *Linum perenne* |
| Flowering rush | *Butomus umbellatus* |
| Frogbit | *Hydrocharis morsus-ranae* |
| Greater reedmace | *Typha latifolia* |
| Great willowherb | *Epilobium hirsutum* |
| Hawthorn | *Crataegus monogyna* |
| Marsh marigold or kingcup | *Caltha palustris* |
| Monkey flower | *Mimulus guttatus* |
| Nettle | *Urtica dioica* |
| Oak | *Quercus robur* |
| Perennial ryegrass | *Lolium perenne* |
| Pondweeds | *Potamogeton spp.* |

| | |
|---|---|
| Purple loosestrife | *Lythrum salicaria* |
| Ragged robin | *Lychnis flos-cuculi* |
| Reed sweetgrass | *Glyceria maxima* |
| Rigid hornwort | *Ceratophyllum demersum* |
| Rough stalked meadow grass | *Poa trivialis* |
| Rowan or mountain ash | *Sorbus aucuparia* |
| Sedges | *Carex spp.* |
| Soft rush | *Juncus effusus* |
| Southern beech | *Nothofagus spp.* |
| Starwort | *Callitriche spp.* |
| Stonewort | *Chara spp.* |
| Timothy | *Phleum pratense* |
| Thistles | *Cirsium spp.* |
| Water crowfoot | *Ranunculus aquatilis* |
| Water fern | *Azolla filiculoides* |
| Water forget-me-not | *Myosotis scorpioides* |
| Water milfoil | *Myriophyllum spp.* |
| Water mint | *Mentha aquatica* |
| Water plantain | *Alisma plantago aquatica* |
| White clover | *Trifolium repens* |
| White water lily | *Nymphaea alba* |
| Willow | *Salix spp.* |
| Yellow flag iris | *Iris pseudacorus* |
| Yellow water lily | *Nuphar lutea* |

## Insects

| | |
|---|---|
| Brown aeshna | *Aeshna grandis* |
| Great diving beetle | *Dytiscus marginalis* |
| Great silver beetle | *Hydrophilus piceus* |
| Green lestes | *Lestes sponsa* |
| Midge | *Chironomus plumosus* |
| Pond skater | *Gerris lacustris* |
| Red eyed damselfly | *Erythromma najas* |
| Ruddy sympetrum | *Sympetrum sanguineum* |
| Screech beetle | *Hygrobia herrmanni* |
| Southern aeshna | *Aeshna cyanea* |
| Water boatman or common backswimmer | *Notonecta glauca* |
| Water cricket | *Velia caprai* |
| Water measurer | *Hydrometra stagnorum* |
| Whirligig beetle | *Gyrinus natator* |

## Appendix 6

# Useful Addresses

Agricultural Development and Advisory Service (ADAS),* MAFF, Great Westminster House, Horseferry Road, London SWIP 2AE
Tel: 01-216 6311

Agricultural Training Board (ATB),* Bourne House, 32–34 Beckenham Road, Beckenham, Kent BR3 4PB
Tel: 01-650 4890

British Association for Shooting and Conservation (BASC)
(a) Marford Mill, Rossett, Wrexham, Clwyd LL12 0HL
    Tel: 0244 570881
(b) Michael McMeekin, 7 Douglas Road, Glenwherry, Ballymena, NI
    Tel: Glenwherry 435

British Crayfish Marketing Association, Riversdale Farm, Stour Provost, Nr Gillingham, Dorset SP8 5RZ
Tel: 0747 85495

British Trust for Conservation Volunteers (BTCV),* 36 St Mary's Street, Wallingford, Oxon OX10 0EU
Tel: 0491 39766

John Chambers (wild flower seedsman), 15 Westleigh Road, Barton Seagrave, Kettering, Northants NN15 5AJ
Tel: 0933 681632

Conservation Volunteers (Northern Ireland) (CVNI), Operations Manager, The Pavilion, Cherryvale Playing Fields, Belfast BT6 0BZ
Tel: 0232 645169

Countryside Commission,* John Dower House, Crescent Place, Cheltenham, Glos GL50 3RA
Tel: 0242 521381

Countryside Commission for Scotland,* Battleby, Redgorton, Perth PH1 3EW
Tel: 0738 27921

Department of Agriculture and Fisheries for Scotland* (DAFS), Chesser House, 500 Gorgie Road, Edinburgh EH11 3AW
Tel: 031-443 4020

Department of Agriculture for Northern Ireland (DANI),* Water Drainage and Conservation Section, Hydebank, 4 Hospital Road, Belfast BT8 8JP
Tel: 0232 647161

Department of the Environment (NI),
(a) Archaelogical Survey, 66 Balmoral Avenue, Belfast BT9 6NY
    Tel: 0232 661621
(b) Conservation Branch, Hut 6, Castle Grounds, Stormont, Belfast BT4 3ST
    Tel: 0232 768716

* Address given is of Headquarters or Head Office from which addresses of Regional/County Offices can be obtained.

216

(c) Countryside and Wildlife Branch, Calvert House, Castle Place, Belfast BT1 1FY
Tel: 0232 230560

(d) Historic Monuments and Buildings Branch, Calvert House, Castle Place, Belfast BT1 1FY
Tel: 0232 230560

Farming and Wildlife Trust (for FWAGS),* National Agricultural Centre, Stoneleigh, Kenilworth, Warwickshire CV8 2LZ
Tel: 0203 696699

Game Conservancy Trust
(a) Fordingbridge, Hants SP6 1EF
Tel: 0425 52381
(b) ARC Wildfowl Centre, Great Linford, Milton Keynes, Bucks MK14 5AH
Tel: 0908 604810

Health and Safety Executive, Magdalen House, Stanley Precinct, Bootle, Merseyside L20 3QZ
Tel: 051-951 4000

Historic Buildings and Monuments Directorate (Scotland), 20 Brandon Street, Edinburgh EH3 5RA
Tel: 031-556 8400

Ministry of Agriculture, Fisheries and Food (MAFF),* Whitehall Place, London, SW1A 2HH
Tel: 01-233 3000

National Rivers Authority,* see telephone directory for address of local office

Nature Conservancy Council (NCC),*
(a) Northminster House, Northminster, Peterborough, Cambs PE1 1UA
Tel: 0733 40345

(b) Hope Terrace, Edinburgh EH9 2AS
Tel: 031-447 4784

Royal Society for Nature Conservation (RSNC)* (for County Wildlife Trusts), The Green, Nettleham, Lincoln LN2 2NR
Tel: 0522 752326

Royal Society for the Protection of Birds (RSPB), The Lodge, Sandy, Beds SG19 2DL
Tel: 0767 80551

Scottish Conservation Projects Trust, Balallan House, 24 Allan Park, Stirling FK8 2QG
Tel: 0786 79697

Scottish Wildlife Trust, 25 Johnston Terraces, Edinburgh EH1 2NH
Tel: 031-226 4602

Shell Better Britain Campaign (for England, Wales & Northern Ireland)
(a) Red House, Hill Lane, Great Barr, Birmingham B43 6LZ
Tel: 021-358 0744
(b) Shell Better Britain Campaign (Scotland), Balallan House, 24 Allan Park, Stirling FK8 2QG
Tel: 0786 79697

Welsh Office Agriculture Department (WOAD),* Crown Offices, Cathays Park, Cardiff
Tel: 0222 825111

Wildfowl and Wetlands Trust Slimbridge Gloucester GL2 7BT
Tel: 045-389 333

*Appendix 7*

# References & Sources of Further Reading

Baines, J. C., *How to Make a Wildlife Garden* (Elm Tree Books 1985)

Beresford, J. E. and Wade, P. M., *Field Ponds in North Leicestershire: Their Characteristics, Aquatic Flora & Decline* (Trans. Leicester Literary & Philosophical Society Vol. 76 1982)

Bregazzi, P. R., Domaniewski, J. C. J. and Jones, J. G. W., *Carp Farming Project—Final Report* (University of Reading 1984)

British Trust for Conservation Volunteers, *Waterways & Wetlands* (BTCV 1981)

Bryant, P., Jauncey, K. and Atack, T., *Backyard Fish Farming* (Prism Press 1980)

Burton, R., *Ponds, Their Wildlife & Upkeep* (David & Charles 1977)

Chinery, M., *The Living Garden* (Dorling Kindersley 1986)

Clegg, J., *British Naturalists Association Guide to Ponds & Streams* (Crowood Press 1985)

Cooke, A. S. and Scorgie, H. R. A., *Focus on Nature Conservation No 3. The Status of the Commoner Amphibians & Reptiles in the British Isles* (Nature Conservancy Council 1983)

Day, P., *Ponds (Marl Pits) in the Lower Dee Valley of Clywd—a Preliminary Appraisal* (Nature Conservancy Council 1981)

de Feu, C., *Nest Boxes* (British Trust for Ornithology 1985)

Dyson, J., *Save the Village Pond* (Ford Motor Co. Ltd 1974)

Game Conservancy Trust, *Sporting Fisheries in the Making* (The Game Conservancy Trust)

Game Conservancy Trust, *Ponds and Lakes for Wildfowl* (The Game Conservancy Trust)

Hampshire & Isle of Wight Naturalists Trust, *The Hampshire Pond Survey* (Hampshire & Isle of Wight Naturalists Trust)

Haslam, S., Sinker, C. and Wolseley, P., *British Water Plants* (Field Studies Council 1982)

218

Hertfordshire County Council Countryside Group, *The Hertfordshire Pond Project* (Hertfordshire County Council 1987)

Kabisch, K. and Hemmerling, J., *Ponds & Pools—Oases in the Landscape* (Croom Helm 1984)

Lewis, G. and Williams, G., *Rivers & Wildlife Handbook* (Royal Society for the Protection of Birds 1984)

Martin, E. A., *Dew Ponds: History, Observation & Experiment* (T. Werner Laurie 1915)

Ministry of Agriculture, Fisheries & Food, *Bulletin 202: Water for Irrigation* (MAFF 1977)

Ministry of Agriculture, Fisheries & Food, *Booklet 2078: Guidelines for the Use of Herbicides on Weeds in or near Watercourses & Lakes* (MAFF 1985)

Michaels, V. K., *Carp Farming* (Fishing News Books Ltd 1988)

National Farmers Union (Stanton Branch), *The Countryside—Farmers Care Too* (NFU 1985)

Nature Conservancy Council, *Nature Conservation in Great Britain* (NCC 1984)

Nature Conservancy Council, *The Ecology & Conservation of Amphibian & Reptile Species Endangered in Britain* (NCC 1985)

Norfolk Farming & Wildlife Advisory Group, *Farm Pond Management* (Norfolk FWAG 1987)

Palmer, M. and Newbold, C., *Wetland & Riparian Plants in Great Britain* (Nature Conservancy Council 1983)

Pugsley, A. J., *Dewponds in Fable & Fact* (Country Life 1939)

Rackham, O. *The History of the Countryside* (J. M. Dent & Sons 1986)

Relton, J., *Disappearance of Farm Ponds*, Monks Wood Experimental Station Report 1969–71, pp. 32–33

Seagrave, C. P., *Aquatic Weed Control* (Fishing News Books Ltd 1988)

Severn Trent Water Authority, *Freshwater Fisheries Management* (Fishing News Books Ltd 1984)

Spencer-Jones, D. and Wade, P. M., *Aquatic Plants—a Guide to Recognition* (Imperial Chemical Industries—Professional Products 1986)

Sterry, P., *Pond Watching* (Severn House 1982)

Street, M., *The Restoration of Gravel Pits for Wildfowl* (ARC and Game Conservancy Trust)

Wells, T., Bell, S. and Frost, A., *Creating Attractive Grasslands Using Native Plant Species* (Nature Conservancy Council 1981)

# Index

# FARMING PRESS BOOKS

The following are samples from the wide range of agricultural and veterinary books published by Farming Press. For more information or for a free illustrated book list please contact:

**Farming Press Books, 4 Friars Courtyard**
**30–32 Princes Street, Ipswich IP1 1RJ, United Kingdom**
**Telephone (0473) 43011**

## A Way of Life: Sheepdog Training, Handling and Trialling

H. GLYN JONES AND BARBARA COLLINS

> *A complete guide to sheepdog work and trialling, in which Glyn Jones' life is presented as an integral part of his tested and proven methods.*

## The Blue Riband of the Heather

E. B. CARPENTER

> *A pictorial cavalcade of International Sheep Dog Society Supreme Champions from 1906, including information on pedigrees, awards and distinguished families of handlers.*

## Farm Woodland Management

JOHN BLYTH, JULIAN EVANS, WILLIAM E. S. MUTCH, CAROLINE SIDWELL

> *A compendium in which all aspects of trees on the farm—both upland and lowland—are considered. Covers the full range of woodland size from hedgerow to agroforestry.*

## Outbursts

OLIVER WALSTON

> *A provocative series of articles by 'a boisterous know-all of great charm' and one of Britain's best-known arable farmers, written over a twelve-year period starting a few months before the Great Drought of 1976.*

Farming Press also publish three monthly magazines: *Dairy Farmer*, *Pig Farming* and *Arable Farming*. For a specimen copy of any of these magazines, please contact Farming Press at the address above.